JACK GA~

travel times: p.257
Venice to London

The Writer's Guide to

Everyday Life

in

Renaissance

From England
1485-1649

Kathy Lynn Emerson

W
WRITER'S DIGEST BOOKS
CINCINNATI, OHIO

This hardcover edition of *The Writer's Guide to Everyday Life in Renaissance England* features a "self-jacket" that eliminates the need for a separate dust jacket. It provides sturdy protection for your book while it saves paper, trees and energy.

Other fine Writer's Digest Books are available from your local bookstore or direct from the publisher.

00 99 98 97 96   5 4 3 2 1

Library of Congress Cataloging-in-Publication Data

Emerson, Kathy Lynn.
   The writer's guide to everyday life in Renaissance England / Kathy Lynn Emerson.
      p.   cm.
   Includes bibliographical references and index.
   ISBN 0-89879-752-7 (alk. paper)
   1. England—Social life and customs—16th century—Handbooks, manuals, etc. 2. England—Social life and customs—17th century—Handbooks, manuals, etc. 3.—Great Britain—History—Tudors, 1485-1603—Handbooks, manuals, etc. 4. Historical fiction—Authorship—Handbooks, manuals, etc. 5. Renaissance—England—Handbooks, manuals, etc. I. Title.
DA320.E48   1996
942.05—dc20   96-22416
                                                                          CIP

Edited by Jack Heffron and Roseann S. Biederman
Illustrations by James B. Bishop
Cover designed by Sandy Conopeotis Kent
Interior designed by Amy Schneider and Sandy Conopeotis Kent

DEDICATION

The Writer's Guide to Everyday Life in Renaissance England is dedicated to Ethel Emerson, for being a great mother-in-law as well as a first rate resource person.

ACKNOWLEDGMENTS

I would like to acknowledge the assistance of several people who were kind enough to read over early versions of various chapters and make suggestions. Thanks go to Shirley Martin (who read the whole thing), Sandy Emerson, Carol Backus and Terry Gerritsen.

PART THREE:

RENAISSANCE SOCIETY

INTRODUCTION

The Renaissance began in Italy, flowered in France and slowly made its way to England. In the year 1500, Henry VII was on the throne of England. His son, the future Henry VIII, was receiving the education that would make him one of the great Renaissance princes of Europe. For the purposes of this volume, then, Renaissance England refers to the reigns of Henry VII (1485–1509), Henry VIII (1509–1547), Edward VI (1547–1553), Mary I (1553–1558), Elizabeth I (1558–1603), James I (1603–1625) and Charles I (1625–1649), and the period comes to an abrupt end with the execution of King Charles.

It is impossible to do justice to a century and a half in a single book, but *The Writer's Guide to Everyday Life in Renaissance England* offers two services to writers of historical romance, historical mystery, time travel and other historical fiction. First, it gives starting points in the form of introductions to a number of specific subject areas. Second, it indicates which of the many volumes of social, economic, literary and political history are most likely to provide the sort of information novelists need.

In-depth studies have been done on exceedingly narrow subjects. Many of their authors, however, were more interested in presenting statistical data or proving some obscure thesis than in supplying interesting anecdotal material. All of the books listed in my select bibliographies are available through interlibrary loans. Most were published during the last thirty years. I've tried to reflect the most recent research while avoiding radical interpretations (although I have included, annotated, a few of the more interesting ones). "Lost" documents are always coming to light and older records are constantly being reexamined. Therefore, assume that all statistics are approximate and that almost any "fact" can and will be debated by scholars.

In addition to the select bibliographies in each chapter, this volume contains time lines, quick reference lists and sidebars to aid in finding specific details. The chapters are arranged by broad subject areas. Material which falls into more than one category is cross-referenced in the text.

A NOTE ON DATES

Some dates may seem contradictory. This is because, in 1582, in order to ensure that church holidays occurred in the proper seasons, Pope Gregory XIII issued a decree dropping ten days from the calendar. By 1583, Italy, Portugal, Spain, France and the Roman Catholic German States were all using "New Style" dates. England, however, as a Protestant nation, continued to use the "Old Style" Julian Calendar until 1752. Thus, English reports on the Spanish Armada of 1588 record events as taking place ten days earlier than Spanish reports do. The day of the week also differed. May 1, 1593, for example, was a Tuesday in the Julian calendar but a Saturday in the Gregorian calendar.

In England, the new year began on Lady Day, March 25, although the holiday called New Year's Day, on which gifts were presented to the monarch, was already being celebrated on January 1. Thus you may find dates for events which took place between January 1 and March 24 written 1588/9. Leap years, as now, added a February 29th every four years; 1584 was a leap year.

PART ONE

Everyday Life

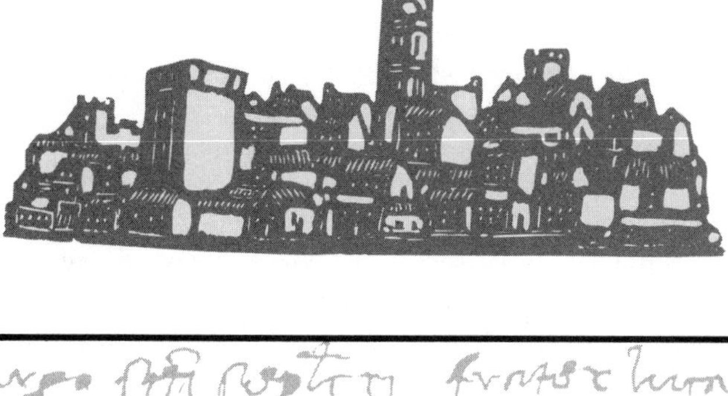

CHAPTER ONE

CLOTHES AND ACCESSORIES

Both fashions and the terms used to describe garments underwent many changes during the period from 1500 to 1650. Meanings have also changed since. When we read that a woman went to church in 1617 in her "rich night-gown and petticoat," it raises eyebrows, but it didn't then. Also called slops (which can refer to any loose-fitting garment), the female nightgown dates from the beginning of the fifteenth century. It could be made of silk, velvet, satin or taffeta faced with fur. It fell to the ankles and had long sleeves. Although it usually served as a dressing gown, it was also worn outside the house. A man's nightgown was a dressing gown, taken off when he went to bed.

It was customary to will articles of clothing to friends and family. Thus, styles decades out of fashion at court would often be seen elsewhere. Only the wealthy could afford a wide range of styles and fabrics.

Portraits are full of detail, showing the texture and color of fabrics, but in general they show subjects wearing the most formal of attire. At home or in the more informal setting of the country, many of the layers, both outerwear and underwear, would likely have been shed. No simple country housewife ever cooked a meal or cleaned her house wearing a wheel farthingale!

Some clothing had specific social implications, identifying the wearer as a member of a profession or as the servant of a particular nobleman. For more details on this function of clothes and accessories, see chapter fourteen.

MEN'S CLOTHING

From the late fifteenth century through about 1590, the codpiece, a fabric pouch which covered the penis, existed as a separate article of male outerwear. It was padded and elaborately decorated throughout the period from 1514 to 1575, after which it gradually began to diminish in size. The codpiece sometimes doubled as a pocket, in which men kept their handkerchiefs and other small items. It was secured by buckles or tied up with points, points being any ties which attached various articles of dress to each other. Points might be either visible or concealed. The wealthy had points of linen or silk thread or ribbon. The poor used strong cord or leather.

Theories about the origin of the codpiece abound. Some say it was worn as underwear first. Another possibility is that it was designed to give extra protection in battle. A third theory suggests that the codpiece was supposed to keep the oily, mercury-based cream many men applied as a treatment for syphilis from staining doublet and hose.

After the codpiece, the doublet was the most striking part of a man's clothing, and usually the most expensive. This close-fitting garment, worn over a shirt or waistcoat and fitted to the waist, was usually made by professional tailors. In various styles it was in fashion from 1450 to 1670.

Sleeves were a separate garment. Most had wrist-ruffs or turned-back cuffs. The armhole joint was concealed by a padded roll of material or a double or single roll of tabs called pickadils. Sleeves were often a contrasting color to other garments. They changed in shape to match the fashion in doublets.

Before 1530, doublets and sleeves were "slashed" so that the layer beneath could be pulled through and "puffed." Until about 1550 the doublet had a square silhouette from shoulder to mid-thigh and a high neck. In the period from 1550 to 1560, padded, pleated bases (a skirt) hung about six inches below the waist. From 1560 the fitted body of the doublet was longer, more padded, and had a V-shaped point in the front. It usually fastened with close-set buttons.

From 1575 to 1600, the peascod-bellied doublet was fashionable. This extended well below the hips in a shape something like a pea-pod and was rigid, unwrinkled, and stuffed with bombast (horsehair, flock, wool, rags, flax, cotton or bran) to preserve its square-shouldered shape. Gentlemen of fashion had to be careful. If they snagged a peascod-bellied doublet on a nail, they might leak bran! The back of the doublet was lined with stiff canvas. Most of the buttons were for decoration. This doublet fastened from armpit to waist on each side like a piece of armor. The front might be further stiffened inside with a triangular piece of wood the consistency of thick cardboard.

After 1590 an alternative style was shorter and hollow-bellied instead of convex and after 1620 the rigidity of outline gradually diminished. By 1630, so-called Cavalier dress, with a higher waist, was in fashion. The doublet was usually left unbuttoned from the breast down. Puritans wore doublets similar in appearance but undecorated and looser. After 1640 the doublet was again short and without an obvious waistline.

The wealthy had doublets made of brocade, satin, taffeta and velvet. The poor wore canvas, fustian and leather.

Below the waist, men wore hose, a term used only for the male garment during the years 1400 to 1620. Until around 1570, hose referred to either the breeches (upper stocks) or the netherstocks (lower stocks, also called simply stocks), although after 1545 hose generally meant the netherstocks alone. The term upper stocks went out of use at about that same time. The breeches fastened to the doublet or waistcoat with points and covered the body from the waist around the seat and over part or all of the upper leg.

Gentlemen's stocks were knitted. The hose of poorer people might be sewn of rough textiles and the bottom might be footless, toeless or stirrup-shaped.

The term tights was not in use at all during this period, and until the 1660s the word stockings usually referred to women's hosiery, although records do show that Edward VI received a gift of silk stockings made in Spain.

Underwear was optional. Shirts were underclothing and commonly made of linen, although they might be made of fine lawn or silk. They were also used to sleep in. Stays were worn under some doublets in the period 1603–1625.

WOMEN'S CLOTHING

The female equivalent of the doublet, at times even called a doublet, was the body, pair of bodies or bodice. It had two parts, the stomacher (a triangular front section) and the bodice proper, which was joined to the stomacher at the sides with ties, hooks or pins. Like a corset, the stomacher was stiffened with busks (flat lengths of bone or wood) inserted in pockets. The neckline varied greatly and might show the underclothes beneath or bare skin or be filled with a partlet. The partlet may have gotten its name because it parted the little round face ruff, which could be opened or closed with aglets (laced through eyelet holes) or hooks and eyes. When the partlet had sleeves, they were not sewn on but were rather a separate article of clothing attached with points. After 1550, necklines had either collars or ruffs attached to them. Very low necklines appeared in the late Elizabethan and early Jacobean eras.

The gown, at first an overdress worn open in front and extending from shoulders to ground, came to mean a woman's dress. The word dress was not used in its modern sense but rather to refer to the entire ensemble, as in "court dress." What looks like a dress to us is the kirtle. Prior to 1545, kirtle referred to the combination of bodice or jacket and skirt. After 1545, the two parts were separate and the term kirtle generally meant only the skirt. By 1625 the term was obsolete and the garment was called a petticoat. The early kirtle had openings at the front in both sections, at top to show the stomacher and at bottom to reveal an underskirt called the forepart.

Sleeves were fastened to the bodice at the shoulder line by ribbon bows, or hooks or pins concealed by decorative rolls of fabric known as wings. A ruffle or cuff at the wrist matched the ruff or collar. Sleeves might be in two parts in contrasting colors and came in various shapes. From 1525 to 1560, a funnel shape was common. From 1540 to 1550, sleeves might also be bell-shaped, worn over embroidered undersleeves and tied back to show puffs of the shift beneath. After 1560, sleeves might be gathered, tapered or full. By 1580, leg-of-mutton sleeves, also called trunk or demi-cannon sleeves, were in fashion.

As far as can be determined, women in this period, at least in England, wore neither panties nor underdrawers. In the Middle Ages it had been argued that the wearing of braies (men's pants) by women could provoke, by friction, undesirable "heat" in the female genitals, and the practice was thus discouraged. In Italy and France, women started wearing long, trouserlike drawers in the 1530s, but the fact that this practice still struck English travelers as odd as late as 1617 seems to indicate that Englishwomen did not adopt the fashion. Cloth pads were used during menstruation, but how they were held in place is unclear.

Englishwomen wore a chemise, shift or smock as their undermost garment. Usually of linen and ankle-length, this garment might be gathered at the neck to form a soft ruff, which would then show, instead of a partlet, above the garments worn on top.

Body-stitchets (stays) were an early form of corset. These were made of heavy canvas, boiled leather (called a basquine and worn over a quilted underbodice), and even iron. More than one might be worn at the same time. Trim sometimes showed above the garments worn on top. The busks used for stiffening were made of wood, steel and cane until about 1600, after which whalebone came into fashion.

The farthingale was worn by women of fashion from 1545 through the 1620s. This structure of hoops of rushes, wood, wire or whalebone was used to extend the skirt under which it was worn. It converted the columnar skirt of the fifteenth century into the cone shape of the sixteenth. There were three distinct versions. The Spanish farthingale was bell-shaped. Originally *vertugado*, it was in fashion in Spain in the 1470s and was introduced in England by way of France (where it was called the vertugale from about 1530). The French farthingale was a padded roll worn around the hips to create a cylindrical effect. It was in fashion from about 1570. The wheel, cartwheel or drum farthingale was in fashion in the late sixteenth century. The flat top of the cartwheel above the hoops was made of canvas. It had a hole for the waist and attached with tapes. The skirt fell directly over the drum shape and the material was gathered into a narrow waist.

For home wear, women wore plainer fabrics. An open gown might be worn like a housecoat over a bodice and petticoat of embroidered linen. The word petticoat could be used for any skirt or underskirt and usually several were worn.

OUTERWEAR

In cold weather people simply added more clothing, a long gown, a jacket of lambskins, a fur-lined cloak, padded garments, boot hose with

A gentlewoman of 1570
This rendering of an
Elizabethan gentlewoman,
based on the memorial brass
of Cecily Fortescue of Mursley,
Buckinghamshire, illustrates
the most prevalent style of
dress during the sixteenth century. Note the opening at the
front of the kirtle to show the
forepart. A partlet and face
ruff frame the face. Wings at
the shoulders hide the laces
tying the sleeves to the bodice.
The skirt is held out by a cone-
shaped farthingale.

long boots, and extra petticoats and shirts. Both sexes wore scarves, mufflers and mittens.

There were no special riding habits but some women hunted and hawked in men's clothing, wearing breeches and high boots.

CHILDREN'S DRESS

Infants were swaddled (wrapped in cloth bands), a practice that was encouraged by doctors who subscribed to the theory of humours (see page 77 for more details). Swaddling was believed to prevent the baby from losing too much moisture. Swaddling bands almost completely immobilized children during the first four months of life. At four months the arms were freed but not the legs.

Young children of both sexes were clothed alike, in gowns that fell to the feet, aprons, bibs and caps, until they were four or five years old. Older children were dressed as miniature versions of adults.

COUNTRY DRESS

Crude clothing identified the ordinary countryman: coarse homespun woolen garments of reddish brown for the best garment, worn with kersey or knitted hose and heavy hobnail shoes. Field clothes were fustian tunics with loose breeches and canvas leggings buskined (tied in place) with strips of cloth. Samuel Rowlands (1609) describes a typical countryman's headgear as a "greasy hat that had a hole ate through by some rat." After about 1560, the "thrummed" (fringed or shaggy) hat became associated with the poor. There seems to be no distinctive dress for the poorest class of women, but a country maidservant might wear the bodice of her petticoat "laced before" and a blue or black kirtle.

HAIR, BEARDS AND COSMETICS

Women's Hairstyles

Women dyed their hair, bleached it in the sun and washed it with alkalized water. Golden hair was highly esteemed but all shades of red and auburn found favor at court even though very little hair showed beneath some headgear. From about 1560, hair was curled and pulled back from the forehead, dressed over a pad and interwoven with pearls and jeweled ornaments. In the 1620s, hair was styled "tete de mou-ton"—frizzled at the sides with a high bun at the back and ornamented with ribbon, pearls or flowers. Maids were hairdressers for their mistresses. Women might also wear wigs.

Men's Hairstyles

Early in the sixteenth century, hair was worn shoulder length or bobbed to the bottom of the ears. By 1520, chin level was fashionable and by 1530 styles went even shorter, especially at the back. Hair might be combed forward at the front to form a short fringe over the forehead. In the mid-sixteenth century men added a trimmed beard and mustache to short hair. Later in the century, hair was longer at the sides. From 1625, men of the court party wore ringlets cascading down their backs. When a single ringlet was tied with a ribbon bow and pulled over the shoulder it was called a love-lock. Men did not wear wigs.

Beards

Most men were clean shaven before King Henry VIII set the style for beards and mustaches in the 1520s. Under Mary and Elizabeth there was no one predominant fashion but the trims included the bodkin beard (long, pointed, in the center of the chin only), the Cadiz beard (a large, disordered growth), the pencil beard (a slight tuft of hair on the point of the chin), the spade beard (cut in the shape of an ace of spades and popular with soldiers from 1570 to 1605) and the swallow's tail beard (forked but with the ends long and spread wide). From 1550 to 1600, it was never in fashion to wear a mustache without a beard. After 1600 the clean-shaven look came back into style. The Vandyke beard (a carefully trimmed mustache and pointed chin beard) was popular during the reign of Charles I.

Cosmetics

Puritans disapproved of cosmetics and the poor could not afford them, but women who could used them in an effort to achieve what was considered the "standard" for beauty: very white skin, red lips and lamplike eyes.

A powder made of ground alabaster was used to whiten the skin. Or one could apply a lotion made of beeswax, asses' milk and the ground jawbone of a hog. White fucus, another popular whitener, was made by grinding up the burned jawbone of a hog, sieving it, and laying it on with oil of white poppy. Many of these homemade mixtures were benign but some caused scarring and other skin problems. Ceruse was white lead (a poison) mixed with vinegar. Other whiteners were a mixture of borax and sulphur; a lotion made of white of egg, alum, borax, poppy seeds and powdered eggshell; and a glaze of egg white.

Fucus was a generic term for red dye used to redden the lips. It may have been made of madder or of red ochre or of red crystalline mercuric sulfide (which ate the flesh). To redden their cheeks, women used a mixture of cochineal, white of hard-boiled egg, milk of green figs, alum and gum arabic.

A freckle was any kind of spot and was anathema to the Elizabethan woman. To get rid of spots she applied birch-tree sap or ground brimstone or oil of turpentine or sublimate of mercury (a poison).

Kohl was used to emphasize the eyes, and another poison, belladonna, was put into them (a custom imported from Venice) to produce huge, velvety pupils.

Dental Care
Dental care was primitive, but people did attempt it, usually by vigorously rubbing or washing their teeth with mixtures such as white wine and vinegar boiled with honey. Toothpicks and tooth-cloths were popular gift items. The toothbrush was known by 1649 but was not yet in use in England.

Perfumes
Almost everyone, male and female, wore scent of some kind. Henry VIII's favorite perfume combined musk, rose water, ambergris and civet. Sweet marjoram was the major ingredient in Queen Elizabeth's favorite scent. Other perfumes used aloe, nutmeg and storax. Scents like rose water and lavender water were distilled at home. More exotic scents were imported.

To cover unpleasant odors, the result of infrequent washing, fabrics were also heavily perfumed. The custom extended to accessories, and one seventeenth-century recipe for perfuming gloves advises steeping two spoonfuls of gum-dragon all night in rosewater mixed with four grains of ground musk and eight grains of ground civet before adding half a spoonful of a mixture of oil of cloves, cinnamon and jasmine. This blend was then beaten into a thin jelly and rubbed all over the gloves, after which they were left in a dry, clean place for forty-eight hours. The final step was to rub the gloves with the hands until the gloves became limber.

ASSORTED ACCESSORIES

aprons: Worn by working classes and country housewives throughout the period. From 1600 to 1640, fashionable ladies wore elegant and elaborately decorated versions.

boot hose: From 1560 to 1680, large, loose boot hose were worn inside boots to protect the hose. They were turned down just below the knee.

boots: Boots were well-fitted, sometimes with outside lacing. By the late sixteenth and early seventeenth century, they reached above the knee. They might be of leather or of russet cloth. Those hanging loose about the leg and turned down and fringed were called "lugged boots." Cockers were knee-high boots of rough make worn by laborers and countrymen. From about 1585, brogues were worn by poor people and some soldiers. Buskins were riding boots and reached the calf or the knee.

fans: The hand fan appeared in England by 1572, having previously been in use in both France and Italy, and quickly gained wide popularity. Large feather fans were round or semicircular and often had a small mirror at the center. Others were made of embroidered silk or velvet. Sir Francis Drake presented Queen Elizabeth with one of red and white feathers with a gold handle inlaid with half moons of mother-of-pearl and diamonds.

girdles or waistbands (belts): Women's girdles might be made of silk, ribbon, velvet covered with small plaquettes, embossed metal or metal links. The fashion of wearing a girdle from which was suspended any number of trinkets continued until about 1600. Wealthy men wore girdles of gold, silver, embroidered fabrics, velvet or silk. The poor made do with caddis, a woven tape.

gloves: Worn by everyone and popular as gifts, they were usually gauntleted and embroidered on the backs and cuffs.

handkerchiefs: In use from the sixteenth century on, they were also called muckinders (a slang term which could also mean a baby's bib) and napkins.

hats: Men remained uncovered only in the presence of royalty. Otherwise, if a man removed his hat to greet a lady, he put it right back on, indoors or out. The size of hats increased under James I and large feathers and other objects, such as gloves, handkerchiefs and ribbons might be stuck onto the hat and into the hatband. Hats for both sexes were made of velvet, silk, felt, taffeta, beaver and ermine. Beaver hats were rare until around 1580. During the second quarter of the seventeenth century most men wore either hats with moderate crowns and wide brims turned up at one side or a sugar-loaf-shaped hat called the copotain. Among women, close-fitting linen caps (coifs) were worn indoors and hoods or hats were added on top to go outdoors.

jewelry: Often made from melted-down coins, the most popular types of jewelry were bracelets (made of ornamental gold links, enameled and jeweled; of rows of pearls or beads of amber, coral or agates; of long, black, tubular beads called bugles; or of hair), brooches (worn by men and women to hold feathers to hats and by women to ornament the bodice), carcanets (hanging collars of linked ornamental design set with jewels from which hung little pendants; rarely seen except at court), chains (gentlemen's were frequently enameled; ladies wore long chains of stones or pearls), earrings (not worn until the late Elizabethan period, they were then seen on both men and women), pendants (worn suspended from chains or ribbons to hang just below the chest) and rings. Rings were worn by all classes and ranged from signets to cameos, intaglios, rings set with precious stones and memorial rings.

masks: Worn to shield the wearer from the sun when riding and to hide identity, some had glass-filled eyeholes.

muffs, snufkins or snoskyns: Made of cloth or fur, the smaller models hung suspended from a woman's girdle.

pomander: A hollow perforated sphere containing a waxed perfume ball impregnated with scent. Men wore pomanders suspended from a chain. Women attached them to their girdles. Often constructed of gold or silver and set with jewels, or engraved or enameled, a pomander might be any size and could contain ambergris, musk, cloves or hartshorn. An alternative style was constructed to look like an orange, with quarters secured at the base by hinges that opened outward when the top was unscrewed.

shoes: Men's shoes were generally flat-heeled and might be made of leather, silk, brocade or velvet and decorated with silver or copper gilt buckles or large ornamental rosettes of silk. Under Henry VIII most shoes were duck-bill shaped. Shoes that more closely fitted the shape of the foot came into fashion in 1554 but they continued to have broad toes. Some had ankle straps. Styles of men and women's shoes went by the same names: mule (a slipper with no heel piece), pinson (a light indoor shoe), pump (a single-sole shoe, close-fitting to the ankle, of cloth or thin leather with flat heels) and slipper (a low-cut indoor shoe). Women's overshoes, which raised the wearer out of the mud, included chopines, clogs or pattens (with wooden soles), and pantofles (cork-soled skuffs which became common after about 1570).

spectacles: Eyeglasses were known as early as the thirteenth century and generally available after about 1520. Demand increased after the invention of the printing press. The Guild of Spectacle Makers was chartered in 1629.

stockings: Women's stockings were held up by garters below the knee. Silk, worsted and fine yarn were all in general use for stockings by 1580.

watches: The "Nüremberg Egg," a portable timepiece invented by Peter Henlien in 1502, may be a myth, but "pocket sundials" were in general use by 1545 and "traveling clocks" are frequently mentioned after 1575. Early watches were large and might be octagonal, oval or round in shape. Their outer covers were pierced with elaborate open-work to enable the strike to be heard. After about 1580 the size decreased and watches were used as personal ornaments.

ITEMS OF CLOTHING

arched hood (1580–1620): This hood made an arch over the head and was associated with widows.

beguin or Flemish hood: A rectangle of linen carefully folded into a symmetrical headdress and caught together at the nape of the neck.

biggin: A cap men wore to bed. It tied under the chin with laces or ribbon.

bone grace or bongrace (1530–1615): A flat, square cap with a short flap of velvet on each side.

bonnet: A generic term for the French hood. Low, flat men's hats were also called bonnets.

braies: Leg coverings worn under long robes and tunics, these were the forerunners of hose worn as outerwear.

bum-barrel, bum-roll or waist bolster: A padded roll tied around the waist under the skirt to hold it out.

canions (1570–1620): Tubular, thigh-hugging extensions worn over the area from breeches to knee. Separate netherstocks could be gartered either over or under the canions.

cap: In men's wear, a cap was a hat worn by an inferior person. Women's caps were worn indoors or under hats.

cassock (1530–1660): Worn by men and women, this was a loose, hip-length coat with a small collar or hood.

caul: A skull cap of silk, often worn by maidens. Caul was also used as a term for a bag-shaped hair net (of gold mesh lined with silk or made entirely of silk thread or human hair), which held the hair back in a coil. This could be worn alone or under a hat.

cloak: Long cloaks were worn by both sexes. From about 1545, men also wore, indoors and out, a short, full cloak, richly lined, with a high upstanding collar. The Spanish cloak (1535–1620) was hooded. The Dutch cloak (1545–1620) had wide, hanging sleeves. The French cloak (1570–1670) reached the knees and was worn over one shoulder and gathered up over the arm.

coat: A short-sleeved or sleeveless jacket or jerkin which was worn over the doublet.

court bonnet (1575–1585): A pillbox of velvet trimmed with jewels and feathers and worn over a caul.

drawers: This male undergarment is mentioned as early as 1150 but was not universally worn.

falling band or falling collar (1540–1670): Any turned-down collar, often lace-edged, worn instead of a ruff.

forepart: Any underskirt, usually highly decorated, revealed through the inverted-V opening in the front of a skirt.

French hood (1530–1630): A small bonnet made on a stiff frame and worn far back on the head. Folds of material fell below the shoulders from a short flat panel at the back. Usually dark in color but decorated with biliments (borders of silk, satin or velvet trimmed with gold or jewels), it was worn over a crespin or creppin (a fine linen cap).

gabardine: A long, loose overcoat with hanging sleeves, worn by both sexes and all classes.

gable headdress (1500–1540): Square, it had two long back panels and front lappets.

gown: For men this was either a sleeveless mock-coat or a cloak with ornamental sleeves. In Tudor times gowns were worn primarily by older men and professionals and on ceremonial occasions. For women the gown was an overdress worn for added warmth or greater dignity. It could be close-bodied or loose and have long or short sleeves or sleeves hanging loosely from the shoulder. Ceremonial gowns might have a train.

head-rail (after 1630): A large square of material pinned around the back of the head. Less fashionably, a kerchief might be draped over the head for covering.

hood: The generic term for a head covering. A countrywoman's hood around 1520 was of white linen with lappets, which might be tied over the top of her head.

jerkin or jacket: A sleeveless vest worn over the doublet. The short jerkin (five to six inches below the waist) came to England with Philip of Spain in 1554. The jerkin of cloth or leather was worn by civilians from 1545 to 1575 and again from 1620 to 1630. As military garments throughout the period, "buff" jerkins were made of leather.

jump jacket: A Dutch style favored by Puritans of the 1640s, this was worn with matching Dutch breeches, "bucket-top" boots, a square white linen collar, plain white cuffs and a wide-brimmed black felt hat.

mandilion: A loose, thigh-length overcoat with a standing collar and loose sleeves. It was popular from 1520 to 1560 and again from 1577 to 1620. After 1620 it was called a Manderville and used only in livery.

Mary Stuart hood (1550–1630): Similar to a French hood but of sheer cloth such as lawn, trimmed with decorative fabric and edged with lace. The front border had a V- or U-shaped curve above the middle of the forehead. Widows frequently wore the style in black silk with a falling back section.

Monmouth cap: A knitted wool cap that fit the head and had a brim and a long peaked top that hung over one side and ended in a tassel. These were common from the 1570s to 1625, especially among soldiers and sailors.

nightcap: Any casual indoor headgear. It was not worn to bed.

nightclothes: Any informal morning or evening attire.

night rail: A garment in which some wealthy women slept by the mid-sixteenth century. Sleeping in the nude or in a shift, shirt or smock was more common.

pipkin (1565–1595): A taffeta hat trimmed with ostrich feathers and decorated with jewels. It had a moderate crown, a narrow, fairly flat brim, and was worn over a caul.

rebato (1580–1635): A collar wired to stand up around a low-necked bodice.

ruff (1550–1630): A circular collar of cambric or lawn in the form of a starched and crimped or pleated frill, the ruff or ruff-band came to England from France. From 1562 to 1577, ruffs measured about three inches wide and two inches deep. They were separate articles of clothing by 1570. The cartwheel ruff was in fashion from 1580 to 1610 and the fan-shaped ruff from 1570 to 1625. The latter was made almost entirely of lace. Men's ruffs were generally higher in back than in front, following the line of the jaw to frame the face and set off the shape of the skull. One from 1589 measures nine inches from neck to edge.

sack: A loose dress for country wear.

safeguard (1570–1630): An outer skirt worn for protection against weather and dirt during travel.

slop-hose: Sailor's breeches.

slops or galligaskins: Any wide, loose breeches.

tippit: A short, shoulder cape for women.

trunk hose, round hose or French hose (1540–1625): A style of breeches for men who wanted to show off their legs. Trunk hose consisted of a padded ring from the waist around the hips, to which long nether-stocks were sewn.

tunic: Belted tunics were worn by the working classes.

Venetians or knee breeches: Any breeches fastened at the knee and separate from the netherstocks. They might be distended with vertical rolls of padding down the inside of each side seam. The codpiece was not worn with Venetians, which buttoned or tied in a concealed front opening.

waistcoat (1485–1625): Optional male undergarment, usually quilted, to which the breeches were fastened. A woman's dressing jacket was also called a waistcoat.

wimple: Cloth covering the head, chin and shoulders. In the country a woman might wear a straw hat over a wimple.

FABRICS OF THE RENAISSANCE

Spinning, weaving and knitting were all practiced in England by the sixteenth century. An improved type of spinning wheel, the Saxony wheel, was introduced in the 1530s. Woolen cloth was produced at home but more exotic fabrics (including cotton) were imported. All those listed here were available by 1570.

Blends

bombazine: Variously described as a plain twilled fabric made of cotton and wool, as a silk and wool blend, and as a silk and cotton blend, bombazine was usually black but was available in colors by the end of the sixteenth century.

borato: A thin, light blend of silk and wool.

buffin: Used in doublets and other garments.

camlet or chamlet: Closely woven fabric of camel's hair and silk (or wool or cotton).

damask: Textile woven of silk and linen with light and shade effects. True damasks were silk but the term came to mean any fabric with an elaborate design woven into it.

fustian: Cotton and flax or flax mixed with wool, with a silky finish. Fustian was used as a substitute for velvet.

mocado or mockado or mock velvet: A deep-piled velvet with better grades made in silk and inferior grades in wool, silk and wool, or silk and linen.

Cotton
The word meant any cloth made from the cotton plant. Cotton was imported as a raw material from Smyrna and Cyprus.

Linen
Linen was any cloth made from flax.

beaupers: Linen cloth similar to bunting.

cambric: Fine linen.

canvas: Coarse linen cloth which, early in the sixteenth century, was imported from France.

dorneck: Linen made in Norfolk and used for servants' clothes.

dornicks: A checked table linen. Dornick was the Flemish name for the city of Tournai and dornicks originally applied to any fabrics manufactured there.

Holland: Any fine linen.

lawn or cobweb lawn: Any very fine, semitransparent linen cloth.

sammeron: It was "finer than flaxen and coarser than hempen."

Silk
Produced by silkworms, both silk thread and finished fabric were imported throughout the period. By 1599, looms were being used to knit silk stockings, waistcoats and other garments.

brocade: A rich silk cloth embroidered in gold and silver. Later, brocade meant any fabric with a raised, figured pattern.

caffa: A rich silk cloth similar to damask.

sarcenet: A fine, soft silk of taffeta weave.

satin: A glossy silk fabric with a smooth surface.

sussapine: A costly silk textile.

taffeta: A rich, thin silk used for doublets.

Wool

Woolens are any fabrics made from carded, short-staple sheep's wool and fulled (shrunk, then beaten or pressed). The New Draperies were worsted or semi-worsted fabrics made with combed, long-staple wool and not fulled. They were introduced to England from the Netherlands by Protestant refugees in the 1560s and included sackcloth, serge, frizado, bays (or baize) and says. Later "New Draperies" came to mean any novelty cloth.

broadcloth: A fine woolen cloth of plain weave, two yards wide, produced in England from the twelfth century on.

cotton cloth: A woolen cloth of which the nap has been "cottoned" or raised, such as baft and frieze. This was manufactured in the North, especially around Manchester.

lemister: A fine woolen used for knitting caps.

puke: An imported woolen cloth or any woolen textile dyed before weaving.

russet: Coarse reddish brown, gray or neutral color woolen homespun.

Other Fabrics

buckram: A coarse linen or cotton fabric used in hose and gowns.

calico: A cotton or cotton and linen fabric imported from the East and therefore costly. Calico later became the generic name for any cloth imported from the East. It was *not* the pattern we associate with the term today.

cloth of gold: Cloth woven with gold wire or flat strips of gold or both.

crape: A thin transparent silk, or silk and linen, used in mourning veils.

furs: Amice (gray squirrel), bauson (badger), beaver, cony (rabbit), ermine, fox, lettice (similar to ermine), lizard (lynx) and sable were all used in clothing.

kersey: A double-twilled say of wool or of silk and wool.

rash: A twilled textile of silk or wool.

tripe: Imitation velvet made of wool or thread.

velvet: Imported until the late seventeenth century and made of silk or cotton. Branched velvet was any figured velvet.

SELECT BIBLIOGRAPHY

Cunnington, C. Willett and Phillis. *Handbook of English Costume in the Seventeenth Century.* Boston: Plays, Inc., 1972.
————. *Handbook of English Costume in the Sixteenth Century.* Boston: Plays, Inc., 1970.
Lister, Margot. *Costumes of Everyday Life: An Illustrated History of Working Clothes from 900–1910.* Boston: Plays, Inc., 1972.
Yarwood, Doreen. *The Encyclopedia of World Costume.* New York: Bonanza Books, 1978.

CHAPTER TWO

FOOD AND DRINK

The staples of the Elizabethan diet were bread, beef and beer. Most people ate three meals a day, though their content varied greatly depending on the social status and wealth of the family.

Breakfast was a simple meal for all classes, and eaten early. Even Queen Elizabeth had only bread, ale, beer or wine and a good pottage made of mutton or beef. The children in the earl of Northumberland's household in 1512 got bread, beer, butter, saltfish (on fish days) or boiled mutton bones.

Dinner was the most substantial and most elaborate meal. It was served between 10 A.M. and 1 P.M. and could last three hours in a wealthy household. In the early seventeenth century the nobility, gentry and university students generally dined at eleven while merchants dined at noon.

Supper was a lighter meal than dinner. The nobility, gentry and students ate between 5 P.M. and 6 P.M., merchants between 7 P.M. and 8 P.M., after business hours.

ON THE MENU

Henry VIII and the eight hundred people who made up his court consumed 8,200 sheep, 2,330 deer, 2,870 pigs, 1,240 oxen, 24,000 larks and 33,000 chickens in one year. At the level of the gentry, the Petre family at Ingatestone Hall, Essex, with twenty servants, ate 55 oxen and calves, 2 cows, 133 sheep and lambs and 11 swine in 1548. On an ordinary day with no guests, the Petre household might consume a piece of beef, a loin of veal, two chickens and oranges in a sauce for dinner, and for supper, a shoulder of mutton, two rabbits, cold beef and cheese. The menus Sir William Cecil drew up for his household at Wimbledon in the 1550s indicate that they had boiled beef as part of almost every meal (except on fish days), as well as roast beef, mutton, pork, veal, capons, rabbits and wild fowl.

A "frugal" dinner to entertain a worthy friend might start with a shield of brawn with mustard. Brawn was meat from the forepart of a young, tame boar fed on oats and peas. It was eaten from November to February and as a special Christmas dish. Usually it had beer poured over it and was highly spiced. In addition there would be boiled capon, boiled beef, roasted beef, roast pig, baked chewits (any finely chopped meat), roast goose, swan, haunch of venison, venison pasty, kid with pudding in its belly, olive pie, custard and various side dishes to bring the total number of selections up to thirty-two.

A townsman tended to eat as much meat as he could afford, breakfasting on salted or pickled herring, cold meat, pottage, bread and ale; buying his midday meal at a cook shop or tavern (roast meats, meat pies and stews were available); and supping on cold meat, bread, cheese and ale.

In contrast, the diet of the average husbandman was comprised mainly of black bread and cheese. In addition he might eat eggs, leeks, parsnips, cabbage, peas, beans and parsley. He'd see little beef or mutton, although he might have bacon now and then and taste mutton or pork at public feasts.

TABLE SETTINGS AND MANNERS

At the finer tables, tablecloths and napkins were used and spoons were provided at each place. Guests brought their own knives. Forks existed in England but were not yet used as individual eating implements. That was considered a foreign affectation until nearly the end of the seventeenth century. Finger bowls were used for washing. Venetian glasses and silver tankards were available to the wealthy. Others used pewter mugs.

Early in the period, trencher bread was still in use. Four-day-old loaves made of wholemeal flour were cut into thick slices and used as plates to sop up the juice or gravy from the food. These trenchers were collected and given to the poor after the meal in wealthy households and eaten as part of the meal by the less well-to-do. For a time, wooden trenchers were slipped under the bread. Later the wooden plate (or pewter, silver or gold for those who could afford it) replaced the bread entirely.

Saltcellars held salt. The largest, or Great Salt, was placed in the middle of the dining table and used to indicate social standing. Those above the salt were the most important members of the household and honored guests. Servants and inferior persons sat below the salt. For further details on dining rooms, kitchens, their contents and protocol, see chapter three.

Drunkenness at meals was frowned upon but belching was acceptable, as was wearing hats to the table. Hats were taken off for toasts.

PRESERVATION OF FOOD

To preserve food for the winter, it was dry-salted and smoked in the kitchen, hanging from the rafters. It could also be pickled in brine. For short-term preservation, food received a light dry-salting. Meat could also be dipped in vinegar. Colorings added to food to make it more appealing included sandalwood (to turn it pink), mulberry juice and saffron.

HEALTH PROBLEMS AND DIET

Almost all the English suffered from malnutrition and from chronic vitamin C deficiency. What was then called "land scurvy" could be progressive, seasonally, over as many as thirty years. Lacey Baldwin Smith, in *Treason in Tudor England* (Princeton, New Jersey: Princeton University Press, 1986), suggests that scurvy may have been responsible for the paranoia, irritability and lack of control (all common symptoms) exhibited by many sixteenth-century Englishmen and for the sheer stupidity of some of the treason plots they hatched. For more information on scurvy, see page 84.

Ergotism, prevalent in areas where rye is grown, had not yet been diagnosed but it was certainly the cause of some miscarriages and of nervous disorders such as St. Anthony's Fire (an inflammation of the skin). It may also have been a factor in several localized outbreaks of witchcraft accusations. Witch trials in both Essex and Norfolk coincide with periods of time during which those areas were rye-growing centers. For more on this plausible theory, see Mary Kilbourne Matossian, *Poisons of the Past: Molds, Epidemics and History* (New Haven, Connecticut: Yale University Press, 1989).

FOODS

bread: Baking required a bread oven, which few but the largest houses had. There were communal ovens in rural locations, but in the towns and cities bread had to be bought from the baker. White (manchet) bread was rare outside of London. It was actually yellow in color, made from stone-ground wholemeal flour. "Cheat" was the next finest bread, containing more bran. Dark bread varied according to the grain available in the area. Maslin or "meslin" flour was half rye, half wheat. Bread entirely of rye was black and cheap. Oatmeal was used in the North. When any grain was scarce, then peas, beans and even acorns were ground together with what little grain there was to make flour. Brewis was a North Country breakfast dish consisting of slices of bread with fat broth poured over them.

butter: Butter came in firkins, wooden barrels which held fifty-six pounds. The poor used butter on their food. The rich used it primarily in cooking.

cheese: Hard cheese was made from skimmed milk. It kept well and was a staple among the poor. Soft (cream) cheese was made from whole milk and allowed to age before it was used in cooking. Green or nettle cheese was fresh curd cheese, not fully pressed. It stood upon a bed of nettles to drain. Spermese was green cheese to which herbs had been added. Junket was a curdled dish made of cream and rennet and set out to dry in small baskets made of rush.

fish: Fish days were Wednesdays, Fridays, Saturdays and every day in Lent. Wednesdays were dropped after the Reformation but restored in 1563 in an effort to support the fishing fleet. Noncompliance was so widespread, however, that efforts to enforce the 1563 law and assess fines were abandoned around 1585. Eels, lampreys and shellfish

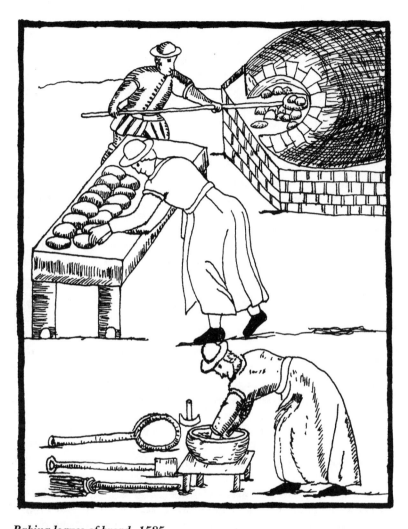

Baking loaves of bread, 1585
Based on a scene from T. F.'s A Book of Divers Devices, *this sketch shows a community oven typical of those found on manors and in small villages.*

(oysters, whelks, cockles, shrimps and crabs) were cheap and plentiful along the seacoast and up river estuaries. Salt and dried fish (especially cod, which was called stockfish) and smoked North Sea herring (sprats) were sold at inland markets. Ling was a large (three to four feet long) cod-like fish. Sturgeon, whiting, roach, dab, thornback, perch, gudgeon, turbot, pike, dolphin (rare, but three were taken in the Thames in 1552), porpoise (young porpoise cost eight shillings in 1509), smelt, salmon (found in the Thames), mackerel, bream, skate, flounder and hake were all eaten in Tudor and Stuart times.

fowl: Wildfowl included pheasant, partridge, plover, pigeon, heron, bustard, titmouse, wren, lark, quail (imported from Flanders), curlew, crane, stork, bittern, shoveller, moorcock, moorhen, woodcock, duck, goose, swan and peacock. Chickens were plentiful. Pigeon pie was a frequent summer dish. Doves were raised in dovecotes for food. The first turkeys were brought to England from Mexico in 1520 but they were still rare in the late sixteenth century.

fruits: By 1549, England grew more fruits than France. Native apples and pears grew in orchards along with quinces, peaches and medlars. For more information on orchards see page 46. Crab apples were used for jelly and verjuice. Verjuice, the juice of any green, unripe fruit (most often grapes) was used for cooking rather than drinking. Strawberries, blackberries and sloes grew wild. England had vineyards in medieval times, but with the closing of the monasteries in the 1530s, the skill to tend the vines was lost. Grapes were still found in the gardens of big houses and many meals were begun with grapes and cherries. By the sixteenth century, every large household had stores of dried dates, figs, prunes and raisins. Currants and oranges were also imported. Orange "season" was autumn, when ships arrived from Spain. Fresh lemons were a luxury. The banana was an oddity in 1633, displayed in a shop window. Pineapples, of which there is mention as early as 1514, were still curiosities in 1640.

herbs: The term herbs included all green things, and thus all vegetables, a word that was not yet in general use. Most of the vegetables we eat today were then considered fit only for the poor. After all, they came out of the ground! In 1542 the only vegetables considered important enough to grace a gentleman's table were rape, onions (originally imported from the Low Countries in about 1420), garlic and leeks. By the latter part of the sixteenth century, there was general growing of melons, pompions (a term used for pumpkins), gourds, cucumbers, radishes, skirrets (a kind of parsnip), carrots, cabbage and white beets. The potato was the sweet potato. The white potato was called the Potato of America and was not a field crop until the eighteenth century. The yam was known as "skirrets of Peru." Turnips came from Caen and were not cultivated in England until the seventeenth century; they were eaten boiled or roasted. Parsnips and carrots were boiled. Artichokes were eaten raw with pepper and salt.

meats: Beef, mutton, pork, rabbit and venison were probably the most frequently served meats. Hugh Platt's recipe for Polonian "sawsedge" (c. 1600) indicates nothing was wasted: "take the fillers of a hog; chop them very small with a handful of Red Sage: season it hot with ginger and pepper, and then put it into a great sheep's gut; then let it lie three nights in brine: then boil it and hang it up in a chimney where fire is usually kept; and these sawsedges will last a whole yeere. They are good for sallades or to garnish boiled meats, or to make one rellish a cup of wine."

pottage: Pottage meant anything from a soup of roots boiled in water to a thick meat stew to oatmeal porridge. The latter was also called frumenty in Dorset, flamery or flummery in Lancashire and Cheshire, and wash-brew in the West Country.

salads: Boiled "sallets" might use leeks, borage, bugloss leaves, hop buds, endive, chicory, cauliflower, sorrel, marigold leaves, watercress, onions, garlic, turnips, rocket, tarragon, radishes, succory, dandelion leaves, beet leaves and roots, spinach, dock leaves, purslane, rampion root, water pimpernel, asparagus and samphire (a type of seaweed gathered off the Norfolk coast). Green salads were just coming into fashion in the late sixteenth century. Lettuce was recommended as a starter to stir appetite and, after supper, to counteract the drunkenness caused by imbibing too much wine. Both "lettuce of the garden" and wild lettuce were available. Chives were not eaten in salads.

seasonings and sweeteners: In addition to herbs, seasonings included mustard imported from Dijon and olives and capers, which were used to flavor mutton and beef. Honey was a native sweetener. Sugar was new in the sixteenth century. Hard and coarse, it came in ten-pound loaves (eight pence per pound in 1546) or packed in chests.

sweets: "Candy" included all comfits (any sweet containing a nut or seed and preserved with sugar) and suckets (fruit preserved in sugar). Marchpane, made with blanched almonds and sugar, was a popular dessert. Florentines (kidney, herbs, currants, sugar, cinnamon, eggs, cream and crumbs) were baked in special pastry and served in deep pewter dishes. Gingerbread was popular, as well as all kinds of puff pastry. Sugar-sops was made from bread, sugar and spices. Green ginger was a sweetmeat in syrup. Succade was an orange conserve. Dry marmalade was a fairly new confection, a quince conserve from Portugal which came packed in boxes. Apple pies were a traditional part of harvest fare and mince pies were served at Christmas. Also popular for dessert were boiled and suet puddings, egg custards and all kinds of tarts and cakes. Cardinal Thomas Wolsey (d. 1530), who was also archbishop of York, is credited with making strawberries and cream popular in Henry VIII's time. Ice cream was known in Italy from the thirteenth century and introduced to France by Catherine de' Medici, but in England it remained a rarity. Charles I is said to have given his cook a yearly stipend of twenty pounds to keep the recipe for "iced cream" a secret.

white meats: This was the contemporary name for dairy products, including milk, cream, butter, curds, whey, cheese and eggs. All were looked down upon as inferior foods, to be eaten only by the poor.

odds and ends: Rice was known, but rare, since it had to be imported from Italy and was very expensive. At the other extreme, anyone could gather field mushrooms and nuts. Filberts and walnuts were particularly popular.

ALEHOUSES

A 1577 survey of thirty counties counted 17,595 drinking houses. Hertfordshire alone had 125 inns, 14 taverns and 333 alehouses. Inns (12 percent of the 17,595) were the most respectable establishments, offering lodging and food as well as drink. The majority of inns sold wine and brewed their own ale and beer. Taverns (2 percent) were drinking houses which did not offer lodgings, but they might still be sizable establishments. The set meal provided by London taverns (which were not included in this survey) consisted of a hot meat dish, bread, cheese and ale. Alehouses were also called tippling houses. Up until 1750, the word "tippler" referred to an alehouse keeper. Alehouses had to be licensed by the local justice of the peace until 1618. After that a patent was granted for a monopoly on alehouse licenses. Alehouses accounted for 86 percent of the survey, but many small, unlicensed alehouses were also in operation. In Lancashire in the early seventeenth century the village of Prescot had one alehouse to every twenty inhabitants.

Drinks available at an alehouse varied by region but might include cider, perry, mead, aqua vitae, ale and beer. After 1553, wine could not be sold in alehouses. By the early Stuart period, beer was more popular than ale and after 1700 all alehouses were actually beer houses.

Drinkables were stored in casks. A kilderkin held 18 gallons of beer and a hogshead held 54. There were two hogsheads in a butt (also called a pipe or a piece) and two butts in a tun, which held 252 wine-gallons. A puncheon held 84 gallons. A tierce was one-third of a pipe.

DRINKS

ale: Brewed from malt infused in water with the addition of spices (but not hops), or from barley mash, yeast and water, ale was the common breakfast drink of all classes. A heavy, thick drink, it did not keep well. It was usually served when five days old.

aqua vitae: This was whiskey and was used more as medicine than as drink. In Scotland in 1505, barber-surgeons were granted the sole right to manufacture and sell aqua vitae.

beer: Produced by the addition of hops to fermented malt and water, beer was introduced into England as early as 1420 but was still regarded with suspicion as a "foreign" and adulterated drink until the mid-sixteenth century. The English called hops the "wicked weed." Beer made from barley eventually caught on all over England, however, both because it kept better than ale (the hops had a preservative effect) and because it was cheaper to make. It was generally served between eight days and one month after it was brewed. Royalty drank beer aged for one to two years. In 1608–10, when William Cecil, Lord Cranborne, was on his Grand Tour of Europe, he traveled with his own brewer because by then the English did not believe they could find good beer abroad. Small or single beer was made by pouring water over the wort in the vat after the "strong" or double beer was drawn off. Double beer could also refer to beer made with twice the quantity of hops to the normal amount of liquid. March beer was another stronger brew.

chocolate: Introduced earlier than coffee or tea, chocolate was drunk in Spain from about 1600. No chocolate at all was imported into England until the middle of the sixteenth century and that was solid chocolate. Chocolate as a drink appeared in England in the late seventeenth century but as it was extremely expensive only the wealthy could afford it.

cider: Made from apples, cider was a popular country drink.

coffee: Not available in England, although the drink had been sampled in Europe. The first coffeehouse in England opened in 1650 in Oxford.

metheglin: Spiced or medicated mead (mead was made from fermented honey), this drink was popular in Wales. Plain mead was more widely consumed.

milk: Considered suited only for children and the aged, milk was blamed for sore eyes, headaches, agues and rheums. If milk was required, asses' milk was preferred. For the aged, milk was heated and mixed with fruit or spices to make a posset. Most milk went into making cheese.

perry: This was made from pears and drunk by country people.

spiced beer: This was beer seasoned with cinnamon, resin, gentian and juniper.

swish-wash: This was made with honey and water with a dash of pepper or other spices.

tea: Not available in England, although the Dutch East India Company introduced it to London at the end of the period. In 1657 tea sold for sixteen shillings per pound in coffeehouses.

water: Water was drunk at risk because of the pollution.

whey: The watery part of milk which remains after the formation of curds during the cheesemaking process, whey was the drink of poor country people who could not afford better; buttermilk was another.

wine: Wines were poured from the barrel into jugs to serve at the table. They were not aged. The term "bastard" in regard to wine meant sweet and spiced and could refer to any wine sweetened with honey, sugar or spices. Other sweet wines were Osney (from Alsace), Compolet, Romney (from Hungary), Malmsey (from Crete), Vernage or Verney (a white wine from Italy) and Mount Rose (a red wine from Gascony). King James I drank sweet Greek wines. Clary was a kind of claret, mixed with clarified honey, pepper and ginger. Both red and white claret were imported. From Bordeaux came Gascoigne, Anguelle, Rochelle and Galloway wines. Rhenish wines included Brabant, to which honey and cloves were added. Piment was a sour, thin wine sweetened with honey. Sack began to be popular early in the sixteenth century and by the seventeenth was the most popular of all wine drinks. The best came from Xeres, which the English mispronounced as sherry. "Sherry sack" made in Bristol was also known as "Bristol milk." Hippocras was red wine spiced with ginger, pepper and "grains of paradise." Raspes was a raspberry wine.

SELECT BIBLIOGRAPHY

Clark, Peter. *The English Alehouse: A Social History 1200–1830.* London and New York: Longman, 1983.

Drummond, J.C. and Anne Wilbraham. *The Englishman's Food: A History of Five Centuries of English Diet.* London: Jonathan Cape, 1939.

Emmison, F.G. *Tudor Food and Pastimes: Life at Ingatestone Hall.* London: E. Benn, 1964.

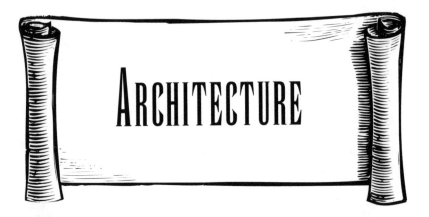

CHAPTER THREE

ARCHITECTURE

Some claim that the introduction of gunpowder to Europe led to the decline of the castle. By the mid-fifteenth century this was a moot point. People wanted not only comfort but luxury in their homes. Large country houses might be built with the same floor plan as castles and have moats and towers that at first glance made them appear to be fortified, but they were no longer constructed with the idea that they would have to hold off a siege.

The quadrangular castle, which evolved in the second half of the fourteenth century, integrated both military and residential needs. Bolton-in-Wensleydale, built in 1379, included accommodations for eight households and had twelve single-chamber apartments for individuals such as the priest. At Tattershall in Lincolnshire, completed in 1448, the house was shaped like a traditional keep but it had large windows and was built of red brick.

MANOR HOUSES AND MANSIONS

The typical medieval manor house had a two-story hall at center and a smaller room at each end. The first floor over the ground floor was reached by a ladder or staircase. Throughout the sixteenth century this arrangement continued as the basic floor plan for all houses. The room at one end usually developed into a kitchen and that at the other into a parlor or a cellar.

Sir William Cecil's house at Wimbledon (ten miles southwest of London) in the late 1550s contained a hall, parlor and two smaller rooms on the ground floor, together with a kitchen, pantry, larder, buttery and two dairy rooms. The upstairs consisted of a gallery and ten chambers. Among the outbuildings were a brew house, a bake house, a barn and a stable with stalls for fourteen horses and two sleeping rooms above for the grooms.

Brick and terra-cotta houses were built in the early 1520s by a number of Henry VIII's courtiers. Examples of early Tudor manor houses are Barrington Court, Somerset, and Compton Wynyates, Warwickshire. Stanstead Hall in Halstead, Essex, was rebuilt by 1553 into a two-story brick "courtyard house" (one built around a central courtyard). It boasted the latest in architectural fashion: octagonal chimney stacks, ogee-topped corner turrets and a brick-lined moat over 180 feet square.

The dissolution of the monasteries, Henry VIII's seizure of lands and buildings which had previously belonged to the Roman Catholic church, led to a building boom in the 1540s. Many of those who acquired former religious houses either remodeled them or used the stone from their walls to build new residences. William Sharington purchased Lacock Abbey in Wiltshire for less than a thousand pounds in 1540 and spent the next ten years rebuilding it. The duke of Somerset's London house (built 1547–1552) was constructed from material taken from forfeited ecclesiastical buildings in the city. The new Somerset House occupied a site (six hundred feet of river frontage) formerly taken up by three episcopal residences.

Between 1570 and 1640, rebuilding and new building were widespread among all social classes save the poorest and in all counties but the four most northerly. Thousands of farm and manor houses were modernized. Ceilings were put in two-story halls to create another chamber above. New staircases gave access to upper apartments, replacing loft ladders and the cramped stairs built into the thickness of the wall in some medieval houses. Chimneys proliferated, as did the use of glass in windows.

THE ITALIAN INFLUENCE ON ENGLISH ARCHITECTURE

An early attempt to learn about classic architecture was made in 1550 when the duke of Northumberland sent one John Shute to Italy to study the subject. Most building in England in the sixteenth century, however, was what has been called "artisan mannerism" and it was the result of workmen with a slight grasp of Flemish building styles adding on to existing English designs. Inigo Jones, in the reign of King James I, was the first to try to integrate into a building the classical principles of balance and proportion. One of his greatest accomplishments was the renovation of Somerset House into a palace for James's queen. Completed in 1612 and renamed Denmark House, it was demolished in 1776.

BUILDING MATERIALS

Building materials varied from one region to another. Most houses in the Southeast and West were timber-framed, but few houses were constructed entirely of wood. Boards were expensive (imported from the Baltic) and reserved for siding and wainscoting the interior walls. The majority of half-timbered buildings had a steep, thatched roof and upper stories which projected over the ones below.

In Kent and Essex and in London, Southampton and Hull some builders used bricks arranged in a herringbone pattern and tile instead of thatch for the roof, but this was fairly rare. Bricks simply cost too much until the second half of the seventeenth century. The brickmaking season was short, lasting only during the warm months. Bricks were made in clamps (burned in stacks in the open) rather than in kilns. Tilemaking, which did use kilns, was also seasonal.

In the west, wattle and daub was whitewashed and timbers were coated with tar to create a black-and-white effect. Wattle and daub was fill made of earth, sand, straw and sticks or reeds. The light wooden wattle core was covered with daub or plaster, instead of with wood.

Stone had always been used for castles, monasteries and churches, and stone-built and stone-roofed houses proliferated along the belt of limestone that runs from Dorset to the North Riding. Clay houses were built in Devonshire, Buckinghamshire, Northamptonshire, Leicestershire and Warwickshire. Flint was used for building in East Anglia.

Those who could afford to had building materials brought to their sites. Fine white stone came from Caen, but the freight costs were higher than the cost of the stone. Blue slates came from Plymouth. Black paving stone came from the Isle of Purbeck and also from quarries near Berwick, from which it was shipped already squared and polished. When Hatfield House was built early in the seventeenth century, fine white marble from the Carrara quarries in Italy was imported for the fireplaces.

ROYAL RESIDENCES

In 1526, King Henry VIII's properties were designated as either "greater houses," capable of accommodating the entire winter court of some eight hundred people, or "lesser houses," big enough for the traditionally smaller summer court of four hundred to five hundred. They did not require that many rooms, but even with dormitory-style quarters a great deal of space was needed for beds. The greater houses included Westminster Palace, Greenwich, Eltham, Richmond, New Hall in Essex and Woodstock in Oxfordshire. There were fifty or so smaller manor houses on the "lesser" list. Henry VIII also acquired Whitehall and Hampton Court (from Cardinal Wolsey) and built one new palace, Nonsuch, in 1538. Nonsuch was demolished in 1682 for building materials.

PRODIGY HOUSES

Prodigy houses, built with a royal visit in mind, kept grand apartments intended for use only by the monarch, who might never pay a visit at all. They were generally built according to one of two plans. The old-fashioned courtyard house continued to be built well into the seventeenth century. Theobalds, Holdenby and Audley End follow this plan. The alternative was to do without courtyards, creating one massive, compact house. Hatfield is one of these.

Theobalds, in Hertfordshire, built by Lord Burghley between 1564 and 1585, had five courtyards and a gallery that was 123 feet long and 21 feet wide. Queen Elizabeth visited there regularly. In 1607 King James persuaded Burghley's son, Robert Cecil, earl of Salisbury, to exchange Theobalds for the old palace at Hatfield. Salisbury kept that building for extra lodgings and constructed his Hatfield, another great prodigy house, right next to it.

SPECIALIZED ROOMS

banqueting house: A separate building used for banquets, which at this time usually meant not a great feast but rather a sort of dessert party. Size varied greatly, from very small to one, at Holdenby, which was three stories high and had six rooms to a floor.

bedchamber: References to bedchambers became common in the mid-sixteenth century, indicating that there were now rooms used mainly for sleeping. In most houses this inner room was accessible only by going through other rooms. In royal residences one entered the presence chamber and passed through the privy chamber to reach the bedchamber. Locks, incidentally, were not fastened to doors but rather screwed on when needed. One could also use padlocks, which went through a hasp, or bar the door.

cellar: The cellar was a storage room and was not necessarily underground. It was usually a wine cellar, but plate (utensils for table and domestic use, often of silver or gold) and other valuables might also be kept there.

closet: A room used for private study and business and sometimes for prayer. In some houses the closet (also called a study) was constructed as a gallery on the second level of a chapel so that the family could attend services without going downstairs. In some houses this room functioned as a library.

gallery: The gallery as a place to take exercise was a development of the sixteenth century. Originally any covered walk, sometimes open on one side and sometimes enclosed completely, it was usually constructed adjacent or close to the great chamber, or sometimes on the next floor. As collecting portraits became fashionable, the gallery was used to display them. In 1601, Lord Petre's gallery at Ingatestone in Essex contained six pictures, nine painted shields, and a few chairs and stools. There generally was not much furniture.

great chamber: The late sixteenth and early seventeenth centuries were the period when the great chamber became the center of the house. Early on, the chamber was a bed-sitting room used for sleeping, playing games, receiving visitors and taking meals. Around 1500, changes began. In smaller houses the great chamber was the principal lodging chamber. The owner ate in the hall or in the parlor. In larger houses the high table had been moved from the hall to the great chamber but there was still a bed there, too. In the grandest houses, the great chamber was used only for eating. This eventually became its chief function and by 1600 it was sometimes called the dining chamber. The great chamber might also be used for playing cards, dice and backgammon; for music, dancing, putting on plays and masques; for the lying-in-state of corpses before funerals; and for family prayers in houses that did not have a chapel.

great hall: The old "great hall" was a communal gathering place and had an open hearth at the center. The smoke from the fire was supposed to escape through a hole in the roof above. At the upper end of the hall was a dais, a raised platform for the table where the family and principal guests dined. A bay or oriel window to one side provided light. In other rooms there was at first no heat, but by the fourteenth century fireplaces were becoming common. Wall chimneys eventually spread into the hall. As the sixteenth century advanced, the hall had less importance and would eventually become little more than the entrance the word implies today.

In the oldest arrangements, one door behind the dais led to the cellar and another to stairs which went up to the great chamber above, which was also called the solar. At the lower end of the hall were "the screens" which formed a sort of inner porch with doors through which servants could enter with food. Screen meant not the small, fragile, easily moved piece of our day but a solid partition attached to the ceiling. The screen end of the hall often had a minstrel gallery above. In addition to shielding those in the hall from drafts from an entrance (often covered with a porch), screens separated the hall from the buttery (from which a butler served drinks) and pantry (originally "bread room" but by now the room from which food was served) and the passage between them which led to the kitchen.

As the century advanced, some halls were ceiled over to insert a first floor above. The earliest conversion that can be dated was at Hookwood Manor in Surrey in 1571, but this practice became increasingly common. In some cases, open halls ceased to be built in new buildings at all, and where a through passage had once been, there was now a central chimney stack that heated two back-to-back rooms. Beyond the chimney stack was a staircase, and these became grander and grander.

In the poorest houses, the hall continued to be the only room and, as in medieval times, it served all purposes, from cooking to sleeping to, on occasion, sheltering the family's animals.

kitchen: This room was sometimes in a separate building because of fire danger. It tended to be huge, with vaulted ceilings and several arches that held the hearths. Kitchens also contained a brick oven for baking, a large working table, and a variety of equipment including spits, pots, chafing dishes, graters, mortars and pestles, boilers, knives, cleavers, axes, dripping pans, pot racks, pothooks, gridirons, frying pans, sieves, kneading troughs, fire shovels, barrels and tubs. In some cases a scullery, where platters and pots were washed, was attached to the kitchen. If so, sinks usually emptied into a ditch beyond the outer wall, as did any washbasins set into the walls. Sometimes dirty water was carried off through pipes to be discharged out of a gargoyle's mouth on the exterior wall.

lodgings: Private accommodations, whether a suite of six or seven rooms or a single chamber, were called lodgings. At a great house, the steward (and one or two other household officers) might have a chamber of his own. Other gentlemen servants would share a room while the lowest orders had dormitory chambers. A few servants slept outside their master's chamber on woven straw mats called pallets. In a suite of rooms, like a hotel suite, there was considerable privacy. Personal servants might literally be underfoot, but others were kept out. Private family lodgings might also contain a closet, an inner chamber, an outer chamber, a wardrobe and at least one privy, in addition to the principal chamber.

parlor: A bed-sitting room early in the sixteenth century, after about 1550 it became only an eating and reception room. It was usually on the ground floor, behind the dais end of the hall and under the great chamber, unless the great chamber was over the hall. Large houses might have more than one parlor, and a small winter parlor near the kitchen, used in winter when a small room was easier to keep warm, was common from the early seventeenth century.

privy: Inside a house, this was usually a small, windowless cell set in an outside wall in which a pierced seat was placed over a shaft connected to a pit or drain, or to the slope outside the building. Some houses had "stool houses" or "houses of office," equipped with a close-stool and pewter pan instead. Lord Lisle's bedchamber in Calais had an adjoining room in which there was a "round curtain of green" and "a close-stool for a Jaques."

The French word garderobe, which means wardrobe, was used for the privy in the same way that cloak room is used for toilet today. Other euphemisms were "seat house" and "jakes." On the first floor of the Bell Tower at the Tower of London, a passageway opposite the door to a vaulted chamber with a fireplace and three narrow windows leads to three latrines set in high niches overhanging the moat. At Greenwich, garderobes were provided en suite in most of the principal lodgings but there were also "pissing places" in the courtyards. At Hampton Court there was a common latrine which seated twenty-eight. Privacy was not a high priority.

The royal privy chamber probably started out as the room between the privy and the great chamber but by this era had evolved into the room where the monarch took meals and held private meetings.

withdrawing rooms: As large rooms were broken up into smaller ones for greater privacy, the great chamber often led into an adjoining withdrawing chamber with a bedchamber beyond. In the sixteenth century withdrawing chambers took over the functions of a private sitting, eating and reception area. Servants still slept in them, at least until the end of the century. In some houses the inner chamber off the lord's chamber belonged to his wife. The wife's chamber might have a chamber for her gentlewomen off or close to it. The wardrobe might also be a separate room off the chamber and, if so, it usually had its own fireplace.

ORNAMENTAL GARDENS

Gardens laid out at Hampton Court by Cardinal Wolsey in figured flower beds started a national style which later borrowed heavily from Italian gardens. One aim was to have as much color as possible all year long. Another was to make the garden an extension of the house. The four-plot design applied to both the garden and its relationship to the

Diagram of a small country estate, 1618
This sketch is based on a plan by William Lawson in A New Orchard and Garden. *The goal of such designs was to make the garden an extension of the house. The various symbols shown here indicate (moving clockwise from the top) the location of the courtyard, knot garden, orchard, kitchen garden, maze and raised flower beds.*

house. The house was the center with a forecourt in front, a kitchen garden on one side and an orchard on the other. At the back (faced by the chief rooms of the house) was the garden.

The first English gardening book, Thomas Hill's *Profitable Arte of Gardeninge*, came out in 1563 and discussed walks, mazes and arbors. By the 1580s, a formal garden was part of almost every new house of any size. Pleasure gardens were usually enclosed, often by a high, clipped hedge of cypress, hornbeam or juniper. Windows and arches were sometimes cut through the hedge, and sweetbriar, whitethorn, privet and roses might be interlaced along the hedge. A square or circle was at the center of the garden, containing a statue, obelisk, fountain, mount (an artificial hill of earth surmounted by steps or a winding path—from the top one could see out of the garden) or sundial. A garden might contain:

- Flower beds—open beds raised above the level of the paths and surrounded by wooden fences. Closed or knotted beds were outlined with low, close-growing plants like hyssop and germander and formed elaborate designs. The open spaces in the patterns might contain daffodils, primroses or hyacinths.
- Mazes—hedge mazes were low, even those of evergreen rarely reaching a man's height, and if they were made of hyssop, lavender cotton, thyme, germander or winter savory they were "dwarf" mazes.
- Small turfed areas—these might contain seats (which might also be found in recesses of wall or hedge or under an arbor), carved wooden figures or works of topiary. Heraldic designs were popular, worked into both topiary (generally done with yew or privet) and knot beds.
- Pleached bowers—formed of trees which branched overhead and entwined, such as willow, lime, wych-elm, hornbeam, privet, whitethorn and maple. They were planted with sweetbriars, honeysuckles, roses and rosemary and made into "covert" walks.
- Arbors—built along the enclosure wall with climbers of rosemary, jasmine or musk roses on wooden latticework. Some had windows.
- Walks—wide and sometimes bordered by brick or stone, walks were rarely turfed but might be sanded, graveled or planted with herbs such as burnet, wild thyme or water mint, which gave off an aroma when trod upon.
- Paths—narrower than walks, paths went between beds. They were sanded (often mixed with pebbles and coal dust, which killed weeds) and bordered by low-growing hedges of lavender, box, rosemary, sage or lavender cotton.
- Other additions—streams (dells) and trout brooks and bridges might be put in if there was space. Wooden galleries might pass through to connect the house with the chapel or some other building. Flights of steps might connect several levels of terraces with garden walks and the garden levels with each other.

ORCHARDS

Orchards were fenced in with brick or stone or with a low hedge of cornelian cherry trees and rose, gooseberry and currant bushes. Inside one might find apricots, peaches nectarines, plums, quinces, damsons, bullaces, cherries, apples, pears, filberts, cornelian cherries and medlars. Orchards were rare outside of Worcestershire, Shropshire, Gloucestershire, Somersetshire, Kent and Essex. Apricots, peaches and quinces did not grow well in Yorkshire or farther north.

NATIVE AND NEW: FLOWERS AND FRUITS

In and around London were a number of botanical gardens in which far more varieties of flowers, trees and other plants grew than were generally available in England. The herbalist John Gerarde (1545–1612) published a catalog of his garden in Holborn in 1597. It contained woodcuts of some 1,800 plants.

Native English flowers included primroses, marigolds, daisies, violets, columbine, roses and gilliflowers (stock gilliflowers were stocks, wall gilliflowers were wallflowers, queen's gilliflowers were hesperis or sweet rocket and clove gilliflowers were carnations and pinks). Also very common were sweet williams, sweet johns, bachelor's buttons, snapdragons, poppies, star-of-Bethlehem, star-of-Jerusalem, eglantine, hollyhocks, lilies, valerian, columbine, carnations and geraniums (not, however, the kind we have today; these were spotted or striped and other names for them were stork's bill and crane's bill).

New flowers imported into England and present in some gardens by 1640 included daffodils, fritillary, hyacinth, crocus (saffron flower), tulip (from Armenia; tulips grew in Holland as early as 1560 but did not reach England until 1600), flower-de-luce (all irises came from Spain), anemone, French cowslip (bear's ear), candytufts, Persian lilacs, sunflowers (from Peru), crown imperial, everlastings, Persian marigolds and tobacco. There was considerable variety in roses, including the damask rose (introduced into English gardens around 1520), musk rose, canker or dog rose, rose of Provence, rose of York and Lancaster, crystal rose, dwarf red rose, Frankfort rose, Hungarian rose, velvet rose, cinnamon rose and apple rose.

Apple trees were native and varieties included Davy gentle, Master William, summer and russet pippins, pomewater, flower of Kent, gillyflower, Kentish codling ("a flat, insipid apple"), pound royal, leather-coat, and spicing. Hertfordshire apples were used to make "redstreak" cider. Other native fruits were crab apples, strawberries and pears. Varieties of the latter included the poperin, the warden or stewing pear, saffron, bon cretien, Windsor and bergamot. Worcestershire was famed for pears, Kent for cherries. Peach trees had come to England with the Romans. There were also vineyards but these were disappearing in this period. Lemon trees were imported as early as 1562, when they cost fifteen crowns apiece. Orange, pomegranate and myrtle were also early imports, and apricots, almonds, gooseberries, raspberries, melons and currants first appeared in English gardens in Tudor times.

SELECT BIBLIOGRAPHY

Girouard, Mark. *Life in the English Country House: A Social and Architectural History*. New York: Penguin Books, 1980.

Howard, Maurice. *The Early Tudor Country House: Architecture and Politics 1490–1550*. London: George Philip, 1987.

Platt, Colin. *Medieval England: A Social History and Archaeology from the Conquest to 1600 A.D.* New York: Scribner, 1978.

Reed, Michael. *The Age of Exuberance, 1550–1700*. Boston: Routledge and Kegan Paul, 1986.

Williams, Neville. *The Royal Residences of Great Britain*. New York: The Macmillan Company, 1960.

CHAPTER FOUR

FURNISHING A HOUSE

T he inventories regularly taken at householders' deaths have left a record of furnishings at all levels of society. One of the most complete is of Petworth House at the time of the death of the ninth earl of Northumberland in 1632. All references to furniture at Petworth are from that list, which is printed in its entirety in G.R. Batho, ed., *The Household Papers of Henry Percy, Ninth Earl of Northumberland (1564–1632)* (London: Royal Historical Society, 1962).

An inventory taken in 1584 of the possessions of a Worcester barber listed six tablecloths, five pairs of sheets, brass pots, a frying pan, a framed table, joined stools, a feather bed, carpets, cushions, a pewter chamber pot, eight pewter flowerpots and a lute. Other records of furnishings also survive, indicating that in a typical hall one might find bankers (bench covers), dorsers (drapes for benches), cushions, a dining board and trestles, an "iron fireplace with tongs," basins, washbowls, candelabra, side tables, a chair, benches, a cupboard, candles and oil lamps.

Lady Lisle, in 1540, had in her bedroom a Flanders chair, a cupboard with a piece of tapestry as a cover, four red carpets worked with blue crewel, two old Turkey carpets and two cushions, one of embroidered Bruges satin and the other of cloth-of-gold. Bess of Hardwick, the wealthiest woman in Elizabethan England after the queen, decorated her bedroom with a bed hung with black velvet with gold fringe, curtains of black damask trimmed with gold lace, and chairs of crimson velvet. Even a musician, in 1603, had hangings of green say, a type of wool, on his plain corded bedstead, as well as window curtains, a trestle table and "a staff to beat the bed with."

ITEMS OF FURNITURE

beds: The boarded bed was a shallow wooden box standing on four short legs. It had a straw mattress and might have a narrow shelf for a candle. The flock bed, with a stack of chaff for the head, was considered a step up. "Stump" bedsteads had no valances or side curtains. A new type of bed introduced in the early sixteenth century replaced the boards supporting the mattress or feather bed with rope mesh. A mattress might also rest on interwoven strips of leather. There were no bed springs. Heavy foot posts (to match the tall head posts) were also added at this time and the tester was no longer suspended from the ceiling but rather rested on the four posts, all of which were elaborately carved. Cardinal Wolsey had a bed with eight mattresses, each stuffed with thirteen pounds of carded wool. The beds were made up with sheets, blankets of fustian or wool, and coverlets. Down pillows replaced bolsters in wealthy homes.

When Lord Lisle was arrested for treason in 1540, an inventory of his bedding revealed fourteen pairs of blankets and eighteen feather beds. He and his wife slept in field beds (portable folding bedsteads) but they managed a four-poster effect by adding a tester and ceiler of blue satin and tawny velvet and bed-curtains of blue and tawny sarcenet. One 1568 bed had a headboard of carved limewood panels and posts of French walnut. At Petworth, feather beds were numerous, as were down pillows. Along with the fine linens, however, those taking the inventory also found an "old Holland quilt" and two old taffeta quilts "not fit for use."

Small beds, usually used by servants, included the trestle bed, the truckle bed, which ran on truckles (solid wheels), and the straw pallet. The poorest folk had only a rough mat with a sheet and coverlets of dagswain or hop-harlot. The poor man's pillow might well be a log.

benches: High-backed benches were in use and so were benches set into window alcoves. Chests and trunks also doubled as benches.

chairs: Reserved for the head of the household, chairs were generally heavy and uncomfortable, even when the wooden seats were covered with cloth. Early designs included the Erasmus chair, the X-shaped or Glastonbury chair, the bobbin-frame chair and the box-chair, which at first was plain but later was carved and ornamented and eventually evolved into the armchair. The carved oak chair of about 1615 had arms and a high back. Upholstered and leather chairs were not unheard of before 1600 but were rare. Upholstery became common only after about 1640. The farthingale chair (c. 1610) was cushioned, usually in velvet or "turkey work." Matching sets of chairs began to be made in the seventeenth century, fashioned of walnut with velvet backs and padded seats. At Petworth there were numerous "elbow chairs."

chests (also called coffers): Chests were often made of cedar and were used both to store things and as seats. Coffers listed in a 1551 inventory held eight pairs of sheets, three tablecloths, one towel and miscellaneous clothing.

chimneys: This was the name used for movable firebacks and grates, much in use before the stationary fireplace became common. Chimneys were included as furnishings in inventories and wills early in the period.

couches: Along with the settle (a long bench with arms, a back and a storage box under the seat), the couch first appeared in England during the reign of Charles I.

cupboards: One type was a flat-topped stand with a shelf and a top covered by a cloth, on which plate (household articles covered with precious metal) was displayed. Another type was a dresser with a carved back and a canopy of wood, a flat top for the display of plate, and a lower half enclosed by doors, below which might be another shelf for the display of ewers and jugs. A food cupboard or hutch was usually enclosed, the doors perforated to let air in. A buffet had three tiers on each of which plate or food was displayed. The "court cupboard" was rarely seen before 1550. Bedroom cupboards held toilet articles, including a basin and ewer, cosmetic jars and a chamber pot. A cupboard in Queen Elizabeth's apartments at court, used to store dried and candied fruit, was big enough for a man to hide in. The wainscot press (used for storing linen and clothes), wardrobes called fripperies, and chests of drawers all came into style in the seventeenth century.

At Petworth there was "a cupboard of cipresse open, but closed with glasse." Clocks were sometimes displayed on cupboards. One clock, at Hatfield House, was made in the shape of a tortoise.

daybeds: Introduced toward the end of the sixteenth century, one daybed at Hardwick Hall is 7'3" long, padded with a long, loose mattress and covered with red damask embroidered in colored silks and gold. Paneled ends of oak rake outward and are painted chocolate red with floral arabesques and the arms of the Talbot and Cavendish families.

stools: Early stools were solid, flat-seated and plain. By mid-century, joined stools commonly had four legs. In the seventeenth century wrought stools were high, four-legged and usually had cushions trimmed with fringe.

tables: Dais tables might have a fixed top, often of elm, and might measure 20' × 3'. The table could be framed, with four to six solid legs and very solid, low-set stretchers (to hold down the rushes and keep the legs steady). The draw-top table was imported during the 1550s. In the seventeenth century, the gate table was coming into style, especially in private parlors. Petworth had a little table with a drawer in it in the earl's closet and a pair of playing tables with ivory men in the dining parlor.

trunks: The great trunk of the Russell family (earls of Bedford) served as the family bank. It was made in the Netherlands, its exterior painted with roses and tulips, and had a Spanish-style double lock. Francis Russell, second earl, also had a long trunk and a great chest bound with iron in which he kept his books.

COVERINGS FOR FLOORS, WALLS AND CEILINGS

carpets: Although some people used these expensive decorative items on their floors, as we do, most carpets were draped over tables and cupboards. In one wealthy mid-sixteenth-century merchant's country house, however, an oblong green carpet covered a waxed and polished oak floor. The Petworth inventory lists a yellow rug, "old and stayned, belonging to the yellow printed saye bed."

ceilings: Plaster ceilings and walls were often painted with ornate designs. Painted canvas ceilings might grace a banqueting house. Friezes and Italian stucco-work were popular in the Elizabethan era. At Cowdray, five episodes from the life of Sir Anthony Browne were painted in the dining parlor.

embroidery: Everything that could be decorated, was, from pillows and wall hangings to clothing, coverlets and bed hangings. In many houses embroidery frames (also called tents) were set up so that anyone in the household with free time could work on the current project.

maps: More expensive than portraits, mounted maps were collected as wall hangings throughout the period. They also came in book form, the word atlas having first been used in 1575. Tapestry maps of counties were popular as decoration. Petworth had a large map of the world in the lower gallery.

mirrors: Polished metal was used for mirrors until the end of the sixteenth century, but wall mirrors of any kind were rare until well into the seventeenth century.

portraits: Painting was called picture-making in the sixteenth century. The word picture was also used for a figure painted on stone or plaster. "Painting in little" meant limning portraits in miniature.

John Rastell's *A Pastyme of People*, published in 1529, contained woodcut illustrations of portraits. It was extremely popular. So were ornate genealogies illustrated with portraits. Copperplate engraving came to England under Elizabeth, producing a more refined look than blocks, and this technique was used for both portraits and maps.

Popular subjects for portraits, aside from one's own family, were the monarchs of England. Hardwick Hall in the seventeenth century had on display twenty-six portraits of family members and a set of portraits of the kings and queens of England, starting with Edward II. Many English homes also had pictures of two other popular subjects, the defeat and capture of Francis I at the Battle of Pavia in 1525 and portraits of "Lucretia," which seems to have referred to any depiction of a female nude.

Among the premier portrait painters of this era were Hans Holbein, Lucas Hornebolte, Levina Teerlinc, Nicholas Hilliard, Isaac Oliver, William Scrots, Hans Eworth, Steven vander Meulen, Cornelius Ketel, George Gower, John Bettes the Younger, Hieronimo Custodis,

Sir William Segar, Robert Peake the Elder, John de Critz, Marcus Gheeraerts the Younger, William Larkin and Sir Anthony Van Dyck.

rushes: Throughout the sixteenth century, even in the royal palaces at Greenwich and Hampton Court, floors were strewn with rushes, reeds and straw mixed with lavender and rosemary clippings. Rush-mats began to replace rushes in the seventeenth century.

tapestries: Real tapestries were woven, but the English also used the word for needle painting (embroidering a picture in wool on a linen ground). Painted cloths were the poor man's tapestries. Lord Lisle's chamber at Calais had eight pieces of tapestry to decorate it and Lady Lisle's had nine. The walls of the dining chamber were hung with "a painted cloth of Olyfernis" (Holofernes decapitated by Judith, a popular subject for tapestries!), and the Great Chamber had six pieces of tapestry and two pictures. Petworth had, among others, nine pieces of hangings of "forrest work" (sylvan scenery) and six pieces of hangings of "imagery" (figured work). Arras, France, was famous for magnificent woven hangings, which gave the name arras or arras-work to some tapestries. Sheldon tapestries were produced from 1561 in Warwickshire, and under James I tapestries were made at Mortlake.

wainscot panels: Wainscoting was a popular way of decorating walls. There was also widespread use of linen-fold paneling.

windows: Included as furnishings in wills and inventories because they could be removed and stored when a house was not in use, windows might contain oiled paper, leaded panes or glass. Curtains, curtain rods and curtain rings were used in some houses but not universally.

LIGHTING

Candles were made of beeswax and tallow (which stank and dripped great quantities of fat into grease pans). They came in various weights and sizes, from tall, fat ones that burned for nearly an hour to slender tapers. Candles were set in wood or iron supports known as candle beams, suspended from the ceiling and operated by a pulley. Individual candlesticks of iron, brass or latten stood on a tripod or a solid round base. Flares were used to light passageways. The poor had only rush dips, or were guided by the light from the fire in the hearth.

SANITATION AND BATHING HABITS

Throughout this period, sanitation was primitive. For a discussion of the privy as a separate room, see page 43. Most houses were furnished with close-stools, which were box-like affairs, lidded, with pierced wooden or padded seats and removable pans in the box beneath. The inventory of Petworth lists several bedrooms with both a close-stool (some covered with cloth) with "one pan unto it" and a chamber pot. Other bedchambers have neither item among the furnishings. The chamber pot was also called a jordan and was most commonly made of earthenware or pewter. For the upper classes there are records of chamber pots of hammered silver with elegant handles and thumb pieces.

Although chamber pots, close-stools and privies were provided at convenient locations (there were even chamber pots in the withdrawing room), many gentlemen still used the chimney or a convenient corner as a urinal. The ladies who came with Catherine of Aragon from Spain remarked upon this fact, complaining that they could scarcely walk down the corridor of an English palace without coming upon such a scene.

Sir John Harington invented the hydraulic water closet, the earliest flush toilet, at the end of the sixteenth century, but although it cost only 30s. 8d. to construct (see chapter ten for more on the value of money), it was regarded as a novelty in England and did not find general acceptance there until the Victorian era. In France the idea caught on more quickly. In 1750, French water closets went by the name "lieux a l'Anglaise."

Toilet paper had not yet been invented. Renaissance men and women, ever resourceful, kept containers of salt water handy and made use of such varied substances as bunches of herbs, moss and sponges on sticks. In 1249 a royal privy was supplied with "downe or coton for wiping."

Water supplies were of varied quality. Rainwater was stored for use, but most water came from wells. Hand pumps were in use and water could be pumped to the ground floor of a house, but not much above that. Pumps powered by waterwheels had appeared in England by the late sixteenth century and were also used to get water to a hilltop site and into a cistern. Cisterns were made of stone, wood or alabaster, and pipes of lead or copper. The Franciscan friary in Southampton had a

Elizabethan bedchamber furniture
Shown are a typical upper-class bed, a "maid of honor" chair wide enough to accommodate a farthingale, and a close-stool of the type used by royalty.

conduit which provided running water to the cloister, the refectory, the infirmary and the kitchen, where a "goodly" lead trough held water. Some Southampton houses also had piped-in water by 1535.

Bathing facilities were limited. In the home, total immersion was infrequent, though the face and hands were washed regularly, often in perfumed water. Fennel and endive were added to water used to wash the feet. When baths were taken, a wooden tub was generally set up in the bedchamber, near the fire which was used to heat the bath water. Queen Elizabeth took a portable bathtub with her when she traveled and insisted on a higher level of cleanliness among her courtiers than was found elsewhere. Fennel and bay were frequently added to bathwater. For details on the soaps available, see page 191.

Rivers and ditches were used for washing bodies as well as laundry.

Steam baths were known in the Middle Ages and became fairly widespread because they were believed to cure venereal disease, but the hot house for bathing was rare in private homes.

Public baths were little more than brothels. London had Turkish steam baths called "Hummums" which also provided private rooms, wine and women to their clients. "Bagnios" provided hot- and cold-water baths. Communal baths at spas were popular in Europe before they caught on in England, but they were taken more for social and medicinal purposes than to achieve cleanliness.

MUSIC AND MUSIC ROOMS

Henry Percy, fifth earl of Northumberland, paid his taborette player four pounds a quarter in 1512, the same wage earned by his Dean of the Chapel. He also kept a lute player and a rebec player on his household books.

Even if a gentleman did not have a separate music room in his house or keep professional musicians, he was likely to own a number of musical instruments and music books. To entertain themselves, most people sang, especially part songs and madrigals, and often accompanied themselves on the lute or on the cittern, which was similar to the lute but easier to play. Songbooks contained collections of dance music as well as songs of four to eight parts.

The virginal, a keyboard instrument similar to the harpsichord which was placed on a table or stood on legs, came in various sizes and was popular in England. A "pair of virginals" referred to only one virginal. The spinet was popular in Italy in the sixteenth century but does not seem to have caught on in England. The third most common instrument after the lute and virginal was the viol.

Other instruments included the bandora (a bass guitar), cornets, the curtall (bassoon), drums, flutes, the hautboy (oboe), the lysarden (a deep-toned bass wind instrument eight inches long with three U-shaped bends), nakers (small kettledrums of Arabic origin), recorders, the sackbut (trombone), shawms (these had a double reed of dried cane and were similar to the modern oboe but were usually played in pairs), tabors (drums) and violins.

Irish harp music became popular during the reign of James I. The sound was believed to soothe melancholy. Organ music was also popular and in addition to the organs found in churches, many stately homes boasted of owning a small "pair of organs set upon a cupboard" (also called "a case of regals").

LIBRARIES AND COLLECTORS

John, seventh Baron Lumley (1534–1609) was the most notable collector of his times, acquiring not only pictures but also books and manuscripts. There had been libraries in some eight hundred monastic houses. Many volumes were destroyed when they were dissolved, even though Henry VIII built three libraries in his palaces to preserve rescued books. The private library Thomas Cranmer built from the dissolved monasteries was later acquired by Lord Lumley, who had a total of 1,000 printed books and 150 manuscripts in 1579 and eventually amassed some 7,000 volumes. These went to Henry, Prince of Wales, on Lumley's death and thus became part of the Royal Library. The keeper of the libraries at Whitehall and Windsor during the reign of Elizabeth was paid 6s. 8d. a day, which may reflect the great value the queen put upon the collection in his care.

Archbishop Matthew Parker had a library at Lambeth, but only a dozen nonclerics seem to have owned more than a hundred books at anytime during the sixteenth century. Some booksellers kept exceptionally large stocks. Roger Ward of Shrewsbury had 2,500 volumes in 1585. John Foster of York had some 3,000 in 1616. This is not so surprising considering the number of books printed in England every year; 259 separate titles are listed in 1600, 577 in 1640. In 1623 the total of 309 included 120 religious works, 89 books on current events and 100 volumes on other topics. Among the other large private libraries were those of Lord Burghley (more than a thousand books); Sir William More at Loseley, Surrey, whose collection numbered over 400 in 1556; and John Dee at Mortlake. At his death in 1618, Sir Thomas Knyvett of Ashwellthorpe, Norfolk, had 1,400 volumes in five languages.

In the earl's closet at Petworth there were 44 books in folio, 28 books in vellum, 33 pamphlets and a wainscot box containing maps and other writings. The library contained fifty-two chests of books and enough books to fill another twelve small chests. Also in the room were a cupboard with mathematical instruments, one large globe and two small ones, antique pictures of the emperors of Rome (purchased in 1586 for £24), a table with a folding frame, two little wainscot tables and a bedstead.

SELECT BIBLIOGRAPHY

The Diagram Group. *Musical Instruments of the World: An Illustrated Encyclopedia.* New York: Paddington Press, 1976.

Edwards, Ralph and L.G.G. Ramsey. *The Connoisseur's Complete Period Guide to the Houses, Decoration, Furnishing and Chattels of the Classic Periods.* New York: Bonanza Books, 1968.

Strong, Roy. *The English Icon: Elizabethan and Jacobean Portraiture.* New Haven: Yale University Press, 1969.

CHAPTER FIVE

MARRIAGE AND FAMILY

F rom 1536, parishes were required to keep records of christenings, marriages and deaths. A variety of scholarly studies of these and of extant wills and inventories have yielded the statistics given in this chapter.

BIRTH

Lying-in

A tradition among those who could afford it, the mother's lying-in was as impressive as she could manage. Friends who came to visit during the lying-in brought gifts, often of money. It was at best a celebration and at worst a final, grand gesture. Three-quarters of gentry wives who died within ten years of marriage did so in childbirth.

Churching

In Catholic homes, husband and wife were supposed to abstain from conjugal relations during pregnancy and for a period of forty days after childbirth (and during Lent). Women were churched after giving birth. This service of thanksgiving was a prerequisite for renewed participation in church rituals and services.

Christenings and Baptisms

Done as quickly as possible in this age of high infant mortality, these ceremonies began with the carrying of the child into the church on a cushion. The father named the child and usually selected the name from the Bible, the family, or the royal family. Godparents were essential, to look out for the child if the parents died. A feast generally followed the ceremony, traditionally featuring sugar and biscuits, comfits and carraways, marmalade, marchpane and sweet suckets. Each guest brought a gift for the child.

Life expectancy was much shorter then than now, but statistics show that children born between 1566 and 1586 actually lived longer than those of any other generation until the nineteenth century. Between 1588 and 1640 up to 50 percent of all children died before reaching adulthood. In one parish, St. Leonard's, Eastcheap (in London), a record of 190 burials between 1602 and 1611 lists the age at death for 171 persons. Leaving out deaths due to plague, 30 percent died before reaching age one, 44 percent were dead before age ten, and 59 percent died before reaching twenty-one. Although the average life expectancy at birth for a child born in the 1640s was only thirty-two, any of those children who lived to see the age of four would probably survive childhood.

Treatment of Babies and Young Children

Perhaps because so many children died young, one theory asserts that there was little overt affection between parents and their offspring in this era. Another disagrees. Family size averaged five to six children of whom three to five survived past early childhood. Most families sent children away from home during their teens if not before, either to school, to apprenticeships or to live with foster families.

Since people were aware that suckling a baby inhibited conception, many mothers breast-fed their own children. They also did so to prevent the child from sucking in evil. Milk was believed to transfer the qualities of the nurse. Some of those who did not nurse their own children sent them out to a wet nurse while others had the nurse live in. Infants were rarely weaned earlier than one year and many continued to nurse as long as two years. They were not toilet trained very early, either, as this was not considered important.

Those children who survived infancy had toys, including dolls, hoops and balls. Just as children today use rhymes to jump rope,

A woman and child, mid-sixteenth century
Portraits of children outside the royal family were fairly rare unless children were shown with one or both parents. This child, a boy, wears skirts, as both sexes did during their early years.

Renaissance children also chanted verses. A typical children's rhyme of 1632 was "Tell-tale, tit! / Thy tongue shall be slit, / And every dog in the town / Shall have a little bit."

MARRIAGE

Only about 13 percent of the population (a 1590 figure) never married at all. The average age of marriage in England during the period from 1536 to 1650 was somewhere in the mid- to late twenties for both men and women. One study shows that early in the period, only one in six men and one in four women married before the age of twenty. Another, for the seventeenth century, reveals that it was one in twelve for men and one in fifteen for women. Men were usually two to three years older than their brides.

The nobility did tend to marry earlier in order to safeguard inheritances, but even among the upper classes there were few child marriages during this period. The son and heir was expected to put in a few years at university, perhaps spend a few at the Inns of Court, and tour the Continent before he married in his early twenties. Younger sons married even later, often not until their thirties. The brides usually reached the age of twenty before they wed. We know about exceptions primarily because they *were* events exceptional enough to be recorded for posterity.

The age of consent for marriage was much younger than the age at which most actual marriages took place. A girl could agree to an espousal at seven, could receive a dowry at nine, and at twelve could confirm or deny prior consent to marry. If she confirmed consent, she was bound forever to the arranged match. Boys were required to be fourteen to consent to marriage. Twenty-one was full age to make a will or sign a contract.

Courtship
The ideal was a well-planned love match. Parents had a duty to provide their children with a good marriage, which meant one which was economically sound. Among apprentices and servants, marriages were discouraged. Even when they were not, the parties frequently put the wedding off until they had money saved. There was no one pattern of courtship, but a record from Yorkshire in 1641 is indicative. First a man wrote to a maid's father to ask permission to court his daughter.

If she was willing, he gave her a ring on his first visit. On the second visit, he gave her gloves, and each time he called thereafter he brought some toy or novelty until the wedding. The parents set the date and arranged the dowry. Once the parents of both agreed, the betrothal took place, with the wedding soon after.

Affinity and Consanguinity

The major obstacles to marriage involved the church's rules on affinity and consanguinity. From 1215 on, no one was allowed to marry a person within the fourth degree of consanguinity. That meant that great-grandchildren of a common ancestor were forbidden to marry. Each degree of consanguinity had a corresponding degree of affinity, acquired by marriage. Thus a widow could not marry anyone related to her late husband up to the fourth degree of consanguinity. Affinity resulted from illicit as well as marital relations, which meant that a woman who had been one man's mistress was not permitted to marry his brother, cousin, second cousin or third cousin. Spiritual consanguinity extended the ban to godparents. Until the Reformation, a papal dispensation could be obtained for a fee.

Types of Marriage

By the sixteenth century, there were five distinct and necessary steps to achieve a legal marriage. First was a written contract between the parents of the bride and groom, setting up financial arrangements. Then the spousals (betrothal ceremony) occurred, a formal exchange of oral promises before witnesses. Next there was public proclamation, the reading of banns in church on three successive Sundays or holy days. This procedure was intended to allow claims to be made of pre-contract (a previous betrothal to someone else) or any other impediment to the marriage. Banns could be omitted with a special license. Step four was the church wedding. Step five was sexual consummation.

There were a few specific places exempt from episcopal jurisdiction, where a couple could go to be married without going through all the steps or obtaining a special license. These included Lincoln's Inn, Southwark Mint and Newgate Prison. The Anglican Church also recognized a contract without a wedding as a marriage, making any sort of exchange of promises before witnesses a valid marriage, even though it wasn't "legal" in the strictest sense. Under English law irregular marriages committed the participants for life, but they carried with them no legal guarantee that a surviving spouse or children would have any rights to inherit the deceased party's property, since civil courts recognized only church weddings.

To add to the confusion, there were two kinds of spousals. "Per verba de futuro" was a promise to marry in the future and was not binding unless the couple consummated their relationship, at which time it became binding for life. The other type was "per verba de praesenti," which was regarded, under ecclesiastical law, as an irrevocable commitment. The revelation of this kind of pre-contract would nullify a later church wedding to someone else.

Premarital Sex

Between one-fifth and one-third of all brides were pregnant on their wedding day. A child born between troth plight and marriage was considered legitimate. The main objection to premarital sexual activity seems to have been practical rather than religious. The birth of a bastard created an expense for the community.

The case of William Shakespeare is illustrative. In November 1582, at age eighteen, he obtained a special license to marry three-months-pregnant Anne Hathaway. There was no time for the banns to be called three times before the beginning of Advent, one of the prohibited seasons for marriage. He paid his fee to the local bishop's officials at Worcester; gave his bond to pay forty pounds if the requirements for a lawful marriage were not satisfied; and swore an oath that he'd told the truth in statements concerning his name, residence and occupation and those of the bride and both their parents, and the reasons for seeking the license. They then married, after the banns were called only once.

Knowledge of methods of birth control was limited. Popular belief held "hard pissing" after sex to be effective. Although a description of a linen condom was published in Italy in 1563 (the word does not appear in print until 1665), such protective sheaths were in wide use only after 1844. The abortifacient properties of the herb savin, however, were widely known, as were those of tansy, willow leaves, ivy and the bark of white poplar. The use of abortion as a means of birth control may have been made more acceptable by the contemporary belief that the fetus did not acquire a soul until eighty days after conception.

Wedding Customs

Weddings were normally held between eight and noon, a requirement which became law after 1604. The usual place for a wedding was at the church door, where the bride (dressed in white or russet, her hair loose) was given away by her father or by friends. There was a formal grant of dowry by the bridegroom and pennies were set aside for the poor. Promises were exchanged, the ring was blessed, and the groom placed it on three successive fingers of the bride, to protect her from demons, before leaving it on the third finger of her left hand. Before the Reformation, a nuptial mass was then said inside the church. A sermon was substituted in the Anglican Church.

Puritans preferred weddings to take place on Sundays before the entire congregation and encouraged the use of plain gold rings. Until about 1650, however, most wedding rings were elaborate. In some cases a gimmal ring, consisting of two rings that could be separated, was divided at the betrothal ceremony and rejoined at the wedding. It was not yet the fashion for the groom to receive a wedding ring.

A chaplet was a circlet set with gems that was sometimes worn by brides. Bride lace was a length of blue ribbon binding sprigs of rosemary and used as a wedding favor. Tied to the bride's arm, these were pulled off by male wedding guests after the ceremony and worn in their hats. Men also wore nosegays in their hats at weddings in the late sixteenth century.

The wedding party feasted after the ceremony. Later the bridal chamber was blessed and the bride and groom were put to bed by all their friends. A great deal of ribaldry accompanied this traditional "bedding" ceremony. One custom which had not yet evolved was the honeymoon. Newlyweds usually spent the first few weeks with her family and then went to his home to set up housekeeping.

A Forced Marriage

In 1617, Sir Edward Coke, hoping to win royal approval, insisted his fifteen-year-old daughter Frances marry Sir John Villiers (later Viscount Purbeck), older brother of King James's favorite, the duke of Buckingham. Her mother (who still called herself Lady Hatton, her title from her first marriage) attempted to prevent the marriage by spiriting Frances away, but Coke found them hiding in a closet and abducted his daughter. Lady Hatton pursued them in a coach until it lost a wheel. Frances was eventually coerced into going through with the wedding, but the match was not a happy one. In 1624 she was convicted of adultery, imprisoned, and ordered to do penance, barefoot and wearing a white sheet, in the Church of the Savoy. She later escaped from prison, wearing male attire, and joined her lover in Shropshire. When she made the mistake of returning to London, she was caught and returned to prison. Following a second escape, Frances went into self-imposed exile in France.

Divorce

Marital infidelity was fairly common in England during this period. In 1604, running out on a family was made a felony. Divorce, however, was not an option in an unhappy marriage. Because of England's peculiar laws on marriage, combined with the break with Rome, it became impossible to set aside one spouse and remarry. Unless there were grounds for annulment, the best one could do was to obtain a legal separation, unless one spouse was absent beyond the seas (out of the country) for more than seven years. In that case, the spouse was presumed dead and the husband or wife at home was exempted from any penalty for remarriage.

A nullity could be granted for incest (common because of affinity and consanguinity), because of a pre-contract, because of lunacy or male impotence (which prevented intercourse and therefore took away the official reason for marriage, the production of heirs), in cases of bigamy, or in the case of the kidnapping and marriage of an heiress by the use of force (a criminal offense).

Margaret Kebell, twenty-five, was a widow abducted from her uncle's house in Staffordshire by one Roger Vernon and 120 armed men. Roger took her back to Derbyshire and forced her to marry him, even though she had planned to wed Ralph Egerton. The Court of the King's Bench would not help her, but she appealed to King Henry VIII in person. When the matter came before the Star Chamber, Vernon was fined heavily and Margaret was freed from her forced marriage and permitted to wed Egerton instead.

The case of John Stawell illustrates the pitfalls of trying to get rid of a legally married wife. Stawell wed Mary Portman in 1556. In 1572, because of Mary's flagrant infidelity, Stawell convinced Archbishop Parker to grant him a license to marry Frances Dyer. Mary then sued him for "cohabiting with a gentlewoman as his wife, his former wife being alive." She was bribed to withdraw the suit, but after Stawell's death, Mary put in a successful claim for dower rights. Under the law she was his first and only wife.

Death

For the period 1550–1700 about 30 percent of the population was under 15 and about 10 percent over 60. Seventy was considered to be "very old age" but there are a fair number of cases, especially among the upper classes, of women who lived into their 80s (Bess of Hardwick, Anne Cooke Bacon and her sister, Elizabeth, Lady Russell) and 90s (Ann Stanhope, duchess of Somerset). In the parish of St. Botolph without Aldgate from 1583 to 1599, forty-three deaths were attributed to "great age." Twelve of those persons were reportedly over 100. Other records report that one Agnes Sadler, buried on April 26, 1576, was 126. Alice George, born in 1572, was still living in 1681, when she claimed her father had lived to be 83, her mother to 96 and her mother's mother to 111. One rough estimate indicates that at least half of those people who reached the age of 25 had lost at least one of their parents by then, but another study suggests that those who reached the age of 21 might reasonably hope to live to be 62.

Causes of Death

Along with disease, war, murder, suicide and childbirth, accidents were a leading cause of death. Of fifty-five accidental deaths in the parish of St. Botolph without Aldgate from 1573 to 1624, the most common causes were drowning and falls.

Funeral Customs

Death was announced by the tolling or ringing of bells. Each parish had its own customs concerning death knells, but bell ringing usually included the number of years in the age of the deceased.

Both the lying-in-state and the funeral of a nobleman were lavish, expensive productions. The courtyard and entrance of the house and the staircase and first room leading to the coffin were all draped in black baize. A second room was hung with black cloth. The room beyond that, where the coffin stood, was shrouded in black velvet and the coffin itself covered with a black velvet pall. Less important corpses did not get black velvet, but the tradition of covering everything in sight with black was followed. Mirrors were turned to the wall. In the funeral procession, coaches, saddles, bridles and so forth were also all in black and the church was draped in black from the floor to the roof beams.

An exception to the use of black was made for children and unmarried girls, who might be buried in a coffin covered with a white pall and accompanied to church by bands of young people dressed in white. An infant less than a month old was usually buried in the white chrisom cloth that had been laid over the baby at his or her baptism.

Catholic ritual provided for sustained intercession on behalf of the deceased's soul before, during and after the interment. In 1533 the burial of the duchess of Suffolk, daughter and sister of kings of England and former queen of France, began with a mass before the coffin (the body had been embalmed and wrapped in lead because the lying-in-state lasted three weeks). After offerings to the poor, a procession formed. The coffin was on a funeral car canopied in black velvet embroidered with her coat of arms. A carved likeness of her lay on top. The procession was led by one hundred poor men who were recruited as mourners and given black gowns and lighted candles. Then came the priests and attendants from her own chapel, members of her household, knights and gentlemen of the court. Drawn by six horses, draped in black, the hearse was surrounded by one hundred yeomen with torches and followed by the family and servants and "all other that would." At Bury St. Edmunds the body was blessed and a ceremony followed. The next morning there were a requiem mass, a sermon and a second mass.

By 1552 a funeral service was much simpler and might conclude with a reading of the exploits of the deceased, sometimes composed by himself. Amye Robsart died on September 8, 1560. On September 22 her body was buried beneath the choir of St. Mary's in Oxford. Her husband, Lord Robert Dudley (later earl of Leicester), who was rumored to have wanted his wife dead so that he might marry the queen, was not present, but that was acceptable in the etiquette of the times. The duke of Suffolk had not attended his wife's rites, either. Margery Norris, a friend of the queen's, was chief mourner, her train carried by a Mrs. Butler, assisted by Sir Richard Blunt. Also in the procession were Lady Dudley's family and friends, gentlemen, yeomen, the mayor of Oxford and his brethren, heralds, the choir of St. Mary's, miscellaneous members of the University, and numerous poor men and women. Eight tall yeomen and four assistants bore the coffin to

St. Mary's and at each corner walked a gentleman bearing a banner. The widower's chaplain preached a sermon. The total cost was more than £500.

The funeral of playmaker Robert Greene in 1592 cost 10s. 4d. That of the second earl of Bedford in 1585 cost nearly £700. The family had to sell their furniture to pay for it. Mourning for family and servants when Edward Russell, fourth earl of Bedford was buried in 1641, cost nearly £500. More than three hundred coaches followed that funeral procession to the church.

After a funeral, food and drink were traditionally served, sometimes at a great feast. Presents of scarves and gloves were given to friends and relatives. Other mourners were given gifts of money, and many had already received mourning robes. Sir Thomas Gresham left money to clothe two hundred such mourners, providing 6s. 8d. per yard for material. The total cost of his funeral in 1575 was £800.

Burials

Most burials were in the churchyard, where the request for a grave was made to the sexton. The north side was unpopular, as that was the burial place of unbaptized children. No burial service was said for papists after the Reformation, and they were sometimes buried at night. Suicides were buried in a public highway between 9 P.M. and midnight, after a stake had been driven into the body!

Ordinary folk were buried without a coffin and their bones might be dug up again in a few years to make room for new bodies. In plague time in cities, special rules governed burials. The 1548 plague orders prohibited burials between 6 P.M. and 6 A.M. In the seventeenth century, corpses were covered with a winding sheet and flung, without burial rites, into a common pest-pit.

The wealthy, who could afford to be "chested," also tended to raise elaborate monuments to themselves. Sometimes they were designed well in advance. The entire family might be represented in marble or stone and it was not at all uncommon for a man to be shown with several subsequent wives. At first these monuments were erected only inside of churches, but during the sixteenth century, headstones began to appear in most churchyards. In a case unusual for that county, Sir Thomas Walmesley of Dunkernaugh, Lancashire, arranged for an alabaster tomb to be erected after his death in 1613.

To prevent the return of the deceased, folk rites involving candle flame, salt and fire were carried out in the Durham region even late in the Elizabethan period. Of Norse origin, the custom also included singing to the dead body of the journey to the afterlife.

Mourning

Men wore long black gowns and hoods to funerals. A poor man might wear a "rat's color" gown. On at least one occasion, doublets and hose of frieze were worn as mourning dress at Elizabeth's court, probably as an affectation of simplicity.

The mourning period for a parent was three to four years. A surviving spouse usually wore black until he or she remarried or died. Sir Ralph Verney not only slept in a black bed after his wife died, he had black nightclothes and nightcaps, a black comb and brush, and slippers of black velvet. Mourning jewelry was customary from the Middle Ages on. Lockets, brooches and rings were designed as containers for a lock of the dear departed's hair. Rings might also be fashioned as skeletons, coffins and skulls.

The term widow's weeds dates from the sixteenth century and was used to denote all mourning garments. Black was the usual color of mourning although the widow of a king of France customarily wore white. Catherine de' Medici broke with tradition by wearing black.

A mourning barbe, often of pleated linen, was worn by widows until the late sixteenth century, under whatever headdress was then in fashion. The barbe covered the neck in front and in the late sixteenth century was worn below the ruff like a bib. The gorgette was similar to a barbe, but unpleated. The wimple (described on page 21) was another alternative style. The widow's peak was a flap projecting in front from the hood or headdress. It could also be indicated by a dip in the center-front edge of the headdress.

Widows' Rights and Remarriage

About 30 percent of marriages were second marriages. On occasion, discussions about the next spouse began as soon as the funeral of the first was over. One well-to-do gentleman took his wife to visit London in 1639. While there, at eight o'clock one evening, he died. Before noon the next day, his widow was married to the journeyman woolen draper who had come to sell her material to make her mourning clothes. Such exceptional cases aside, a bereaved spouse did not ordinarily stay single, even though, in the case of widows, this state gave them, for the first time, control over their own lives and property. A widow's own property reverted to her and she also enjoyed a life interest in her husband's lands. She lost these rights only if her husband had been convicted of treason, or if she committed treason, felony or adultery.

Widows had to have permission to remarry if they held land under the old feudal system. A license cost one-third of the annual value of her dower. To remarry without a license might incur a fine three times that high and might also cause her new husband to be fined for contempt of court. Such complications aside, between 50 and 70 percent of all widows remarried. Those whose first marriage had lasted less than ten years were more likely to remarry, particularly if they had small children to provide for. Those who had no children were least likely to remarry. Statistics also indicate that the average marriage lasted ten to twelve years and that the average length of time between marriages was about two years.

A number of prominent persons married more than twice. King Henry VIII is infamous for his six wives. His sixth wife, Catherine Parr, had four husbands, as did Bess of Hardwick. So did Catherine Gordon, whose first was the impostor Perkin Warbeck, who claimed to be Richard IV, rightful king of England.

EXTENDED FAMILY

Wards

Until 1646, heirs to land held by knight service and other feudal military tenures became wards if their fathers died before the heirs reached the age of twenty-one. Sale of wardships was a source of considerable profit as was holding one. A child's guardian was entitled to the profits of a portion of that child's lands and had the right to arrange his or her marriage.

English law provided that the eldest son inherit all lands, but if there were no sons, lands and goods were equally divided among the daughters. At sixteen a girl was out of wardship if she was under fourteen when her father died. If she was already fourteen at his death, she did not become a ward at all.

When Sir John Basset died in 1528, his son John was just nine. The king granted the purchase of his wardship and marriage to John Worth of Compton Pole, Devon, for 200 marks. Worth then made a private deal with Lady Basset to allow her to raise her own son. In some cases, the child's mother bought the wardship of her own son or daughter outright, but it was just as likely to be sold to a stranger.

Charles Howard bought the wardship of Henry Wriothesley, third earl of Southampton (1573–1624) for £1,000 in 1581. He transferred the care of the boy and the right to arrange his marriage to Lord Burghley but continued to administer Southampton's lands. Burghley had previously had several other wards in his household. One of them, the earl of Oxford, he married to his own daughter. When he tried to force Southampton to wed one of his granddaughters, however, the earl refused, and ended up having to pay Lord Burghley a hefty fine.

Poor Relations
In addition to other people's children taken in as wards or for fostering, households might also include various relatives. A stint as a servant was regarded by some young people as a useful educational experience. For others it was an economic necessity. Waiting gentlewomen, companions, nursemaids and governesses were usually recruited from the ranks of unmarried female relations who had nowhere else to go.

Pets
At Calais, Lord Lisle and his family kept, at various times, spaniels, mastiffs, a greyhound called Minikin, a young hound called Hurll and a dog called Wolf. Dogs were among the most popular pets, especially spaniels, which were kept by Queen Elizabeth's maids of honor. In addition to lapdogs, house pets included English shepherd dogs, whippets (good watchdogs), "dancing dogs," mastiffs, and a woolly dog called a shough which was imported from Iceland and apparently tended to eat candles. Sir John Harington, inventor of the water closet, had a portrait painted of his dog, Bungey.

Other pets included tame foxes, squirrels, ferrets, marmosets, monkeys (a good one cost £60) and birds. Parrots came into fashion with increased overseas trade. One given to Sir Robert Cecil by Sir John Gilbert came with instructions. It could eat bread, oatmeal groats and all meats and should be put on the dinner table so it could choose. Salt was to be avoided, but it should drink water or claret wine. It was put in a cage at night, which was covered to keep it warm, but during the day it liked to sit in a gentlewoman's ruff. Cecil later paid £15 10s. for a "bird of Arabia" in a cage and £20 for a white parrot. In 1607 he sent a man to the East Indies to collect parrots, monkeys and marmosets. He also had "little artificial parakeets in a cage of silver wire." Lady Lisle had a linnet sent to her in Calais. After almost being lost in a shipwreck during the channel crossing, this bird survived for a time in a cage, but it was eventually eaten by a cat.

Although cats had an unfortunate link to witchcraft, they were still popular as pets. Two famous prisoners in the Tower had cats with them: the earl of Northumberland (who also kept a dog and a parrot during his captivity) and the earl of Southampton. Southampton even had his cat painted into the portrait done of him during his imprisonment. English cats came in many colors but at this time were all of the domestic short-hair variety.

SELECT BIBLIOGRAPHY

Clark, Alice. *The Working Life of Women in the Seventeenth Century*. New York: Augustus M. Kelley, 1968. (Note: this is a reprint of the 1920 text.)

Fraser, Antonia. *The Weaker Vessel: Women's Lot in Seventeenth-Century England*. New York: Knopf, 1984.

Fussell, G.E. *The English Countrywoman: A Farmhouse Social History, 1500–1900*. London: A. Melrose, 1953.

Hogrefe, Pearl. *Tudor Women: Commoners and Queens*. Ames: Iowa State Press, 1975.

Houlbrooke, Ralph. *The English Family, 1450–1700*. London and New York: Longman, 1984.

Kelso, Ruth. *Doctrine for the Lady of the Renaissance*. Urbana: University of Illinois Press, 1956.

Marshall, Rosalind K. *Virgins and Viragos, A History of Women in Scotland from 1080–1980*. Chicago: Academy Chicago Ltd., 1983.

Prior, Mary, ed. *Women in English Society 1500–1800*. New York: Methuen, 1985.

Thompson, Roger. *Women in Stuart England and America: A Comparative Study*. Boston: Routledge and Kegan Paul, 1974.

Of Special Interest in Women's Studies
Goulianos, Joan, ed. *by a Woman writt*. Indianapolis: Bobbs-Merrill, 1973.

Hull, Suzanne W. *Chaste, Silent & Obedient: English Books for Women 1475–1640.* San Marino, California: The Huntington Library, 1982.
Stanford, Ann. *The Women Poets in English: An Anthology.* New York: McGraw-Hill, 1972.
Travitsky, Betty, ed. *The Paradise of Women: Writings by Women of the Renaissance.* Westport, Connecticut: Greenwood Press, 1981.
Woodbridge, Linda. *Women and the English Renaissance: Literature and the Nature of Womankind, 1540–1620.* Urbana: University of Illinois Press, 1984.

CHAPTER SIX

PHYSIC AND PHYSICIANS

D isease at this time was believed to have supernatural as well as natural causes. No one linked illness to malnutrition or to lack of sanitation. The first suggestion that washing hands and removing rings before examining a patient might be wise did not appear in print until 1560, and that was in France, not England. Epidemics were regarded as God's punishment for man's sins. Prayers were frequently part of the cure.

Every household also had herbal home remedies, which were the first choice in treating illnesses. There is a letter extant from Lord Edmund Howard to Lady Lisle in which he thanks her for sending him one of her own medicines. "It hath done me much good," he writes, "and hath caused the stone to break, so that now I void much gravel. But for all that, your said medicine hath done me little honesty, for it made me piss my bed this night, for the which my wife hath sore beaten me."

PRACTITIONERS

The "Physicians Act" of 1543, also called the "Quacks Charter," defended the right of cunning men and women to use herbs, roots and waters to treat diseases, but throughout this period an effort was made to control, by licenses, all those who gave medical aid to others. From 1511, bishops had licensed practitioners who were not university graduates, including surgeons. After 1560 they also regulated the activities of midwives.

The Barber-Surgeons became the first recognized medical guild in England in 1540. The barbers had been incorporated in 1462 by a charter that allowed them to let blood, engage in minor surgery, pull teeth, cut hair and shave. Thus, at a barbershop, a man could have his hair and beard washed and trimmed, his teeth cleaned (by scraping) or drawn, his nails pared, his ears picked or syringed, and his blood let. After 1600 the barbershop also sold tobacco. Surgeons wore long robes while barbers' robes were short.

Apothecaries, whose numbers increased dramatically after Henry VIII closed down all the monasteries, were affiliated with the Grocer's guild, since both apothecaries and grocers dealt in medicinal herbs. Many apothecaries used a Turk's head with a gilded pill on his extended tongue for a tradesman's sign. Pills were made by mixing powdered herbs into a stiff paste with honey, rolling this on a board, and pinching off small pieces which were then rolled into shape with the palms. Most drugs were kept in stoneware jars, the mouths or spouts closed by a piece of parchment that was tied in place. Moist drugs were stored in glass or horn containers. Dry roots were hung from the ceiling. In 1617 the Apothecaries' Guild was chartered and began to use Cobham House in Blackfriars as a school for teaching physic.

The best trained physicians spent seven years in England obtaining a master of arts, then acquired the M.D. degree at a foreign university, which they then "incorporated" at Cambridge or Oxford. Montpellier was the greatest medical center in Europe early in the sixteenth century. Bologna, Padua, Pavia and Pisa all offered lectures in both medicine and anatomy. In the sixteenth and seventeenth century, "an anatomy" was a skeleton and the idea of studying the body by dissecting a corpse was regarded with great suspicion. In 1565, however, following Continental practice, the College of Physicians (which had been chartered in 1518) was granted up to four bodies of executed criminals a year in order to do dissections. The College of Physicians also licensed all physicians practicing within a seven-mile radius of London and examined any they considered either astrologically or medically unqualified.

A physician, 1562
This likeness, said to be Dr.
William Bullein (d. 1576),
provides a good example of the
social implications of clothing.
People could tell at a glance,
from his coif (here worn beneath
a flat cap) and long gown, that
he was a professional. The skull
is included here to indicate
which profession, although a
urine flask was the more usual
symbol for doctors. The walking
stick was a common accessory,
especially among older men and
women. Dr. Bullein was the au-
thor of several books on health,
diet and medicine.

Medical students did not often come in direct contact with patients. They read old books, attended lectures and got their degree by "spoken disputation." A man's humour (sanguine, choleric, phlegmatic or melancholic) played an important role in treating his ailment. Physicians relied heavily on watercasting, the diagnosis of the balance of the humours by examination of the patient's urine. The urine flask was used as a symbol of the physician's profession. Administering purgatives and clysters and bleeding a patient were also common medical procedures. Each large English leech was able to suck three-eighths of an ounce of blood from a patient, and several were usually applied. There were specific bleeding points for some ailments, such as the outer side of the ankle for sciatica, even though the chronic pain would have been at the hip or thigh. The standard fee charged by a doctor was an angel, valued at ten shillings in Elizabethan times.

WOMEN IN MEDICINE

Female physicians had existed in previous centuries but were extremely rare by the sixteenth. Women barbers and surgeons had guild membership in some places. A woman surgeon was licensed in Norwich in 1568 and in 1572 York's council supported Isabell Warwick's case to continue doing surgery, but more common was the case of Ann Dell, a butcher's wife of Shoreditch, who was accused of practicing surgery without a license in 1615.

Midwives were the most numerous female practitioners. The birthing stool was in general use but obstetrical forceps (introduced in England in 1569 by a refugee doctor, William Chamberlen) were not. After 1610 the Barber-Surgeons licensed surgeons to assist at dangerous and difficult confinements, but in caesarean sections, the woman always died.

Nurses working in St. Bartholomew's Hospital in 1551 included a matron and eleven "sisters," the name a holdover from the days when nuns and novices did most of the nursing. The Savoy paid its matron £4 6s. 8d. a year. The women on her nursing staff were required to be unmarried and over the age of thirty-six (past the age when they might be inclined to seduce the patients). For 10d. a week they not only did the routine nursing work, they also did all the laundry, cleaning and cooking.

Another type of nurse was anyone hired to care for plague victims who had no family or servants to look after them. One woman, who nursed a Dutch family in Sandwich in 1638, received 8s. a week for her trouble.

A physician treated only the living. "Ancient matrons," sworn to their office, were employed as searchers and called in to examine any dead person to determine the cause of death. If a death was suspicious, only then was a coroner called in. The parish records we have which specify what a person died of are thus based on the conclusions of an untrained observer who did no more than ask a few questions of the family.

HOSPITALS

All English hospitals were closed when the monasteries were dissolved, but a hospital at this time meant any refuge or shelter. In London,

Bridewell sheltered vagabonds and beggars and was also a house of correction. Christ's Hospital was for homeless children under the age of six. Only St. Bartholomew's and St. Thomas's actually took in the sick. The former closed in 1539 and was refounded in 1546. The latter closed in 1540 and reopened in 1551 with 260 beds. The Savoy Palace on the Strand, rebuilt as a hospital for the poor on Henry VII's orders, opened with 100 beds, each of which was equipped with three pairs of sheets, two blankets, a linen cover and a counterpane. By Elizabethan times, however, the Savoy had become little more than a sanctuary for criminals.

Bethlehem, better known as Bedlam, housed lunatics from 1403 onward. It was given to the city of London as a hospital "for distracted people" in 1546. In 1600, Bedlam housed some twenty patients supported by parishes and filled the rest of the space with private cases whose families were charged anywhere from sixteen to sixty pence a week. Inmates were classified as either "fools" (feeble-minded) or "madmen."

THE PLAGUE

There were significant outbreaks of the plague in 1518, 1563, 1578, 1582, 1593, 1603, 1625, 1630 and 1636 and smaller epidemics in other years in specific areas such as Manchester, where 2,000 died of the plague in 1605. Usually outbreaks of plague started in early summer and were over by November. Bubonic plague, the most common form, had a fatality rate of 60 to 85 percent.

The first plague orders, in 1518, provided that infected households in London be marked by bundles of straw hung from the windows for forty days. Inmates were to carry a white stick if they went out into the

ESTIMATES OF PLAGUE DEATHS IN LONDON	
1563	20,000
1578	6,000
1582	7,000
1593	11,505–18,000+
1603	30,583–34,000
1625	35,428–50,000
1636	12,102

streets. The book of plague orders issued by the Privy Council in 1578 was printed in 1583. By then houses were marked with a painted white cross. Still later a wooden cross, painted red, was nailed to the door, since it had proved too easy to wash away white paint. The first pest-house (a hospital for people with an infectious disease) did not open in London until 1594.

The College of Physicians was scarcely more advanced than the local cunning woman when it came to preventing or curing the plague. Doctors often advised the use of a large onion, hollowed out and filled with fig, rue and Venice treacle, as a preventive. Treacle, at least one variety, was made of sixty-four "drugs" including viper's fat. Onions, peeled and left for ten days in the house, were also supposed to absorb all the infection in the air.

Other advice for avoiding infection included drinking four ounces of mummy (dead man's flesh, dried) mixed with ten ounces of spirits of wine, drinking unicorn's horn (swordfish blades) mixed with angelica root, wearing a bag of arsenic next to the skin, and burning old shoes to create purifying fumes.

HEALING WATERS

Drinking or bathing in the waters of the warm spring at Buxton, especially as a cure for gout, became fashionable in Elizabethan times even though the accommodations there were poor. The therapeutic powers of the waters at Bath were lauded in print as early as 1562, but the old Roman baths there did not begin to achieve new popularity until after Queen Anne visited them in 1615. In 1646 there were complaints of rowdies throwing dogs, cats and even pigs into the water while people were bathing. In 1606 the springs at Tonbridge Wells were found to have medicinal value, especially for splenetic distempers. Queen Henrietta Maria visited there. Knarlesborough was discovered, in 1620, to have waters which, while "vitroline" in smell and taste, did wonders for the stomach, bowels, liver, spleen, blood, veins and nerves. The waters at Epsom may have been known as early as 1618 but the spring there tended to dry up. The twin springs at Leamington (one fresh and one salt water) and the spring at Newnham Regis were also in use in the early seventeenth century. In Wales, there was a healing well at Holywell in Flintshire.

AILMENTS

Although plague was the most memorable of the killer diseases and as such has been much studied, a man could die as easily from a cut, a bit of spoiled meat, or the cure mandated by his doctor. Chronic ill-health was normal at all levels of society once middle age was reached. Some of the most common ailments included bronchitis, gout, griping in the guts (gastric upsets), jaundice, kytes (chilblains), lice, rheumatic disorders, runny noses, shingles, sore eyes, sores and worms.

ague: Various intermittent fevers (agues) were probably forms of malaria, which had been endemic in Europe for centuries. The cure (Peruvian Bark) was brought to Spain in 1639 but was not available to the general public. Symptoms of typhoid and of pneumonia may also have been mistaken for malaria. Blackwater fever and Lurden fever were two other names for the condition. The traditional cure in the Fenland was "the stuff," opium poppy juice coagulated into pellets. Spider's web was also recommended as a cure.

apoplexy: "A cold humour which stops the brain" (Andrew Boorde, *Brevyary of Helthe*, 1547), this condition was treated by blowing white hellebore, pepper and "castery" into the nostrils.

asthma: Supposedly cured by wine in which woodlice had been steeped.

bleach: A skin disease that caused a whitening of the skin, bleach was sometimes mistaken for leprosy.

broken limbs: Oil of swallows (made with twenty-one herbs, neat's-foot oil, cloves, wax, butter and twenty live swallows all beaten together) was rubbed on a break after it was set. In 1610, when the earl of Northumberland broke his leg, leaden plates tied on with ribbon were used to set it right. The large, hollow-crowned root of comfrey was used as a bone-setter. The pulp was drawn through a linen cloth, then packed around the straightened bone as it lay in a wooden trough.

chaudepisse (gonorrhea): Believed to arise as a side effect of bladder stones, this venereal disease acquired the name *clap* during the late sixteenth century.

chincough: Whooping cough, known as "the kink" in Scotland.

consumption (tuberculosis): An infection spread most easily in close quarters such as small, smoky houses. Tuberculosis carried off large numbers of young women between the ages of fourteen and twenty. Those who were malnourished were least resistant to the infection. Modern researchers think tuberculosis, undiagnosed at the time, was the probable cause of death of Henry VIII's brother, Arthur, their father, Henry VII, and Henry VIII's illegitimate son, Henry Fitzroy, duke of Richmond. His other son, Edward VI, definitely died of acute pulmonary tuberculosis. Restoratives and cordials were prescribed, including those made of stewed pig, cock in jelly, and raw eggs. One drink said to cure consumption was made by only very slightly roasting half a leg of mutton, a piece of veal, and a capon and squeezing all their juices together with a dash of the juice of an orange.

dropsy: Spoken of as a disease caused by superfluous cold and moist humours, this term was used for some of the symptoms of scurvy and to describe ascites, the accumulation of free fluid in the peritoneal cavity because of colonic cancer or liver failure. As a preventive, blood was let on September 17.

English disease (rickets): Daniel Whistler (1619–1684) got his medical degree at Leyden in 1645 for his treatise on rickets, then known on the Continent as "the English disease" because the first recorded case of death by rickets seems to have been in England in 1634. James I may have suffered from rickets as a child. It is caused by lack of vitamin D in the diet.

falling sickness (epilepsy): Cured by drinking spring water at night from the skull of "one who has been slain." Also useful were cramp-rings, rings hallowed by the monarch on Good Friday. When worn, these rings were also believed to ward off convulsions, rheumatism and muscular spasms. The last blessing of cramp-rings was done by Mary I. Migraine or "megryn" was believed to be closely related to epilepsy.

flux: Probably dysentery and also called scouring and bloody flux and the Lask. Outbreaks often followed famine.

French pox: Early in the sixteenth century, syphilis was at its most virulent in Europe and it reached epidemic proportions in England in 1506 and 1546. The name syphilis came into use only after 1530, derived from the name of a character in a poem by Girolamo

Fracastoro. It was generally referred to in England as the French pox or Great Pox. Early warning signs were the appearance of small lesions followed by a rash. Later manifestations were loss or thinning of hair and a distinctive stench that included bad breath. The favored treatment was the application of a mercurial ointment, although mercury was also administered orally and by fumigation. One salve contained "oldbane, oil of roses, quicksilver, bitterage of gold and turpentine." Turpentine was also popular as a dressing for wounds and serious cuts. As a preventive measure against French pox, men were advised to wash the genitals in vinegar or white wine and engage in "hard pissing" after sex. Women did the same—to avoid getting pregnant. Superior brothels provided separate chamber pots for the whore and her customer.

gaol fever (typhus): Common after the Wars of the Roses, some three hundred people died at the "Black Assizes" at Oxford in 1577. Other outbreaks occurred at assizes at Cambridge in 1522, Exeter in 1586 and Lincoln in 1590, carrying off judges and jurors as well as prisoners. The fatality rate was about 50 percent.

green sickness (chlorosis): Anemia from lack of iron, this was common in young women.

heart disease: Nuts, milk, cheese, meat and fruits were known to be "evil for this."

immoderate pissing (diabetes): Treated with a purge and by forcing the patient to drink cold water until he vomited. Also recommended: eating four eggs prepared with powdered red nettle and sugar every morning.

impostumes: This could include any kind of abscess.

infertility: An infertile woman was advised to swallow an elixir of mare's milk, rabbit's blood and sheep's urine.

insomnia: For insomnia, Andrew Boorde (1490–1549) advised eating lettuce seeds, white poppy seeds or mandragora seeds. Laying a mixture of one ounce of oil of violets, one-half ounce of opium and woman's milk on the temples with a fine linen cloth was also supposed to cure insomnia.

inward burning distaste: Possibly a stomach or duodenal ulcer.

jawfallen: This was the Tudor name for tetanus.

King's evil (scrofula): This disease was really tuberculosis of the soft tissues, generally the lymph nodes in the neck. Supposed to be cured by the royal touch, the form for this ceremony was included in the *Book of Common Prayer* until the reign of George I.

leprosy: This disease had almost died out in England by Tudor times, but the term was also loosely used for skin conditions resulting from lupus, cancer, scabies ("the Scotch disease"), pellagra and scurvy.

measles: Epidemic in 1517, this was dangerous because it often led to pneumonia. The term was also used for any condition in which the skin had spots or pustules.

mother: Disturbances of the mother (uterus) were thought to cause hysteria and could be fatal if swelling caused respiratory difficulty and suffocation. "Heaving of lights" (lungs) was sometimes listed as cause of death.

planet, planetstruck, moonstruck: Any sudden attack of illness, including stroke, catalepsy, paralytic seizure and sunstroke, resulted in a diagnosis of "struck with a planet" or "taken in a planet" because the victim was supposed to have come under the hostile influence of a heavenly body.

pox: This usually meant smallpox rather than French pox or swinepox (the Tudor name for chicken pox). Smallpox was a disease new to England in the sixteenth century, but it became more widespread and increasingly virulent with each passing decade. One of the worst epidemics was in 1562, when Queen Elizabeth nearly died of smallpox. There was about a 30 percent fatality rate. Doctors recommended hanging the patient's bed with red curtains. The worst seventeenth-century outbreak was in 1634–1635. To fumigate Woburn after the countess of Bedford's recovery from smallpox in 1641, pitch and frankincense were burned in both house and yard.

putrid throat (diphtheria): Epidemic in 1517.

scaldhead: A skin disease, possibly ringworm (which was also called tetters).

scurvy: Mentioned on page 27 as a diet-related ailment, scurvy resulted from a lack of vitamin C. It was common at sea (see page 158) but also prevalent as "land scurvy." Symptoms included a cough, shortness of breath, lack of strength, swollen limbs, loose teeth, and pains in the loins, stomach and bowels. Fresh air and fresh food helped and most people believed the coming of spring was the cure. One early seventeenth-century medical guide advised frequent gargling with lemon juice and the "honest company" of one's lawful wife as remedies. The juice of scurvy-grass (mustard and cress) or limes also helped. In the mistaken belief that the more sour the taste, the more effective the cure, vinegar (which had no beneficial effect on scurvy) was substituted for juices in the seventeenth century.

spleen: This term could refer to either migraine or severe depression. Depression, anxiety or concern was also described as "taken in a thought" and was listed as the cause of death in twenty-one cases in the parish of St. Botolph's without Aldgate from 1583 to 1599.

stone: Kidney, bladder or gallstones. One early Tudor remedy was made of white wine and salad oil followed by "carp's eyes in powder with the bone in the carp's head." This was followed by toasted cake buttered with sugar and nutmeg, taken with two draughts of ale. Another cure for the stone was saxifrage root (the "stone breaker"), steeped in the blood of a hare, baked, powdered and taken morning and night. Dried samphire (seaweed) was another remedy.

stytche: Probably appendicitis.

sweating sickness (the English sweat): Possibly a viral infection, but probably not a form of typhus or influenza (which was epidemic in 1557–1559 and 1579–1580). Epidemics of the mysterious disease called "the sweat" afflicted England in 1485, 1507–8, 1517, 1528 and 1551, with a 40 percent mortality rate, then never appeared again. Only in 1528–9 did it affect any other country. All the outbreaks began in summer. Victims might be dead in as little as two hours. Sleep was believed to be fatal, so sufferers were kept awake, usually in a closed room with a fire, until the sweat ran its course. The only food they were allowed was a crust of bread soaked in ale, whole mace and sugar. Among the preventives for the sweat, all of which could be kept in glass boxes up to thirty years and improved with age, were:

1. A mixture of endive, sowthistle, marigold, mercury and nightshade

2. Three large spoonfuls of water of dragons and half a nutshell of unicorn's horn

3. Philosopher's egg ("crushed egg, its white blown out, mixed shell and all with saffron, mustard seed, herbs and unicorn's horn")

toothache: Believed to be caused by worms, or by unbalanced humours. Chewing horehound root was recommended.

tympany (gas): To avoid wind after meals, it was recommended that one take, one hour before eating, a draught of sugar, coriander, conserve of roses, margaret, galanza root, aniseed and cinnamon. Tympany could also refer to a more serious condition that developed from excessive gas in the abdomen. This was thought to be a form of dropsy and was also called wind colic.

watery humours: Inflammation of the kidneys.

MEDICINES

One apothecary list included preservative lozenges, cinnamon comfits, liquorice pastilles, suppositories made from olive oil ointment, a lozenge cordial, plasters for the spleen, sponges for fomentation, and pills of mastick and of Elsham ginger. The physic border recommended for a kitchen garden included eringoe (sea-holly), mandrake, blessed thistle, wormwood, plantain and valerian. The kitchen garden itself would probably include harefoot, blood-wort (or bloody dock), pennyroyal, marigolds, sea-blite, burnet and tansy. Thomas Tusser's mid-sixteenth-century "Essential Home Remedies" included aqua vitae, tart vinegar, rosewater, treacle, cold herbs, white endive, succory, "water of fumitory" and conserves of barberry and quince.

The new "chemical medicines," metals and mineral salts introduced in the late sixteenth century (such things as oil of vitriol) included many poisons, such as arsenic. The Grocers and Apothecaries' Act of 1557 specified that no one could sell poison unless he was sure of the honesty of the buyer. Buyers' names and the dates of their purchases were to be recorded.

Theriacs were any herbal compounds effective as antidotes to poison. They were also used as cures for other ailments. Mithridate or mithridatium was a compound of seventy-two ingredients and was itself an ingredient in many medicines. Oliver Cromwell took mithridatium as a preventive for plague and it had the happy side effect of clearing up his acne.

Home remedies which were widely known and used included taking "purging beer" in the spring for general health. This drink was made of scurvy grass, watercress, liverwort, rhubarb (Andrew Boorde sent the first rhubarb seeds back to England from the Barbary Coast around the year 1540), red dock, raisins and oranges. Hazelnuts, rue and garlic mashed with treacle and taken in beer were believed to rid a person of the venom of an adder bite or that from the bite of a mad dog. Also, the key to a church door was said to be effective against a mad dog. For a bad bruise, tradition urged the prompt application of fried horse dung.

HERBAL CURES

comfrey (Saracen's root): Together with calamint, liquorice, enula, campana and hyssop, comfrey was good for the lungs. Its juice was used to wash wounds, and as a bone setter.

lavender: Good for catalepsy, "a light megrim," the falling sickness and swooning. It was also prescribed for apoplexy, with dire results.

lettuce: Supposed to cure both insomnia and gonorrhea. Those who believed eating lettuce interfered with sexual intercourse and weakened eyesight mixed it with celery to avoid those side effects.

periwinkle: Holding two leaves between the teeth would stanch the blood flowing from a wound.

saffron: Believed to cure stomach problems and strengthen the heart, dried saffron was also an antidote for poison and a cure for smallpox. It grew at Saffron Waldron and other locations. The leaves and flowers were most potent if they were gathered between Lady Day (March 25) and Midsummer (June 24), the stalks and fruits between Midsummer and Michaelmas (September 29), and the roots between Michaelmas and Lady Day.

sassafras: A sovereign remedy for the pox, this should not be confused with saxifrage. Sassafras was native to North America and unknown in Europe before 1528.

MAGICAL STONES

amethyst: Counteracts drunkenness.

bezoar stone: A stony mass found in stomach of goats; used in a variety of medicines.

chelidonius: Found in the belly of a swallow, this stone was wrapped in a fair cloth and tied to the right arm to cure lunatics and madmen of their lunacy and madness and make them "amiable and merry."

coral: Used for diagnostic purposes, it turned pale when the person wearing it was sick and returned to its former color as the patient recovered.

jet: A hard, compact black form of lignite (a fossil deposit), jet was polished to a high gloss and worn to ward off phantasms due to melancholy.

sapphire: Held in the hand, sapphire was effective against the sweating sickness.

toad-stone: The stone in the marrow of the head of the earth toad. Also called borax and lapis bufon, this was taken when the moon was waning and put in a linen cloth for forty days, then cut from the cloth. The stone was a powerful amulet, hung at the girdle to cure dropsy and the spleen. It was also, when swallowed, a remedy against all sorts of poison.

SELECT BIBLIOGRAPHY

Copeman, W.S.C. *Doctors and Disease in Tudor Times.* London: Dawson's of Pall Mall, 1960.

Evans, Joan. *Magical Jewels of the Middle Ages and the Renaissance, particularly in England.* New York: Dover Publications, 1976.

Slack, Paul. *The Impact of Plague in Tudor and Stuart England.* Boston: Routledge and Kegan Paul, 1985.

Thomas, Keith. *Religion and the Decline of Magic: Studies in Popular Beliefs in Sixteenth and Seventeenth Century England.* New York: Scribner, 1976.

Webster, Charles, ed. *Health, Medicine and Mortality in the Sixteenth Century.* Cambridge: Cambridge University Press, 1979.

PART TWO

Government and War

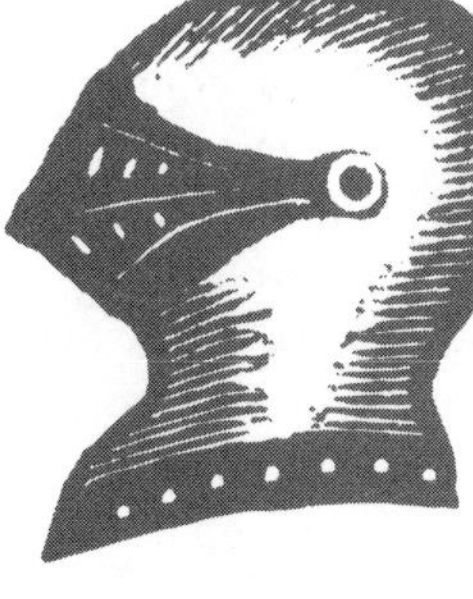

CHAPTER SEVEN

GOVERNMENT

Engla nd was a personal monarchy in Tudor and Stuart times. Some four million English men and women were subjects, not citizens. Civil servants worked for the Crown, not the state. In fact, the term "state" in its modern sense did not even exist much before 1540.

Although England claimed Ireland (English-Irish relations will be discussed in chapter eleven) and was, after 1603, united with Scotland, only with Wales was there a real blending of government and legal systems. With the Act of Union of 1536, all distinctions were abolished between the old pricipality and the marches (border lands). English law was extended into Wales, and Welsh counties were thereafter represented in the English parliament.

In 1603, 20 percent of England's people were living in the Thames valley, most of them in London. Those counties close to the center of government tended to be more closely regulated. Those at some distance, such as Lancashire and Northumberland, with small populations and little wealth, were often neglected by the central government and consequently allowed to go their own way. Everywhere in England, however, keeping "order" was the most important function of government. Until the Book of Orders of 1630 attempted to reorganize the administration of counties into a divisional system, a fairly straightforward pecking order prevailed.

THE PRIVY COUNCIL

The power of the realm centered on this body. What had been a large, unwieldy King's Council was reduced under Henry VIII to the Privy Council, rarely numbering more than twenty. It was essentially a cabinet made up of experts chosen by the monarch. Usually only eight to ten key members regularly attended meetings. Decisions were actually made by only two or three trusted advisors. The Principal Secretary was the most influential Privy Council post under Elizabeth I. Her Privy Council of 1601 consisted of one archbishop, five peers, five knights, one judge and one gentleman. Of those, six held offices of state, including Lord Chancellor, Lord Admiral and Lord Treasurer.

DEPARTMENTS OF CENTRAL GOVERNMENT

Four departments handled government business for the monarch. Chancery drafted royal grants, treaties, appointments and acts. This office was headed by the Lord Chancellor, who was Speaker of the House of Lords, head of the law courts, presiding judge in the Star Chamber and the Court of Chancery and, frequently, also Keeper of the Great Seal. The functions of Chancery and Star Chamber as law courts will be covered in chapter nine. Chancery also made documents official with the Great Seal. The Privy Seal office, which employed four clerks and several deputies, drew up and sent instructions to royal officials and used the Privy Seal. The Signet office handled personal correspondence for the monarch and the Signet was held by the principal secretary. The fourth department was the Exchequer, which handled royal revenue and also served as an income tax tribunal.

Offices in the central government were distributed through a system of patronage. Elizabeth I had about twenty-five hundred offices at her disposal, of which about twelve hundred were "worth a gentleman's having." Those eligible to serve by reason of being gentlemen, knights or peers, numbered above twenty thousand.

PARLIAMENT

Parliaments were summoned and dissolved at the monarch's pleasure, and were usually summoned only when the monarch needed them to approve taxes, legislate on a specific topic (such as declaring that

Elizabeth possessed supreme authority in all matters ecclesiastical) or to give advice on policy. Under Henry VII there were eleven sessions, most at the beginning of the reign. Henry VIII, Edward VI and Mary called another thirty-nine parliaments, but one, the Reformation Parliament of Henry VIII, stayed in session from 1529 to 1536. Under Elizabeth, Parliament met thirteen times. The Stuarts were even less fond of Parliament, particularly because by then statutes (acts of Parliament) had been established as the highest form of law and could even override a royal proclamation. This was not the case in Scotland, where James I had already been king, as James VI, since 1567. The English Civil War was immediately preceded by eleven years without Parliament, Charles I's "personal rule." The Long Parliament of 1640 was overwhelmingly opposed to the king's policies and by Christmas 1641, hostilities were imminent. On August 22, 1642, King Charles formally declared war on Parliament. When he was later tried and condemned to death, he refused to acknowledge Parliament's right to do either, but in spite of his objections to the proceedings, he was executed on January 30, 1649.

During the Tudor period there was a gradual shift in importance away from the House of Lords (predominantly a lay assembly after the break with Rome) to the House of Commons. At the same time, the size of Commons grew. There were still only 2 members for each county, each city and each borough but the number of municipalities increased. When Wales was incorporated into England, twelve counties and eleven boroughs were added, each returning 1 member, and 2 new English counties (Monmouthshire and Cheshire) were formed. Only one "county" had no representation, the Palatinate of Durham. After that the number of county members was fixed at 90, but the number of borough members continued to increase. Henry VIII added 14 borough seats, Edward VI 34, Mary 25 and Elizabeth 62. Between 1547 and 1584, 119 new borough seats were added, some created at the request of courtier peers.

Although M.P.s were supposed to be residents of the constituency they represented, this was one of those laws that was ignored. Gentlemen were regularly elected at the request of the local nobility to represent boroughs they might never even have visited.

The Speaker of the House of Commons was formally elected by the House, but was in reality selected by the Crown. There were two Clerks of Parliament, the senior clerk, who served the House of Lords, and the underclerk, who served the Commons. They compiled journals, kept custody of draft bills, and read the texts to the House.

LOCAL (COUNTY) GOVERNMENT

William the Conqueror divided England into forty-two counties. There were thirty-eight counties (also called shires) in 1515. William Harrison's *Description of England* (first published in 1577 but written in the 1560s) names forty shires in England and thirteen in Wales. In 1630, Bristol, Durham, Gloucester and Worcester were all county boroughs; in other words, each was a county as well as a city. Each county had certain local officials who were appointed by the Crown. Sheriffs, justices of the peace, chief constables and petty constables will be discussed in chapter nine. In addition, the monarch chose a Lord Lieutenant and a Deputy Lieutenant.

The Lord Lieutenant was a Tudor invention and served as the monarch's personal representative. One Lord Lieutenant might have more than one county to oversee, and he might also be a Privy Councillor. The Lord Lieutenants and Deputy Lieutenants were responsible for supervising the trained bands, a county militia officially established in 1573. Between 1605 and 1614, the trained bands numbered about 5,850 men and 150 horses, but only 2,000 were armed with muskets and pikes.

Deputy Lieutenants oversaw the impressment of men for service in expeditionary forces, provisioning these men with a good coat and eightpence a day for food while they were marched to the nearest port. Troops for service abroad were levied on an ad hoc basis and taken from the bottom of society. About 10 percent deserted and another 50 percent were found to be unfit for service. A total of 106,000 men were sent to Ireland, the Netherlands, France and Spain during the reign of Elizabeth, 12,600 of them in 1601 alone.

TREASON

When Henry VII won the throne at the Battle of Bosworth in 1485, he consolidated his claim by marrying Elizabeth, eldest daughter of Edward IV, and uniting the warring factions of Lancaster and York. There were, however, rival claimants to the crown, and whether the

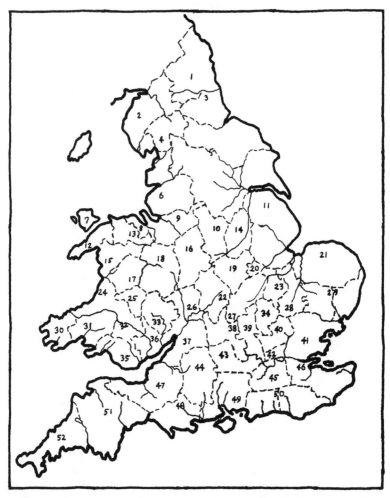

A map showing the counties of England under Elizabeth I

Key to map of counties:

1. Northumberland
2. Cumberland
3. Durham
4. Westmorland
5. Yorkshire
6. Lancashire
7. Anglesey
8. Flintshire
9. Cheshire
10. Derbyshire
11. Lincolnshire
12. Caernarfonshire
13. Denbighshire
14. Nottinghamshire
15. Merionethshire
16. Staffordshire
17. Montgomeryshire
18. Shropshire (Salop)
19. Leicestershire
20. Rutland
21. Norfolk
22. Warwickshire
23. Huntingdonshire
24. Cardiganshire
25. Radnorshire
26. Worcestershire
27. Northamptonshire
28. Cambridgeshire
29. Suffolk
30. Pembrokeshire
31. Carmarthenshire
32. Breconshire
33. Herefordshire
34. Bedfordshire
35. Glamorganshire
36. Monmouthshire
37. Gloucestershire
38. Oxfordshire
39. Buckinghamshire
40. Hertfordshire
41. Essex
42. Middlesex
43. Berkshire
44. Wiltshire
45. Surrey
46. Kent
47. Somerset
48. Dorset
49. Hampshire
50. Sussex
51. Devonshire
52. Cornwall

threat they posed was real or imagined, some of them ended up being charged with treason.

The first serious rebellion came in 1487 and was settled by Henry's victory at the Battle of Stoke on June 16. There were three pretenders to the throne. In May 1487, Lambert Simnel was crowned "King Edward VI" in Christ Church, Dublin, after claiming to be Edward Plantagenet, earl of Warwick, who had the best claim to the throne. Warwick, however, was a prisoner in the Tower and could be produced. Later, one Ralph Wilsford also claimed to be Warwick. Perkin Warbeck said he was Richard, younger of the two princes who were supposedly murdered in the Tower of London. On September 7, 1497, Warbeck landed at Land's End, Cornwall, with three ships, one hundred men and a royal wife (Catherine Gordon, cousin of Scotland's James IV). Captured, Warbeck was kept at court under light guard. His wife became one of Elizabeth of York's ladies. When Warbeck escaped in 1498, he was quickly recaptured and confined in the Tower of London. In 1499 both he and the earl of Warwick finally were executed.

Others with Plantagenet blood who were executed on charges of treason were Edward Stafford, third duke of Buckingham, in 1521; Henry Courtenay, marquis of Exeter, and Henry Pole, Baron Montagu, in 1538; and Margaret Plantagenet, countess of Salisbury (Warwick's sister) who, after two years in the Tower, was beheaded without a trial in 1541. It was sufficient that she had been declared guilty of treason by an Act of Parliament (a bill of attainder—those affected were "attainted") in 1539. The countess refused to cooperate in her own death and had to be chased around the block by the executioner.

Under Henry VIII a great many more things became treasonous. After 1536 it was treason for anyone with royal blood to marry without the monarch's permission. Because of the charge of treason brought against Arthur Plantagenet, Lord Lisle, an illegitimate son of Edward IV, all the family's letters and papers were seized in April 1540. Lord Lisle and Lady Lisle were both placed in custody, and there was a furor when authorities discovered that Mary Bassett, Lady Lisle's daughter by a previous marriage, had entered into a secret marriage contract with Gabriel de Montmorency, Seigneur de Bours, a Frenchman, without Henry VIII's consent. When Mary tried to get rid of her love letters by throwing them down the jakes, the letters were assumed to contain treason.

Written and spoken words, as well as overt actions, might constitute treason under Henry VIII. As soon as Edward VI took the throne, Parliament repealed all the treason and heresy acts of Henry's reign, but the duke of Somerset, Edward's Lord Protector (Edward was only nine when he became king), pushed through a new act which tightened up the procedure in treason trials. Ironically, he was himself tried and convicted for treason and executed in 1552.

Throughout the sixteenth century, the laws on treason were expanded and refined. Some of the most significant conspiracies and rebellions against the realm, most of which are too complex to address in detail in this book, are listed at the end of this chapter. In addition, there were many treason trials of people like Mary Cleere of Ingatestone, Essex, who was burnt at the stake in 1576 for saying that Queen Elizabeth was baseborn.

Queen Mary I persecuted Protestants as traitors. To be Catholic in Elizabethan England was illegal, but whether it was also treasonable depended upon the individual. Under Elizabeth, most irreconcilable Catholics went abroad. Those called "church papists" by the Protestants and schismatics by other Catholics made a show of attending church, as the law required, but clung to their old beliefs in secret. Recusants were those who refused to attend Anglican services. They were continually fined (twelvepence for each offense) for their failure to do so. Early in the reign, saying mass cost a priest a year's income and sent him to prison for six months for a first offense. The second offense cost him his benefices and sent him to prison for a year. The third offense meant life imprisonment. Similarly, those convicted of hearing mass were fined one hundred marks for the first offense and four hundred marks for the second offense. Their goods were confiscated and they were sent to prison for life for a third offense.

In 1581 the law became much more severe. Those trying to win persons from the Church of England were traitors. Those they persuaded were also guilty of high treason. Those who aided and abetted the others were guilty of misprision (neglecting to report a crime) of treason, which was also a felony. There was still a distinction, however, between being Catholic and becoming Catholic. Those who had been Catholics all along were not traitors, but they now had to pay even greater fines, twenty pounds a month for failure to attend church. The penalty for hearing mass became a fine of one hundred marks and a year in prison.

In 1568, Dr. William Allen had founded a seminary at Douai in

Flanders which sent missionary priests into England. The seminary moved to Rheims in 1578 and continued to train militant Catholics who were prepared to become martyrs. Many were caught and executed for treason (an estimated 180 Catholics were executed between 1570 and 1603) but others were deported. In April 1584, seventeen priests were being held in the Marshalsea Prison in London. In January 1585, some of them were among the forty "Jesuits and seminaries" sent by prison ship to Normandy.

On occasion Puritan extremists also ran afoul of the treason laws. When John Stubbs's *The Discovery of a Gaping Gulf Whereinto England is Like to Be Swallowed by Another French Marriage* was published in 1579, criticizing Queen Elizabeth, she ordered both Stubbs and his printer, William Page, to be hanged, drawn and quartered as traitors. The sentence was commuted to losing their right hands by knife and block. Copies of the offending book were confiscated and destroyed. Those Puritan extremists who operated the so-called Marprelate Press were also guilty of treason for turning out seditious publications.

Religion continued to be a political issue under the Stuarts. The Gunpowder Plot in 1605 was prompted by new anti-Catholic legislation. Under Charles I, it was not Queen Henrietta Maria's Catholicism that concerned the English so much as what was perceived as his subversion of the Church of England by appointing William Laud the new archbishop of Canterbury in 1633. Laud opposed church reforms proposed by the Puritans. In addition, in 1637, he attempted to introduce the Anglican liturgy into Scotland. Riots ensued, the so-called "Bishop's War," and that eventually led to Laud's impeachment by Parliament. He was executed as a traitor in 1645.

CONSPIRACIES AND REBELLIONS

1489: The Yorkshire Rebellion during which the fourth earl of Northumberland was assassinated.

1497: A Cornish Rebellion over being forced to pay taxes to fight Scotland. The rebels were led by Thomas Flamank, a lawyer, and Michael Joseph, a blacksmith. They were joined by James, Lord Audley. All three were executed.

1533: The prophesies of the "Nun of Kent" were used to stir up public feeling against Henry VIII's plans to divorce Catherine of Aragon. The nun, Elizabeth Barton, was executed for treason in 1534.

1534: William, fourth Lord Dacre, Warden of the West Marches, was tried for treason for holding secret meetings with Scots enemies in wartime. He was acquitted by his peers but was not reappointed warden until after Henry VIII's death.

1536: The Lincolnshire Rising over rumors of government control, restrictions and taxes. More than ten thousand marched on Lincoln, then disbanded.

1536–7: The Pilgrimage of Grace, a disorganized rebellion caused in part by disapproval of Henry VIII's dissolution of the monasteries, led to 178 recorded executions.

1540: The Botolf Conspiracy (Gregory "Sweet Lips" Botolf was one of Lord Lisle's chaplains) planned to seize Calais during "herring time" (September 29 to November 30), when the port city was overrun with herring buyers and sellers. It was this conspiracy which led to Lord Lisle's arrest.

1549: Lord Admiral Thomas Seymour was arrested for trying to overthrow his brother, the Lord Protector, kidnap King Edward VI, and marry the princess Elizabeth. He was executed on March 19.

1549: Kett's Rebellion in East Anglia (Norfolk and Suffolk) was just one of several riots and rebellions to protest enclosures and demand justice. Rumor claimed three hundred executions followed, but existing records show only forty-nine.

1553: John Dudley, duke of Northumberland, attempted to put Lady Jane Grey on the throne instead of Mary I. He was executed. For further information on Lady Jane see page 105.

1554: Sir Thomas Wyatt the Younger attempted to overthrow Queen Mary and put a Protestant monarch on the throne in her place. Over six hundred men were arrested. Almost one hundred, including Wyatt and the duke of Suffolk (Lady Jane Grey's father), were executed.

1559: A Protestant rising in Scotland succeeded with English support. In 1560, Protestantism became the official religion of Scotland.

1569: The Northern Rebellion, also called the Revolt of the Northern

Earls, was led by the earl of Westmorland and the earl of Northumberland. The agitators were Richard Norton, age eighty-one, sheriff of Yorkshire; Norton's son-in-law, Thomas Markenfeld; Westmorland's uncle, Christopher Neville; and Dr. Nicholas Morton, an official of the papal court who brought word that Elizabeth was about to be excommunicated by the Pope. Eventually some six hundred persons were executed for their involvement in the rising.

1571: The Ridolfi Plot (named for Robert Ridolfi, a Florentine banker living in London) involved a plan to marry Thomas Howard, fourth duke of Norfolk, to Mary, Queen of Scots. Although Norfolk denied he'd been party to the plot, he was executed for treason in 1572.

1583: The Throgmorton Plot came to light when Francis Throgmorton was arrested and tortured. He confessed that the French duc de Guise intended to invade England in the Catholic cause, financed by Philip II of Spain and the Pope. Throgmorton was executed at Tyburn and the Spanish ambassador, Bernardo de Mendoza, was expelled from England.

1585: The Parry Conspiracy. Dr. William Parry was executed for plotting to assassinate Queen Elizabeth.

1586: The Babington Plot involved fourteen conspirators, including Anthony Babington, who were plotting to put Mary, Queen of Scots on the English throne. The conspirators were executed in September 1586. Mary was beheaded in February 1587.

1591: A Catholic plot to marry Elizabeth's likely heir, Lady Arbella Stuart, to Rainutio Farnese, son of the duke of Parma, was uncovered and prevented by sending Arbella to her grandmother, Bess of Hardwick, in Derbyshire.

1593: The Hesketh Plot sought to make Ferdinando Stanley, fifth earl of Derby, king. Derby himself turned Richard Hesketh over to the authorities.

1594: Dr. Rodrigo Lopez, chief physician to the queen since 1586, was executed for plotting to poison Elizabeth. Lopez was a Jew, and anti-Semitism played a role in the verdict.

1598: Edward Squire was caught trying to kill the queen by putting poison on the pommel of her saddle. It was to have seeped through her gloves and into her skin.

1601: The Essex Rebellion was the attempt by Robert Devereux, second earl of Essex, to protect Queen Elizabeth by ridding her realm of traitors like her Principal Secretary, Sir Robert Cecil. Essex was executed for treason. His fellow conspirator, Henry Wriothesley, third earl of Southampton, was imprisoned in the Tower of London.

1603: The Bye Plot and the Main Plot were separate conspiracies but are usually spoken of together. The plan to put Arbella Stuart on the throne led to the imprisonment of Sir Walter Ralegh. There is some evidence that he was set up and the accusation that he conspired with the Spanish, long his sworn enemies, hardly fits his character.

1605: The Gunpowder Plot, known at the time as the Powder Treason, was an attempt to blow up king, court and Parliament. It was foiled by a last-minute discovery that was probably orchestrated for maximum public-relations effect.

1611: Mary Cavendish Talbot, countess of Shrewsbury, was tried before the Star Chamber for helping Arbella Stuart escape from the Tower. The countess was held until 1618, when she was released on payment of a fine of twenty thousand pounds. Lady Arbella was recaptured and kept in prison until her death.

1629: Grain riots at Maldon, Essex. Food riots were a long-standing tradition. There were smaller riots in 1527, 1551, 1586–7, 1594–8, 1605, 1608, 1614, 1622–3, 1630–31 and 1647–8. In March 1629, some one hundred women boarded a Flemish ship and forced the crew to fill their caps and aprons with grain (rye) from the hold. In May, a large number of people (two hundred to three hundred) attacked ships taking on grain. Four were executed, including a woman, Ann Carter.

1642: The outbreak of Civil War. In 1646, King Charles I surrendered to the Scots. In 1649 he was executed.

SELECT BIBLIOGRAPHY

Fletcher, Anthony. *Tudor Rebellions*. London: Longman, 1968.

Graves, M.A.R. and R.H. Silcock. *Revolution, Reaction and the Triumph of Conservatism: English History 1558–1700*. London and New York: Longman, 1984.

Haynes, Alan. *Invisible Power: The Elizabethan Secret Services 1570–1603*. New York: St. Martin's Press, 1992.

Russell, Conrad. *Crisis of Parliaments: English History 1509–1660*. London: Oxford University Press, 1971.

Smith, Lacey Baldwin. *Treason in Tudor England: Politics and Paranoia*. Princeton, New Jersey: Princeton University Press, 1986.

CHAPTER EIGHT

MONARCHS, NOBLES AND COMMONERS

The reigning monarchs for the period 1500–1650 were Henry VII (1457–1509), Henry VIII (1491–1547), Edward VI (1537–1553), Mary I (1516–1558), Elizabeth I (1533–1603), James I (1566–1625) and Charles I (1600–1649).

THE SUCCESSION

As discussed in chapter seven (see page 95), Henry VII of Lancaster married Elizabeth of York (1465–1503) to bolster his claim to the throne and also systematically eliminated any rival who appeared. His heir, Arthur, Prince of Wales, died in 1502, leaving only one son to carry on. That son, Henry VIII, made his six marriages, at least in part, to secure the succession. The wives were (1) Catherine of Aragon (1486–1536), (2) Anne Boleyn (1507–1536), (3) Jane Seymour (1509–1537), (4) Anne of Cleves (1515–1557), (5) Catherine Howard (1521–1542) and (6) Catherine Parr (1514–1548). Henry ended up with two daughters, Mary and Elizabeth, and one sickly son. The Act of Succession of 1536 declared both Mary and Elizabeth illegitimate, but they were reinstated in the succession by another Act of Parliament in 1544. Henry also devised a will to indicate his preference that, after the succession of his own children, the children of his older sister, Margaret, be passed over in favor of the children of his younger sister, Mary. Lady Jane Grey (1537–1554), granddaughter of Henry VIII's younger sister, was chosen by John Dudley, duke of Northumberland and Edward VI's guardian, to succeed the boy king and prevent the realm from returning to Catholicism, as it was sure to do if Mary I succeeded her brother. Northumberland persuaded Lady Jane's mother to relinquish her own claim to the throne in Lady Jane's favor, then married the girl to one of his own sons, Lord Guildford Dudley, and got the dying king to declare his cousin as his successor. Had Northumberland managed to capture Mary, he might have succeeded in his scheme, but she eluded him, raised an army and took back the throne. Lady Jane's "reign" lasted nine days. She and Lord Guildford were executed in 1554 as a result of Wyatt's Rebellion.

Mary I wed Philip II of Spain (1527–1598) in 1554, but died childless. Elizabeth I never married at all, and refused to name an heir until she was on her deathbed. During the period from 1554 until 1603, when James I (the great-grandson of Henry VIII's sister Margaret) succeeded peacefully, there were a number of contenders.

Lady Frances Brandon, duchess of Suffolk (1517–1559), was the daughter of Henry VIII's younger sister and the mother not only of Lady Jane, but also of Lady Catherine and Lady Mary Grey. After her husband's execution in 1554, the duchess married her Master of the Horse. Lady Catherine Grey (1539–1568) lived at court as heiress presumptive until she disgraced herself by secretly marrying Edward Seymour, earl of Hertford. She bore him two sons while they were both imprisoned in the Tower. Lady Mary Grey (1542–1578) eloped with a commoner, Thomas Keyes, in 1565. They were separated and Lady Mary was confined for the remainder of her life.

Lady Margaret Clifford, Lady Strange and later countess of Derby (1540–1596), was also a descendant of Henry VIII's younger sister. She had an interest in alchemy and was believed to be a Catholic, both factors against Elizabeth considering her or her sons as successors.

Lady Margaret Douglas, countess of Lennox (1515–1578), was the daughter of Henry VIII's elder sister. Her romantic entanglements during Henry VIII's reign got her in trouble more than once. In Elizabeth's reign she was twice imprisoned over the marriages of her children, when Henry, Lord Darnley, wed the queen of Scots in 1565, and again when Charles, earl of Lennox, married Bess of Hardwick's daughter, Elizabeth Cavendish. This second union produced Lady

Arbella Stuart (1575–1615), who was considered by many to be the leading candidate to succeed Elizabeth. Unlike her cousin, James of Scotland, she had been born in England. After James succeeded, Arbella eloped with William Seymour, a grandson of Lady Catherine Grey. As this unauthorized marriage constituted treason, Lady Arbella spent the rest of her life in prison and died childless.

Mary, Queen of Scots (1542–1587) was Elizabeth's most serious challenger for the throne. Mary even quartered the English arms with her own when Mary I died in 1558. At that time, Mary was queen of France. After the death of her husband, Francis II, she returned to Scotland, married Lord Darnley and possibly murdered him, then married the earl of Bothwell. Deposed (she abdicated in favor of her son, James VI, in 1567) and driven out of Scotland, she sought asylum in England and was promptly imprisoned. She was executed in 1587 on very suspect evidence of a plot to seize Elizabeth's throne.

Three other candidates had much more distant claims. Henry Hastings, third earl of Huntingdon (1535–1595), a descendant of the duke of Clarence, brother of Edward IV, had Puritan leanings. The Infanta Clara Eugenia, daughter of the king of Spain, was a descendant of Edward III. She had the backing of the Jesuits. And Robert Devereux, earl of Essex (1567–1601), had a very distant strain of Plantagenet blood, enough to make him believe he could "save" the country with his ill-advised coup in 1601.

Once James VI of Scotland became James I of England in 1603, the succession was clear. He had two sons by Anne of Denmark (1574–1619). Henry, Prince of Wales, died at eighteen but James's second son, Charles, became Charles I in 1625. He married Henrietta Maria of France (1609–1669).

THE COURT

"The court" was everything within a ten-mile radius of wherever the monarch was living, or the "customary precincts" of Whitehall, Richmond or Greenwich. In some respects, the Royal Court was like a small town, or a large family. For most of the year, especially in the summer, it moved about a good deal. This was necessary to allow a royal residence to be cleaned. Between four hundred and eight hundred people accompanied the monarch, most with household servants of their own. The duke of Northumberland, in 1553, had forty gentlemen and thirty yeomen ushers in his personal retinue, while the marquis of Northampton's household at court numbered thirty-four gentlemen and thirteen yeomen.

By 1558 the Lord High Steward and Lord Great Chamberlain were both hereditary offices, ceremonial in nature. The Lord High Steward carried a white staff as a symbol of office and, at the funeral of the sovereign, broke it over his own head before the bier. The "Board of Green Cloth" consisted of the "white staves," the treasurer and the comptroller of the household, the cofferer, and some of the clerks of the counting house. They had responsibility for day-to-day operations in the royal household. The Lord High Steward was in charge of twenty-five "below-stairs" departments, each of which had a serjeant, clerk and purveyor, plus numerous junior assistants.

The Lord Great Chamberlain was responsible for the "above-stairs" servants, who served the monarch in the bedchamber, privy chamber and presence chamber. Henry VII created the concept of a privy chamber, primarily to give the monarch some privacy. When Henry VIII increased the number of gentlemen of the chamber (to 112 in 1526) that original purpose was lost. In 1526 the entire household was reorganized by the Eltham Ordinances, which reduced the number of gentlemen of the chamber to 12 and the number of grooms of the chamber from 69 to 15. At any one time, Henry VIII's attendants now included only 16 gentlemen, 2 gentlemen ushers, 4 gentlemen ushers serving as waiters, 3 grooms and 2 barbers in the privy chamber and 3 cupbearers, 3 carvers, 3 servers, 4 squires of the body and 2 surveyors in the outer chamber. The most important post was that of Groom of the Stool (sometimes written Stole), who was responsible for the royal close-stool.

One important and much-sought-after office was conferred by royal patent. This was the post of Master of the Horse. He had a staff of sixty under Henry VIII. The kennels alone were staffed by ten men, whose only duty was to look after the royal greyhounds, harthounds and harriers.

A special sort of royal servant was the entertainer. King Henry VIII's fool, Will Somers, was the most famous, but there were a number of other fools, and dwarfs, at court. There were also royal musicians, sixty of them in 1547, including fifteen trumpeters and a bagpiper.

Under Henry VIII the number of beds (and horses) permitted to courtiers varied by rank. A duke was entitled to keep twenty-four horses and got nine beds for his retainers. An earl might keep eighteen horses and have seven beds while the Lord Chamberlain was entitled to seven beds. A dowager duchess was allotted seven beds, a queen's maid three and the master of jewels one. Grooms of the privy chamber got two beds for four men.

The king's wife had a separate household. Catherine of Aragon's numbered 160 (she'd had 44 as Princess of Wales), including 8 ladies-in-waiting and 8 ladies of the bedchamber and maids of honour. Anne Boleyn's household numbered 200, as did Jane Seymour's. Anne of Cleves made do with only 126 and the ladies-in-waiting, now reduced to 6, were renamed "great ladies of the household." In Queen Catherine Howard's household were 6 "great ladies," 4 ladies of the privy chamber, 9 attendants "of exalted rank," 5 maids of honour, a mother of maids and several chamberers.

Since the attendants closest to Mary I and Elizabeth I were women and could not become Privy Councillors, the privy chamber lost much of its importance as a political entity after 1554. Mary had 7 ladies and 13 gentlewomen in her private retinue. Queen Elizabeth generally had 4 ladies of the bedchamber, 7 or 8 gentlewomen of the privy chamber (paid £33 6s. 8d. per annum), 6 to 8 maids of honour and 3 or 4 chamberers (paid £20 per annum). There were also 39 unpaid "ladies of honor" during her reign, who appeared with her on ceremonial occasions.

In 1603 the privy chamber of James I consisted of 48 gentlemen, half of them English and half of them Scots. They waited in quarterly shifts of 12. The size of the court increased overall under the Stuarts until, in 1640, the combined households of King Charles, his queen, and the Prince of Wales numbered over 1,700 persons.

THE PEERAGE

The peerage of England under the Tudors was relatively small. Thirty-four peers were summoned to Henry VII's first Parliament in 1485 (two dukes, ten earls, two viscounts and twenty barons). Of a total of fifty-five lords, six were minors under the age of twenty-one and five were under attainder. Between 1485 and 1509, three viscounties and four baronies disappeared permanently from the peerage for lack of heirs. One peer created by Henry VII, Philibert de Chandee, who had been

Henry Wriothesley, third earl of Southampton, in the Tower of London with his cat
Southampton was in many ways typical of an Elizabethan nobleman. He lived beyond his means, secretly married one of Queen Elizabeth's maids of honor, and ended up in the Tower of London for his part in the Essex Rebellion of 1601. Note the long hair, the beard and mustache, the falling band type of collar and the embroidered glove. According to legend, the earl's faithful cat scaled the prison wall to be with him. Southampton was released in 1603. Other domestic animals included in their masters' portraits were horses, dogs, birds and squirrels.

109

captain of Henry's mercenary troops, vanishes from history following his elevation to Earl of Bath in 1486.

In 1509, England had only one duke, one marquis (a prisoner in Calais, accused of treason), ten earls and thirty barons. Although Henry VIII created a number of new peers, the entire peerage had only increased to fifty-one by 1547. The upheaval of Edward VI's minority led to the creation of two dukes, Somerset (1547) and Northumberland (1551), but both were executed for treason and their titles were forfeit. In 1553 there were fifty-six peers. This number had increased to fifty-seven by 1558 when Elizabeth I became queen but she created or restored only eighteen peerages. The only remaining duke, Norfolk, was executed for treason in 1572. No new dukes were created until 1623.

Elizabeth was not only stingy about granting peerages, she was also parsimonious when it came to gifts of land to accompany such honors. In 1572, when Sir Henry Sidney was about to be offered a barony without any property, his wife wrote to Lord Burghley to ask him to dissuade the queen. They could not, she explained, maintain a higher title than they now possessed. Sir Henry, as a loyal subject, was already spending a great deal of his own money in the service of the queen.

The right to succeed to a barony created by writ (writ of summons to Parliament) was not limited to male heirs. A woman could inherit such a barony, but in actual fact was not always allowed to. Baronies granted by patent or charter (rare before the sixteenth century) often limited the succession to male heirs.

In 1603, when James became king, there were 55 peers in England. In need of money, he devised a plan to sell titles and even created a new level, the baronet, in 1611. These were limited to 200 and carried a prerequisite of an annual income of £1,000. New baronets paid the Crown £1,095 for the honor. Several wealthy gentlemen acquired baronies, for £10,000 apiece. In 1623 Elizabeth Heneage, the widow of Sir Moyle Finch and only a knight's daughter herself, paid £12,000 for the title Viscountess Maidstone. Five years later she became countess of Winchilsea for a further payment. Between 1603 and 1629, the peerage doubled in size. James I elevated 46 commoners to the peerage and Charles I elevated 26. In 1641 the number of peers stood at 121. In all, 342 peers held titles between 1558 and 1641. Approximately 87 percent of all peers' wives came from either the peerage or the upper levels of the gentry.

THE GENTRY

Knighthoods followed a pattern similar to that of peerages. During Elizabeth's reign, 878 new knights were created. Of those, the earl of Essex created 21 at Rouen in 1591, 68 at Cadiz in 1596, and 81 in Ireland in 1599. King James I created 1,161 new knights in 1603 alone. He also granted court favorites the right to name knights and baronets and to receive the fees. Charles I continued the practice of selling knighthoods.

Esquires were those gentlemen whose ancestors had been knights. A knighthood was not inherited but a coat of arms could be. There were 2,000 new grants of arms between 1560 and 1589, and 1,760 between 1590 and 1639. The gentry as a group increased dramatically in number during the Renaissance. One estimate gives 16,500 as the number of heads of gentry families between 1590 and 1642.

By the seventeenth century there was little real distinction between the lesser gentry and the upper yeomanry and, in addition to the sons of gentlemen, "gentlemen" included lawyers, physicians, university graduates, captains in the wars, and anyone else who could "live without manual labor and . . . bear the port, charge and countenance of a gentleman."

For forms of address for various peers and commoners, see pages 220–223. There was no equivalent term for social "class" before the eighteenth century. Indeed, there was little sense of classes at all as we know them. An early-seventeenth century list designated the following: rich men, great men, men of quality, sufficient men, men of the better sort, able persons of good estates, persons of the meaner sort, persons of the ruder sort, poor laboring men and men of the common sort.

THE TRADE OF COURTIERSHIP—
SOME NOTABLE WOMEN

A reigning queen's ladies had no official standing as advisors. In practice, however, they might exert considerable influence. A word whispered in the royal ear was worth money to those eager for advancement. Ann Russell, countess of Warwick, and a lady of the privy chamber once turned down a bribe of one hundred pounds (to advance a lawsuit in chancery with Queen Elizabeth) because the sum was too small.

Katherine Champernowne Astley (d. 1565): Appointed waiting gentle-woman to Elizabeth in 1536 and was later her governess. Kat Astley was twice imprisoned for her close connection to the princess. In 1549 she was accused of conspiring with Lord Admiral Thomas Seymour and held for several weeks. In 1554 she was suspected of being in contact with the organizers of Wyatt's Rebellion. She was arrested again in 1556, when a cache of seditious books was found in the house where she was staying. When Elizabeth became queen, however, Kat was made First Lady of the Bedchamber, an influential post she held until her death.

Lady Elizabeth Fitzgerald, countess of Lincoln (1528–1589): She was brought to England from Ireland by her English mother when her father, the earl of Kildare, was accused of treason. She was raised with the princess Mary and was an inspiration to the poet Henry Howard, earl of Surrey. Thomas Nashe's *The Unfortunate Traveler* (1594) later publicized the fact that she had been Surrey's "Fair Geraldine." As the widow of Sir Anthony Browne, she was sent to the household of Queen Dowager Catherine Parr (by that time married to Lord Admiral Thomas Seymour) at Chelsea in 1548 under orders to keep an eye on the young princess Elizabeth, who was also living there. Despite her position as a spy, and her later involvement in Northumberland's schemes (by that time she was married to Lord Clinton) she became one of Queen Elizabeth's closest friends and was much at court during her reign.

Lucy Harington Russell, countess of Bedford (1581–1627): Lucy be-came both a bride and countess of Bedford at thirteen. Family fortunes suffered a severe setback when her husband involved himself in the Essex Rebellion in 1601, but as soon as Queen Elizabeth died in 1603, Lucy was on her way to Edinburgh to ingratiate herself with the new monarch. She was appointed a lady-in-waiting and was soon wielding a great deal of influence at the new court. She is given credit for helping develop the court masque into an art form.

Helena Snakenborg, marchioness of Northampton (1549–1635): She came to England as a maid of honour to Princess Cecilia of Sweden (wife of the margrave of Baden-Rodemachern) in 1565. Sixteen at the time, Helena attracted the attention of William Parr, marquis of Northampton (brother of Henry VIII's sixth queen), then fifty-two.

Northampton's marchioness, Elizabeth, a close friend of the queen's, had died of breast cancer earlier that year, but he had an earlier wife still living (a scandalous story in its own right), and it was necessary for him to wait until she died, in 1571, to marry Helena. The bridegroom lived for only six months after the wedding. As marchioness of Northampton, Helena was First Lady of the Court after the queen's heirs (who tended to be in custody elsewhere). She kept her rank even after she married Thomas Gorges, a Groom of the Privy Chamber. Queen Elizabeth detested change and almost always refused her ladies permission to marry if they asked, so Helena and Thomas followed the established procedure and married without permission. The inevitable result was a royal fit of temper, banishment and imprisonment for the newlyweds, followed by their profuse apologies and payment of a fine, after which all was forgiven. When Elizabeth died in 1603, Helena was First Mourner at the funeral. In 1619, when Queen Anne died and three countesses were quarreling over which of them should have that honor, the threat that the old Lady Marquis of Northampton would be sent for was enough to settle the dispute.

SELECT BIBLIOGRAPHY

General

Akrigg, G.P.V. *Jacobean Pageant*. Cambridge: Harvard University Press, 1962.

Emerson, Kathy Lynn. *Wives and Daughters: The Women of Sixteenth Century England*. Troy, New York: Whitston Publishing Company, 1984.

Hogrefe, Pearl. *Tudor Women: Commoners and Queens*. Ames: Iowa State Press, 1975.

Loades, David. *The Tudor Court*. Totowa, New Jersey: Barnes and Noble Books, 1987.

Mathew, David. *The Courtiers of Henry VIII*. London: Eyre and Spottiswoode, 1970.

Rowse, A.L. *Court and Country: Studies in Tudor Social History*. Athens: University of Georgia Press, 1987.

Starkey, David, et. al. *The English Court: from the Wars of the Roses to the Civil War*. London and New York: Longman, 1987.

Williams, Neville. *All the Queen's Men*. New York: The Macmillan Company, 1972.

——————. *Henry VIII and his Court.* New York: The Macmillan Company, 1971.

Biography

Dictionary of National Biography (DNB). Currently being revised, the present twenty-two volume version (London: Oxford University Press, 1967–8), some of which was compiled more than a century ago, contains inaccuracies. It is, however, always a good place to start and can assist in sorting out family relationships.

Beer, Barrett L. *Northumberland: The Political Career of John Dudley, Earl of Warwick and Duke of Northumberland.* [1502–1553] Kent, Ohio: Kent State University Press, 1973.

Bruce, Mary Louise. *Anne Boleyn.* New York: Coward, McCann & Geoghegan, 1972.

——————. *The Making of Henry VIII.* New York: Coward, McCann & Geoghegan, 1977.

Byrne, M. St. Clare. *The Lisle Letters*, Vol. I–VI. Chicago: Chicago University Press, 1981. This is an account of Arthur Plantagenet, Lord Lisle (c. 1464–1542), and his wife, Honor Grenville (c. 1494–1566). A one-volume edition of the letters was edited by Bridget Boland (Chicago: Chicago University Press, 1983).

Chapman, Hester W. *The Last Tudor King: A Study of Edward VI.* London: Jonathan Cape, 1968.

Chrimes, S.B. *Henry VII.* Berkeley: University of California Press, 1972.

Durant, David N. *Bess of Hardwick: Portrait of an Elizabethan Dynast.* New York: Atheneum Publishers, 1978. This is a biography of Elizabeth Hardwick, countess of Shrewsbury (1527–1608).

Erickson, Carolly. *Bloody Mary: The Remarkable Life of Mary Tudor.* Garden City, New York: Doubleday, 1978.

——————. *Great Harry: The Extravagant Life of Henry VIII.* New York: Summit Books, 1980.

Fraser, Antonia. *King James VI of Scotland and I of England.* New York: Knopf, 1975.

——————. *Mary Queen of Scots.* London: Weidenfeld and Nicolson, 1969.

Gunn, S.J. *Charles Brandon, Duke of Suffolk c. 1484–1545.* New York: Blackwell, 1988.

Harvey, Nancy Lenz. *Elizabeth of York, the Mother of Henry VIII.* New York: Macmillan, 1973.

————. *The Rose and the Thorn: The Lives of Mary and Margaret Tudor.* New York: Macmillan, 1975.

Haynes, Alan. *Robert Cecil, First Earl of Salisbury, 1563–1612: Servant of Two Sovereigns.* London: P. Owen, 1989.

————. *The White Bear: Robert Dudley, the Elizabethan Earl of Leicester.* London: P. Owen, 1987.

Hibbert, Christopher. *Charles I.* New York: Harper & Row, 1968.

Johnson, Paul. *Elizabeth I.* New York: Holt, Rinehart & Winston, 1974.

Lacey, Robert. *Robert, Earl of Essex.* New York: Atheneum, 1971.

Luke, Mary M. *Catherine the Queen.* New York: Coward-McCann, 1967.

Mathew, David. *James I.* London: Eyre & Spottiswoode, 1967.

————. *Lady Jane Grey: The Setting of the Realm.* London: Eyre Methuen Ltd., 1972.

Read, Conyers. *Lord Burghley and Queen Elizabeth.* New York: Knopf, 1960.

————. *Mr. Secretary Cecil and Queen Elizabeth.* New York: Knopf, 1955.

Reed, Evelyn. *My Lady Suffolk: A Portrait of Catherine Willoughby, Duchess of Suffolk.* New York: Knopf, 1963.

Richardson, Walter C. *Mary Tudor: The White Queen.* Seattle, Washington: University of Washington Press, 1970.

Scarisbrick, J.J. *Henry VIII.* Berkeley: University of California Press, 1968.

Seymour, William. *Ordeal by Ambition.* London: Sidgwick and Jackson, 1972. This covers the lives of Lord Protector Edward Seymour, duke of Somerset (1502–1552); Lord Admiral Thomas Seymour, Baron Seymour of Sudeley (1507–1549); and Jane Seymour, queen of England (1509–1537).

Smith, Lacey Baldwin. *A Tudor Tragedy: The Life and Times of Catherine Howard.* New York: Pantheon Books, 1961.

Wilson, Derek. *Sweet Robin: A Biography of Robert Dudley, Earl of Leicester (1533–1588).* London: Hamilton, 1981.

CHAPTER NINE

CRIME AND PUNISHMENT

hroughout this period of English history, people at all levels of society went to the law courts at the drop of a hat. Civil suits and criminal cases and cases brought before the ecclesiastical courts concerned every aspect of everyday life. Between 1560 and 1580, the number of suits tripled in the courts of King's Bench and Common Pleas. In 1580, 13,300 cases were at an advanced stage in these two courts. In 1606 the number was 23,453 and in 1640, 29,162. Similar numbers apply to the other courts. The Western assize judges, whose circuit included six counties, heard 721 cases in 1611 and 1,024 in 1656. The number of lawyers also multiplied at a phenomenal rate.

LAWYERS

A lawyer, to use the most general term, was anyone who handled the legal affairs of another. Estimates place their numbers at 1,400 in 1574. Several thousand men were active in the profession between 1560 and 1640.

By 1600, solicitors and attorneys were the two types of lawyer most often consulted by clients at the beginning of a suit, but there was as yet no rule against direct access to a barrister. Solicitor was a term just coming into use to refer to one who prepared and directed a case, but it was still ill-defined. The qualifications of a solicitor were also vague. An attorney was any lawyer who appeared in place of a litigant in the central courts housed in Westminster. By 1560, attorneys had to undergo some form of examination and take a sworn oath, but there were no specific qualifications. Some attorneys studied at the Inns of Court. Others, including many small-town attorneys, who provided basic legal services to ordinary people, were trained by apprenticeship.

The Inns of Court have been called England's third university. There were four, actually houses where students of common law lived and studied: the Inner Temple, the Middle Temple, Gray's Inn and Lincoln's Inn. In addition, there were eight Inns of Chancery, where lawyers might study before transferring to an Inn of Court, and two Serjeants' Inns, for serjeants at law and judges only. It cost about forty pounds a year for seven to eight years to train a competent barrister, who could then expect to net about six hundred pounds a year in income.

The Elizabethan equivalent of an upper branch of the legal profession included barristers (who served as readers, benchers and pleaders) and serjeants at law. Judges in the Westminster courts were appointed from the latter group.

By the mid-1520s, 100 to 200 barristers were practicing in England. About 50 of them worked only in the courts at Westminster. The number of calls to the bar per year averaged 184 in the 1570s, 383 in the 1580s and 515 in the 1630s. No clear distinction between a barrister and an attorney seems to have been made before 1700, although the professional status of those who were called to the bar at an Inn of Court grew in importance during the sixteenth and seventeenth centuries.

STEPS IN THE LEGAL PROCESS

Common law procedure was fairly straightforward. In civil cases, the plaintiff obtained a writ from Chancery to enable the case to commence and to compel the defendant to appear. Counsel for both sides prepared documents. Until the early sixteenth century, all pleadings were done orally but by the middle of Henry VIII's reign, written pleas were the norm. The central courts usually assigned cases to the local assizes by a writ which ordered the parties to appear in Westminster on a certain day if they had not settled their differences by then.

A judge and jury heard civil cases. In criminal cases, the accused was "presented" and a formal charge (indictment) was placed before a grand jury of up to twenty-four men. If they found a "true bill" the accused was then tried before a judge and a twelve-member petty jury.

CENTRAL LAW COURTS

There were four law terms, when the courts met for four weeks at a time. Even after the Reformation, they continued to be known by names that had their origin in the Catholic calendar: Hilary, Easter, Trinity and Michaelmas. Central Courts housed in Westminster included:

- Court of the King's/Queen's Bench—a common-law court which handled criminal cases and also served as a court of review, exercising jurisdiction over both quarter sessions and assizes.
- Court of Common Pleas—a common law court which handled debt, trespass and other personal actions.
- Court of the Exchequer—actually the royal accounting department, which had a small common-law jurisdiction.

ASSIZES

Judges from the central courts traveled to hold assizes in each county town. They tried all felonies except larceny and added that after 1590. Six circuits held two assizes each per year except in the extreme north, in Middlesex and in London. Two commissioners were assigned to each court. The judges rode their circuit in the Lent and Trinity vacations.

QUARTER SESSIONS

These courts met every three or four months at the county level and provided trial by jury. Quarter sessions generally lasted three days. They were presided over by two justices of the peace. Most cases dealt with minor offenses, but since any theft of property worth more than a shilling was a felony, punishable by death, they did order many executions. In 1599 in Essex, for example, Agnes Osier was hanged for breaking into a house and stealing 60s. and two flaxen sheets (worth 4s. 4d.). After 1590 all capital crimes were referred from the quarter sessions to the assizes. A list of indictments at quarter sessions in Kent at the beginning of the seventeenth century indicates that the offenses were 68 percent administrative, such as keeping an unlicensed alehouse, and 32 percent criminal.

PREROGATIVE COURTS

Created by exercise of royal prerogative in order to remedy shortcomings in the judicial system, these courts also met in Westminster. The Court of Chancery handled trusts, partnerships and mortgages, administered estates and enforced contracts and came to be the body which established case law and legal precedent. Lawsuits began with original writs issued here but the preparation of cases was handled by officials of common pleas. In 1590, Chancery employed at least forty-one different officials, most of whom had assistants. Tips and gratuities to all the minor officials, such as doorkeepers, were customary. By 1600 the Court of Chancery was hearing three hundred cases a year and delays of up to three years were common.

The Court of the Star Chamber (originally the Privy Council in Star Chamber) took its name from the fact that the ceiling in the chamber in which it first met was decorated with stars. Established in 1487, the Star Chamber became a law court separate from the Privy Council around 1540 and was abolished in 1641. The Star Chamber met only on Wednesday and Friday during law terms and claimed to be superior to common law. It was thus the only English court which could order the accused to be tortured. Until 1588 the rack (a frame upon which the victim was stretched by turning rollers attached to his wrists and ankles) was "the accustomed torture" but from 1589 to 1603 torture was generally carried out at Bridewell, which had no rack. At first the Star Chamber dealt primarily with cases involving riots and or other violence but later cases of slander and libel were heard there. Use of defamatory words was a criminal offense solely within the jurisdiction of the Star Chamber and the ecclesiastical courts. The number of cases in the Star Chamber increased tenfold between 1558 and 1603.

The Court of Requests was set up to handle civil matters for poor suitors and evolved into a formal court by 1485. Judges held their seats for life. The Lord Privy Seal was nominal head of this court but no one who held that office sat as a judge during the years 1516–1630. In 1598 the common-law courts refused to recognize the authority of the Court of Requests. It lingered on until the Civil War but had lost much of its influence.

A MISCELLANY OF SPECIALIZED COURTS

Regional Courts operating in restricted jurisdictions during this era were the Royal Palatine Courts of Chester and Durham, the tribunals associated with the Duchy of Lancaster, the Council of the North (which met in York from 1537 on) and the Council of the Marches of Wales. The last two were regional equivalents of the Court of Requests and the Star Chamber. By 1600 the Council of the North was hearing one thousand to two thousand cases a year.

Admiralty Courts: Primarily tried pirates and distributed the booty seized in their capture.

The Court of Chivalry: Tried civil cases under the law of arms. James Tuchet, Lord Audley, was condemned to death by this court in 1497 for his part in the Cornish Rebellion.

The Court of Delegates: A royal tribunal staffed with civil lawyers. They heard appeals from the Bishops' Consistory Courts and the Courts of Admiralty and Chivalry.

The Court of the High Steward: Convened to try peers by common law before a select panel of noblemen. Rarely used, it almost always dealt with treason. An exception was the 1541 trial of Thomas Fiennes, Lord Dacre of the South, for his involvement in the death of a gamekeeper during an illegal hunting expedition. Seventeen peers found Dacre guilty. He was hanged at Tyburn two days later.

The Court of Sessions: Established in 1532 to handle civil cases. It later extended its jurisdiction to criminal cases. The first Old Bailey Sessions House was erected in 1539 next to Newgate Prison at a cost of six thousand pounds. It took its name from a nearby street.

The Court of Wards and Liveries: Established by statute in 1540 to deal with the estates of infant wards of the Crown. It was presided over by the Lord Treasurer, two Chief Justices, the Chief Baron, the King's Serjeant, "divers Surveyors" and an Attorney of the Court. When a male ward reached twenty-one (for a female it was sixteen), he could "sue out livery" with a payment of half a year's profits from his estates.

Ecclesiastical Courts: Administered canon law, dealing in sin rather than crime. The Bishops' Consistory courts, episcopal courts of audience, archdeaconry courts and the courts of some independent parishes and chapelries continued to be active after the Reformation. Proctors, usually notaries public, served in these courts as advocates. Many of the cases dealt with the sexual misbehavior of parishioners and this earned the ecclesiastical courts the nickname "bawdy courts."

The Court Baron: A manorial-level court concerned with customary law to do with tenures, copyhold and freehold issues, trespass and debts up to forty shillings. The manor's steward acted as judge with a jury of tenants.

The Court Leet: Also on the manorial level, it was involved in keeping the peace, enforcing statutes and punishing antisocial behavior. The manor's steward presided as both judge and clerk.

Petty Sessions: An outgrowth of the increased caseload of the quarter sessions. They met monthly by the late 1590s. Here two magistrates dispensed justice without a jury.

The Sheriff's Court (or County Court): Had only one function left in the seventeenth century, the election (by acclamation) of the two members of Parliament for the county.

The Courts of Small Pleas: Met in towns. Some hundreds (the municipal division between a parish and a county) also had their own courts.

LAW ENFORCEMENT PERSONNEL

Justice of the Peace

J.P.s were appointed by the monarch, though actually chosen by the Lord Chancellor, to be responsible for the upkeep of roads; the building and maintenance of bridges; the erection of jails; the control and licensing of public houses and players; the regulation of labor, wages and trade; the administration of the Poor Law; and the determination of paternity when bastards were born. In criminal cases, justices received and investigated complaints, called witnesses and bound them over to appear at a trial, examined accused persons and committed them to gaol or released them on bail. They ran the quarter sessions and served at the assizes as a sort of grand jury.

Although Henry VIII's J.P.s included almost every adult peer, some of whom served in more than one county, J.P.s were usually drawn from the ranks of the landed gentry. Their numbers steadily increased. Kent had 56 in 1562 and 110 in 1604. In 1580, J.P.s numbered 1,738 for the whole of England.

High Sheriff

Elected on the morrow of All Soul's Day (November 2) by the Privy Council, a sheriff served for one year, during which time he was required to live in his county and keep up the dignity of the office at his own expense. Since this usually cost more than the position paid, few sought the honor. In 1609 the sheriff of Worcester had several extra expenses. He had to hire four guards to transport a notorious horse stealer from Westminster to Worcester, and he had to buy faggots, pitch, gunpowder, links of iron and straw and pay six men to tend the fire in order to carry out the sentence of death by burning against one Mary Perkins for poisoning her husband.

In a few cases, the office of county sheriff had a longer tenure. Under Henry VII and Henry VIII, the Cliffords were hereditary sheriffs of Westmorland. Sir Edward Stanley, created Lord Monteagle in 1514, served as sheriff of the county palatine of Lancaster from 1485 until his death in 1523, but his son did not inherit the post. Likewise, in 1534, Henry VIII appointed the sixth earl of Northumberland sheriff of that county for life. Northumberland, who died in 1537, paid the king forty pounds a year for the honor.

By the mid-sixteenth century, sheriffs had few judicial or military powers left (these having gone to the justices of the peace and the lord lieutenants respectively) and were primarily administrative agents for the central government. They collected debts and royal revenues (rent on Crown lands, debts owed the Crown, legal fees, and the tax called ship money under Charles I), served writs of the central courts, impaneled juries, executed judgments of common-law jurisdictions, enforced local penalties, listed prisoners held in gaol, and were responsible for calling and running the assizes and quarter sessions. This included making arrangements for lodging and entertaining the judges, everything from the provision of hogsheads of beer and wine, sugar loaves, a sheep or a calf, and the services of cooks, butlers, a steward, chamberlains and criers, to oats and fodder for some thirty to forty horses.

Norfolk and Suffolk shared a sheriff until 1575, although other joint shrievalties were abolished in 1567. Most sheriffs appointed undersheriffs and bailiffs to do the actual work of serving writs and carrying out arrests. Cities also had an official called a sheriff, but the post bore little resemblance to the high sheriff of a county.

Coroner

The coroner ("crowner" in medieval times) was concerned with sudden death because in cases of murder the property of the murderer was forfeited and a share went to the Crown. Out of this, the coroner received 13s. 4d. He got nothing from a suicide or an accidental death. The coroner had lost much of his authority by the sixteenth century, but he could still make an indictment upon viewing a body and order an arrest. Arraignments, however, now took place before two justices and they, not the coroner, bound the accused felon over for trial.

High or Chief Constable

The local police authority of a hundred (the administrative district betweeen a county and a parish), the high constable maintained the watch, set up beacons, moved vagrants along, oversaw the repairs to roads and bridges, passed instructions from the quarter sessions down to individual parishes, enforced the annual wage scale and returned presentments by parish officers to the quarter sessions. Most served more than one year and a few held the same post for decades.

Petty Constable

Also called parish, village or town constables, these were the most lowly officers in the system. A petty constable was chosen by the steward of a manor or elected by his fellow householders (among whom the job was rotated) to carry out the instructions of the county courts. Duties included collecting taxes, raising the hue and cry after a fugitive, and executing punishments ordered by the magistrates. These included the stocks, whipping post, ducking stools and a "high cage" for rogues and vagabonds. Constables' weapons might include bills (primitive bladed weapons), pikes, bows and arrows, and muskets. As the general-purpose official in charge of all detection and presentment of crime in his parish or manor, the petty constable was responsible for apprehending felons and was liable for a fine for failure to arrest. He could

London watchman, 1608
The watch, like the petty constable of a village, was recruited from the ranks of householders in the neighborhood. Armed with lanterns, bells and pikes, they were expected to call out the hour of the night and arrest any malefactors they came upon. This sketch is based on an illustration in Nathaniel Butler's The Bellman of London.

also be made to maintain a bastard child if through negligence he let the father escape the area.

Common Informer

Although not officials in the law enforcement system, informers played an important role by reporting the misdemeanors of their neighbors. Some informers regularly presented twenty to forty lawbreakers to the quarter-sessions judges. This wasn't difficult when there were laws on the books concerning everything from the sumptuousness of the clothes one wore to the price an innkeeper could charge for ale. For this service, informers received half of whatever fines were assessed. The Crown got the other half. Informers themselves were regulated by an act of 1589.

PROSECUTION OF CRIMINALS

Criminal cases could be prosecuted on behalf of the Crown or the victim. Most offenders were male. The most common charge was theft. Larceny, burglary and robbery accounted for between two-thirds and three-quarters of all appearances in court. Homicides accounted for between 10 percent and 15 percent of all cases.

In the case of a suspicious death, certain procedures were supposed to be followed. Whoever found the body was to raise a hue and cry, which meant he informed his four nearest neighbors of his find. They went for the bailiff, who sent for the coroner and summoned all free men over the age of twelve in the community. From their ranks the coroner picked twelve jurors for the coroner's inquest. This was held as soon as the coroner arrived, usually within three days. The deceased was not buried until after the coroner examined the body for wounds, bruises or signs of strangulation. If an indictment of homicide was made, the coroner ordered an arrest. Arraignment took place before two justices, who bound the accused felon over for trial. In murder cases, this meant holding the accused in gaol until the next assizes.

Murder trials were far different from those today. For one thing, they rarely lasted more than ten minutes. Rules of evidence were unknown. A defendant charged with felony or treason was not entitled to legal representation. Autopsies were considered barbaric and not allowed. Defense witnesses were rarely called and were never sworn in. The theory was that the prosecution's case ought to be unanswerable.

By implication, any defense witness was a liar. Furthermore, that witness meant to speak against the Crown. This was frowned upon. All evidence was given orally in open court, though a written confession might be read. The accused could cross-examine prosecution witnesses, who were sworn in. Verdicts were decided by a jury of twelve men. Women could be tried for a crime but could not serve on a jury. The verdict was usually based on "common knowledge" rather than on the results of detection.

In the case of Philip Wetherick, common knowledge was wrong. After Ambrose Letyse disappeared in December 1537, the parish constables and bailiff believed that Wetherick had murdered him. Apparently hoping to awe him into confessing, they brought him before the earl of Essex as well as to the local J.P., John Spring. Wetherick's wife, Margery, asked for assistance from her uncle, the abbot of St. Osyth's, but when Wetherick's eleven-year-old son, Martin, testified that his father had killed Letyse and burned the body and produced bones and ashes as proof, Wetherick was tried at the assizes in Bury St. Edmunds in March, 1538, found guilty, and hanged. The following month Letyse turned up in a nearby village, alive and well. The bones had been those of a pig.

Trial by battle was still a possibility in this era, and might be used in felonies or in cases involving a contested land title. There were, however, no recorded instances of trial by battle between 1571 and 1639, and in the 1571 case, one of the parties failed to show up on the day appointed for the showdown.

PUNISHMENTS

Death Penalty

Murder was only one of the crimes punishable by death. Any criminal convicted of the theft of goods worth more than twelvepence (one shilling) could be hanged. In 1590, with a population under five million, England had more than eight hundred hangings. The conviction rate rose from 47 percent in 1558 to 68 percent in 1603.

Local studies have produced varied statistics, but a person probably had about a one in four chance of being hanged if he was tried on a felony charge. In Middlesex in the early 1600s, there were an average of seventy executions a year. In Devon in 1598, out of 387 indictments, seventy-four capital sentences were passed (though not all performed). On the other hand, in more than twenty-five Essex parishes, for no discernible reason, there was not a single case of felony during the reign of Elizabeth. Between 1560 and 1650 in the parish of Earls Colne, Essex (which had an average population of eight hundred during that period), there were only two murder cases. In 1608 a woman was hanged for killing her child. In 1626 another woman was acquitted of a charge of having poisoned her husband. Another Essex study, covering the years 1559–1603, reports 129 homicides, 28 infanticides, 110 highway robberies, 320 burglaries, 1,460 simple or compound larcenies, 172 cases of witchcraft, 28 rapes and 8 cases of buggery. At one assize for Exeter in 1598, 134 prisoners were indicted. Seventeen were ordered hung, 20 flogged, 15 pardoned, and 11 who claimed benefit of clergy were branded and set free.

Overall, the number of prosecutions for felony rose in the late sixteenth century, and there was a mounting crime problem throughout the years 1570–1630. It is estimated that in London 150 felons were executed every year during the Jacobean period. Still, only about 10 percent of those convicted of theft were actually executed. Studies of the period from 1550 to 1800 indicate that between 25 percent and 50 percent of those indicted were acquitted. Up to 80 percent of felony suspects escaped trial entirely because they could not be caught and brought into court.

The first permanent London gallows was erected at Tyburn in 1571. Eighteen feet high, it had cross beams that could hold eight at a time. Hangings were accomplished by having the prisoner climb a ladder with the rope around his neck and jump off. Those who refused were "turned" off.

The manner of execution was established by law and determined by the crime. It could not be altered. Most executions were by hanging, but some crimes called for burning and others for pressing to death. Between 1603 and 1621, at least forty-one men and three women were pressed to death in Middlesex.

Execution could be avoided by obtaining a royal pardon, of which about a hundred a year were issued. Transportation (sending a convict to a penal colony in another country) as an alternative to the death sentence was proposed as early as 1611 but was not in regular use until after the Restoration.

Benefit of Clergy

A man who could read had "benefit of clergy," and therefore could get a lesser sentence (usually branding on the thumb) for a first offense. This had ceased to have much connection to the clergy or clerical status by the sixteenth century. At the Essex assizes between 1579 and 1603, 80 percent of those convicted of stealing sheep or cows successfully read the "neck verse" (Psalm 51, verse 1). In 1576 at the Launceston assizes, seven were executed and seven others "had their books" and were reprieved.

A series of statutes severely reduced the use of benefit of clergy. From 1536 on, those suspected of robbery, piracy, murder or other felonies at sea, crimes which had previously been tried by civil law in the Admiralty Courts, were to be tried without benefit of clergy and by common law. Benefit of clergy was later disallowed in cases of petty treason, homicide, burglary, housebreaking, robbing of churches, theft from the person, rape and abduction.

Benefit of clergy had never been available to female felons, unless they could prove they had been nuns before the Reformation. If a convicted felon was pregnant, however, her execution was postponed until after the child was born. A woman who committed murder had a further disadvantage under the law. She could be charged with petty treason if her victim was either her husband or her master. Then the sentence was death by burning rather than death by hanging.

Lesser Crimes

Those who stole items valued at less than a shilling (petty larceny) were publicly whipped. Misdemeanor was at this time a vague term for any nonfelony. In many cases, a jury would deliberately undervalue the goods that had been stolen in order to avoid passing a death sentence.

Imprisonment

Going to prison as a punishment was a relatively new concept and gaols were primarily for holding prisoners until trial. Legislation passed under Edward VI created separate houses of correction for the incarceration of petty offenders. The prototype was Bridewell, a prison, hospital and workhouse from 1556. Public floggings were held there twice a week and prisoners were issued blue uniforms. It housed about two hundred. By the 1630s there was a house of correction in every county. The two daily meals of an inmate in the House of Correction at Bury,

Suffolk, in 1588 included eight ounces of rye bread, a pint of porridge, a pint of beer, four ounces of meat on flesh days and a half pound of cheese or one good herring on fish days.

London prisons specialized in the type of offender they held. Those charged with felonies went to Newgate and were held in "the Limboes," a dungeon lit by a single candle set on a black stone. A bell at nearby St. Sepulchre tolled for Newgate prisoners at ten every night, and at six in the morning of execution days. The great bell also began to toll when the dead cart brought prisoners out to the gallows at ten in the morning and continued to toll until the day's executions were over.

The Tower of London housed traitors, at least those from the upper classes. When the duke of Northumberland's three younger sons were housed there during the first part of the reign of Queen Mary, they had allowances for food, wood, coal and candles. Each had two servants. They were allowed out of their cells to exercise and their wives were permitted to make conjugal visits.

Londoners guilty of any crime but treason or felony were sent to Ludgate. This included imprisonment for debt. The Counter in Poultry and the Counter in Wood Street (moved from Bread Street in 1551) were for offenders against city laws and both stayed open all night. In 1606 the keepers of both Counters were ordered to provide two tables, one on the "Master's Side," which would charge ninepence for a meal, and another in the "Knight's Ward," which would charge fivepence. For a weekly charge of ten shillings a prisoner could dine alone or with friends and be waited on. Beef, veal, capon, bread, beer and claret wine were served, with fish substituted on fish days.

The Fleet and the Marshalsea housed recusants but the Fleet got those committed by the monarch's personal decree. By the late seventeenth century, the Fleet had become primarily a debtor's prison while the Marshalsea held pirates and mariners. The King's Bench took persons brought before that court, the majority of whom were debtors. Bridewell, under Elizabeth, was a political prison.

Furloughs were common. If sufficient bail was provided, a prisoner could leave prison for up to a year. For a day outside prison walls one had only to pay twenty pence, the wages of the prison official who went along. Prisoners could also hire other prisoners as their servants, if they had the funds, and "entertain" lady friends.

In 1602 an experiment in privatization of a prison, at Bridewell, turned its management over to four London businessmen, paying them three hundred pounds a year. Within a few years, most of the prisoners had been released and whores were subletting the premises.

Tudor and Stuart Gun Control—A Summary of Laws

1487   Proclamation vs. unnecessary carrying of weapons.
1523   Act vs. crossbows and handguns.
1557   Proclamation to ban fighting in churchyards and limit the use of long rapiers, swords and "other than bladed weapons."
1559   Proclamation to restrict the use of handguns and dags (similar to pistols) due to their use in crimes.
1575   Proclamation vs. dags and pistols because so many vagrants were armed.
1600   An act against dags, fowling pieces and other guns, linking the common practice of carrying firearms to the high rate of criminal activity.
1612   Law against pocket-dags.
1616   Law against handguns.

A SAMPLING OF CASES

July 16, 1533: John and Alice (Tankerfelde) Wolfe and three accomplices murdered Jerome de George and Charles Benche, two foreign merchants, in a boat on the Thames. John escaped to Ireland but Alice was arrested and was imprisoned in the Tower. She escaped, but since she was "a woman appareled like a man," she roused the suspicions of the watch and was caught. Because of the location of the murder, Alice was tried by the Admiralty Court and sentenced to be hung on the pirates' gallows at Wapping Stairs.

February 15, 1551: Alice (Mirfyn) Arden supervised the murder of her husband, Thomas Arden, by her lover and several hired assassins. The crime was poorly planned. A trail in the snow led directly from her door to the body. Alice was burned to death in Canterbury. An account appeared in *Holinshed's Chronicles* (1577) and the murder was the basis of an anonymous 1592 play.

1576: At Launceston Assizes a schoolmaster was sentenced to lose his ears and spend six months in prison for "repining against the sacrament."

1586: William Painter, Clerk of Ordnance, was charged with embezzling almost two thousand pounds from the Crown. His official wages were eightpence a day.

May 30, 1593: Playmaker Christopher Marlowe was slain in Deptford by Ingram Frizer. Officially, he died during a quarrel over a reckoning (bill) but murder for political reasons has never been completely ruled out. For a full account see Charles Nicholl, *The Reckoning: The Murder of Christopher Marlowe* (New York: Harcourt Brace & Company, 1992).

1601: John Daniel, formerly a servant of the earl of Essex, was tried for "forgery, corrupt cosenages and other lewd practices" in the Star Chamber for blackmailing the countess of Essex with some letters he'd stolen in 1599. He was sent to the Fleet for life and fined three thousand pounds, the same amount he tried to extort.

1612: Mary Frith (Moll Cutpurse) was fined two thousand pounds and made to do penance at Paul's Cross on a Sunday. She had appeared dressed as a man on stage at the Fortune (a theater) and sung bawdy songs while accompanying herself on the lute. She was also a pickpocket, a forger, a fortune-teller and a receiver of stolen goods. In 1610 she had been the subject of a book and in 1611 the model for *The Roaring Girl*, a play by Thomas Middleton and Thomas Dekker.

September 15, 1613: Sir Thomas Overbury died in the Tower of London, poisoned on the orders of the countess of Somerset. For a full account of this case see Beatrice White, *Cast of Ravens: The Strange Case of Sir Thomas Overbury* (London: John Murray, 1965).

1615: Ellen Pendleton was arrested and tried for leading bands of outlaws in the shires of Norfolk, Kent, Lincoln and Leicester. She was convicted of burning the town of Windham, Norfolk, and suspected of conspiring against King James and giving false evidence to the king's council. Because she was pregnant, her execution was delayed until her child was born.

1630: Anne Walton, a pregnant seventeen-year-old, was murdered in Lumley, County Durham, by Mark Sharp on the orders of Anne's uncle, Christopher Walker. The two men were convicted and hanged the following April on the basis of evidence given by the ghost of the murder victim. For a full account see the chapter titled "Anne Walton's Murderers" in Neville Williams's *Knaves and Fools* (New York: Macmillan, 1959).

SELECT BIBLIOGRAPHY

Cockburn, J.S., ed. *Crime in England 1550–1800.* Princeton, New Jersey: Princeton University Press, 1977.

Ives, E.W. "The Law and the Lawyers." *Shakespeare Survey* 17. (1965): 73–86.

McMullan, John L. *The Canting Crew: London's Criminal Underworld 1550–1700.* New Brunswick, New Jersey: Rutgers University Press, 1984.

Sharpe, J.A. *Crime in Early Modern England 1550–1750.* New York and London: Longman, 1984.

CHAPTER TEN

COINS, MONEY AND HOW MUCH THINGS COST

I n England the mark was never an actual coin. Rather it was imaginary money, a unit used only in accounting to indicate one hundred pence ("pence" being the plural of "penny"). In the currency of the day, the mark had a value of thirteen shillings and fourpence (13s. 4d.). The pound (£), shilling (s.) and penny (d.) were also denominations used in accounting, with the pound sterling valued at twenty shillings. Until the first issue of a sovereign in 1489, there was no coin with the value of exactly one pound.

There was no paper money. English coins were either yellow money (gold), white money (silver), red money (copper) or black money (billon). Some merchants used square lead or copper tokens as small change, but England had no authorized coin of pure copper or of billon (mixed copper and silver) except between 1542 and 1551, when the king's economic advisors made the mistake of thinking that decreasing the amount of precious metal in coins and minting more of them would be beneficial to the kingdom. What is now called the "great debasement" reduced the silver content of coins to as little as 25 percent of what it had been and was a leading cause of subsequent problems of inflation and poverty in England.

Between 1551 and 1562, the coinage was restored to its proper value, but at the same time gold coins were almost completely replaced with silver coins. This recoinage had the effect of calling down the value of all coins in circulation.

Under James I, there was a brief attempt to combine the coinage of England and Scotland, using Scots values, but in 1619, England went back to English values and Charles I continued to use separate coinage for England and Scotland.

MINTING OF COINS

Since the value of a coin depended upon the intrinsic metallic value of its gold or silver or copper, this was carefully controlled by the moneyers in the Royal Mints. One of the ceremonial tests devised then is still in use today.

Early in the Tudor era there were two mints in the Tower and other mints operating in Bristol, Canterbury, Dublin, Durham, Durham House in the Strand, Southwark, Tournai (in 1513 only), Waterford and York. For part of the period, only the Tower Mint was in operation. Under Charles I, new mints were opened in York, Edinburgh and Aberystwyth.

Minting was by two methods, hammering or milling. Most English coins were produced by hammering. Milling was done in England only from 1561 to 1571, when the French engraver Eloi Mestrell was hired away from the Paris Mint. He used a screw press powered by a horse-drawn mill. Mint workers complained about the technique, claiming it was less accurate. After Mestrell was let go, he turned to forgery in order to live. He was condemned to death for this crime in 1578 since counterfeiting any coin, English or foreign, had been high treason since the fifteenth century. Clipping, culling, melting or exporting English coins was also illegal.

Sir William Sharington (1495–1553), vice-treasurer of the Bristol Mint, began to manufacture testoons illegally, for his own use, in 1547, clipping coins for the metal and falsifying the books. Over three years he embezzled some four thousand pounds. He was caught only after Lord Admiral Thomas Seymour asked him to coin more money for

Minting coins, 1560
This drawing is based on a sketch in Holinshed's Chronicles *and shows the production of coins by hammering.*

Seymour's use. Sharington was arrested in January, 1549. He confessed, was attainted, and then was pardoned. When he later served as sheriff of Wiltshire (1552), he was praised for his honesty.

DOMESTIC COINS

angel: A gold coin worth 6s. 8d. until Henry VIII and then 10s. In 1565, England was flooded with Flemish-made counterfeit angels.

angelet or half angel: A gold coin worth 5s.

crown: A gold coin first issued in 1526. Worth 5s., it had the royal arms surmounted by a crown on one side. The value was raised to 5s. 6d. in 1611. In 1551 the first silver crowns (worth 5s.) were minted, meant to compete with the *lion daaldre*, a Dutch version of the thaler, which was the standard trade coin of central Europe. In 1601, silver crowns and half crowns were issued for the first time since 1553 and quickly became the primary coins in use.

dollar: There was no English dollar in the regular coinage, but the thistle dollar (a large silver Scots coin also called a sword dollar and worth 30s. under James VI) was in use in England. In 1600 a "portcullis dollar" was struck in London for the East India Company but was legal tender only in the East Indies. By 1610 the word dollar might refer to any silver coin of thaler size and was sometimes used to distinguish the silver crown from the gold crown. A dollar meant a silver crown while a crown generally meant a gold crown.

farthing: A silver coin worth 2s. 6d. under the early Tudors. No farthings were minted between 1553 and 1613, when an issue of copper "patent farthings" went into circulation. This coin was called a "Harington" because the patent to mint it had been granted to John, Lord Harington as a way to repay the debts he had incurred while supervising the education of the princess Elizabeth.

groat: A standard coin worth 4d. as far back as 1279, the groat was considered old-fashioned after the issue of the sixpence under Henry VIII and the shilling under Edward VI. In 1551 it was devalued to 3d. and later to 2d.

half crown: A gold or silver coin worth half as much as the crown of the same metal.

halfpenny: A silver coin. Production was restricted in 1553 but the coin was reintroduced in 1583.

half sovereign or double crown: A gold coin worth 10s. until 1611, when its new value became 11s. "Harry ten shillings" was the slang term for a half-sovereign coin minted in the reign of Henry VIII.

noble: This gold coin was worth 6s. 8d. until it was devalued in 1464. For the sixteenth century version, see under ryal.

penny: The most common silver coin, worth 1d., it was not minted from 1572 to 1583 but was reintroduced after the minting of three-quarter pence and one-and-a-half-pence coins (begun in 1561) was discontinued.

pound: (£) See sovereign.

quarter angel: A gold coin worth 2s. in 1542. It was abandoned for a time, then reissued in 1572 with a value of 2s. 6d.

ryal or rose noble: A gold coin worth 10s. until the reign of Henry VIII and then worth 15s. Under James I it was replaced by the spur ryal, angel, angelet and quarter angel.

shilling: (s.) A silver coin worth 12d., first minted in 1504. It was devalued in 1551 to 9d. and later to 6d.

sixpence, testoon or tester: A silver coin worth 6d.

sovereign: First issued in 1489, this was the first coin to have the value of a pound sterling (20s.) Gold, it showed an enthroned king on one side with the royal arms and Tudor rose on the reverse. The value was raised to 22s. in 1611.

three farthing piece: A silver coin worth 3 farthings.

threehalfpenny piece: A silver coin worth 1½d.

threepenny or three-penny-piece: A silver coin worth 3d.

twopence piece, half groat or twopenny: A silver coin worth 2d.

FOREIGN COINS IN USE IN ENGLAND

cavallo: A copper coin from Naples.

doit: A copper Dutch coin issued in 1580 and after. It was worth less than a farthing.

double plack: The silver Flemish double patard, worth 4d. in early Tudor England.

ducat: The Spanish ducat was worth 4s. 6d. (1522–38), then 5s. (1538–1554), then 6s. 4d. The double ducat was valued at 13s. 4d. in 1554.

ecu a la couronne (French crown): A gold coin valued at 4s. 4d. until 1526, then 4s. 6d. (1526–1538), then 4s. 8d. (until 1554), 6s. 4d. (until 1560) and finally 6s.

florin: A gold Dutch coin. There were two types, one worth 2s. and the other 3s. 3d.

imperial crown: A gold Spanish coin worth 6s. 4d.

korte: A copper coin from the Netherlands.

moidore, moy or cruzado: A gold Portuguese coin which was legal tender in England under Mary I. The "long cross cruzado" was worth 6s. 4d. and the "short cross cruzado" 6s. 8d.

pistolet: A gold Portuguese coin worth 6s. 2d. (5s. 10d. after 1560).

real: A silver Spanish coin in use in England only between 1554 and 1561.

SOURCES OF ROYAL REVENUE

Taxes

Henry VII instituted indirect taxes as soon as he took the throne, in particular customs revenues, both import duties and export duties known as tunnage and poundage. The original tunnage was on tuns of wine, and poundage referred to pounds of wool and leather, but they were collected on many other commodities. Excise taxes were generally levied during the first year of the reign and lasted for the life of the monarch.

Overall, England had fewer resources than France or Spain. France had a population of thirteen to fifteen million in 1560. England was still under five million in 1603. Even with all the indirect taxes, fees, and rents from Crown lands, Henry VII also had to resort to Parliament for money. Since 1483, non-Parliamentary taxation had been illegal. Parliament reasserted this right in 1497 and made grants dependent upon specific military needs.

Taxes were generally in the form of "fifteenths and tenths," a levy on chattel, merchandise, livestock and other moveables. Those in urban areas were assessed a tenth of the value of their possessions. Those in rural areas paid a fifteenth. Parliament could also levy a subsidy, a graduated income tax that was developed to its full potential by Henry VIII's advisor, Cardinal Wolsey. Subjects paid at the rate of 1s. to 4s. on the pound.

There were a number of outbreaks of violence directed against tax collectors. Eleven assaults in the London area alone are recorded between 1485 and 1547. The rebellions in Yorkshire in 1489 and Cornwall in 1497 were the result of excessive taxation. In the latter case, rebels killed a subsidy commissioner at Taunton.

In 1513, when a subsidy and a fifteenth and tenth were levied in the same year, a number of municipalities petitioned Henry VIII to plead poverty. He had to forgive them payment of the fifteenth and tenth. Another subsidy, intended to raise £800,000 over four years, was levied in 1523. It yielded only £151,215 but it did produce statistics concerning the wealth of the population because the tax was levied on all persons with lands, goods or wages worth a pound a year or more. Based on tax collectors' records, it appears that one-third to one-half of the population escaped this tax entirely by reason of poverty. About 25 percent had incomes ranging from £2 to £10 per annum. Only 3 percent were assessed at £40 or more.

The mean taxable income of a peer has been estimated at £801 in 1523 and £921 in 1534. In 1525, Henry VIII and Cardinal Wolsey attempted what has been called the Amicable Grant. This was a levy of one-sixth on the goods of the laity and one-third on the goods of the clergy. There were immediate protests. The Act of 1483 forbade this extraction of "benevolences" (forced loans) from the wealthy. Many noblemen also pleaded poverty. The king, faced with passive resistance rather than open rebellion, eventually backed down.

A new source of tax income after the break with Rome was the church. In 1533 all payments by English churches to the Pope were stopped. In 1535 the old clerical taxes were replaced by a 10 percent tax on the annual income of each benefice. Every new incumbent in a clerical office also paid the full first year's income to the Crown as "first fruits." The sale of monastic lands brought in additional Crown revenue.

The taxes paid to Henry VII during his entire reign totaled £282,000. Taxes paid to Henry VIII between 1509 and 1540 totaled £520,463. Parliamentary taxes during the years 1541–1547 alone yielded £656,245. Direct taxes were levied at irregular intervals during the reigns of the later Tudors and early Stuarts, usually in response to some emergency or to discharge the accumulated government debts of the previous monarch.

Other Sources of Income

The sale of public offices, the profits of justice (court-imposed fines and the fees paid for writs and letters in civil cases) and income from grants of monopoly permits all provided royal revenues. In 1624, Parliament attempted to take control of the lucrative granting of monopolies and banned the king from making such grants to individuals. Corporations, however, could still be granted monopolies.

Feudal Rights and Recognizances

Over a twenty-five-year period, Henry VII managed to double royal revenue without resorting to much direct taxation. In essence, he blackmailed his peers by enforcing laws against keeping more than a set number of retainers (retaining) and by claiming his feudal rights of marriage and wardship.

Retainers could run the gamut from liveried domestic servants to small private armies, and it was at the king's discretion which cases to prosecute. His decisions were generally based upon economic rather than political reasons. In 1504, the duke of Buckingham, the earls of Derby, Essex, Northumberland, Oxford and Shrewsbury, and the Lady Margaret Beaufort, countess of Richmond and Derby (the king's mother), were indicted at the quarter sessions in York for illegal retaining. They were not tried. George Neville, Lord Abergavenny, however, was both indicted and tried at the King's Bench in 1507 for keeping 471 men for thirty months. He pleaded guilty. The penalty was a fine of 100s. per month per man, plus fines. Henry generously reduced the amount, which was unpayable, to a fine of £5,000 to be repaid over the next ten years.

Feudal rights included the fees paid when an heir succeeded, the escheat (reversion of property to the Crown if there was no heir—the escheator was the royal official responsible for protecting the monarch's rights to feudal dues in a county), and the custody of property of widows and idiots. The rights concerning marriage and wardship of a minor heir produced around £6,000 per annum during the later years of Henry's reign. There were profits from the sale of these rights and other, incidental benefits. When Katherine Woodville, dowager duchess of Buckingham and Bedford, married her third husband, Sir Richard Wingfield, without royal license, she was fined £2,000. Henry took further advantage of her oversight by making her son, the third duke of Buckingham, responsible for the debt.

Mabel, dowager Lady Dacre of the North, arranged the marriage of young Richard Huddleston, a royal ward, to her daughter. Her action deprived the king of the income from his right to sell Huddleston's marriage. She was thus charged with "ravishing" Huddleston, imprisoned in Lancaster Castle for nine months, and fined 1,000 marks. In order to pay, Lady Dacre and her son, Thomas, had to undertake four recognizances (bonds by which a person agreed to fulfill a condition or forfeit the amount of the bond). The fine was excessive, but there is some indication that it was also intended to punish Lord Dacre for an earlier exploit. He'd abducted and married Elizabeth, heiress of Lord Greystock. In that case, the king did not take action because he had already sold her wardship and therefore had not lost any money because of Dacre's actions.

In a similar case, Richard Grey, third earl of Kent, abducted one Elizabeth Trussell, probably to marry her to his half-brother, Sir Henry Grey. For usurping the king's rights, he was fined 2,500 marks. As security, he gave a recognizance for 4,000 marks, after which his fine was reduced to 1,000 marks.

There were forty English peers of full age during the period from 1502 to 1509. As many as two-thirds of them at one time were required to give recognizances on their own behalf or to guarantee the good behavior of friends or relatives.

Henry Percy, fifth earl of Northumberland, already in trouble over retaining, usurped the king's right of prerogative wardship when he abducted an heiress, Elizabeth Hastings, the daughter of a wealthy knight. For this he was fined £10,000, which was suspended "during the king's pleasure" in return for Northumberland's agreement to pay 500 marks every Candlemas (February 2) until 3,000 marks had been paid. The payments were to be made under threat of a forfeit of 6,000 marks if he missed one. Northumberland did not do much better under Henry VIII, even though when Henry took the throne in 1509 he cancelled as many as 175 recognizances. In 1516 Northumberland was tried for retaining by the Star Chamber and sent to Fleet Prison, where he remained for twelve days.

INFLATION

Until about 1525, prices were fairly steady and food was relatively cheap. Then inflation began a slow, steady climb. A horse, which might cost 30s. in 1560, was 40s. in 1580, as much as 83s. in 1638 and up to 102s. during the Civil War. Food prices rose as much as 120 percent between 1541 and 1641 while wages, especially agricultural wages, stayed nearly the same. By the end of the sixteenth century, grain cost six times what it had in 1500 and wages were little more than twice as high. In the 1630s, prices had risen another 50 percent over those of 1600. Severe depressions added to the problem, one of the worst lasting from 1620 to 1624. In the economic crisis of 1623, the price of wheat increased in one year from 16s. a bushel to 53s. 4d.

Eight pair of knitted hose cost 3s. 4d. in 1561. In 1576 one pair of white silk hose sold for 25s. In 1635, stockings were 4s. 3d. a pair. A pair of worsted stockings cost 7s. in the 1650s. Points, which sold for 1d. per dozen in 1550 and 6d. per dozen in 1561, were 1s. per dozen in 1589. In 1561 a peach-colored beaver hat, edged with silver with a band of finest lawn, cost £2. In 1603 a plain black beaver hat set the buyer back as much as £4.

WAGES AND PRICES

Two pounds ten shillings a year was considered a marginal but adequate income in the Elizabethan period. The Statute of Laborers and Artificers (1563) mandated that every unmarried person between twelve and sixty, and married persons under the age of thirty, who had income of less than 40s. a year, were to hire themselves out as servants paid by the year. This statute also fixed wages, with some local variation, and specified that household servants were to receive board, lodging and an allowance of clothing in addition to wages. Under this early minimum wage law, a field worker received 2d. or 3d. per day for working from dawn to dusk.

Other laws followed, amending the first. In 1594 laborers were getting 1d. per day in winter, plus meat and drink, and 2d. per day in summer, plus meat and drink. Children, apprentices and women were paid less than men. On average a woman received half to two-thirds of what a man made. In 1515 a woman servant could not be paid more than 10s. per year plus board and lodging. Under Elizabeth's statutes, a woman servant in charge of brewing, baking or malting was not allowed more than 17s. per year plus board and lodging. In the seventeenth century, the wages of female domestic servants were increased again, but never seem to have exceeded 40s. per year.

In the 1590s, when a London artisan earned 7s. per week, the costs of various forms of entertainment ranged from 1d. to see a play (2d. if it was a new one), 3d. for a wherry ride on the Thames, and 4d. for a quart of ale, to 8d. for a quart of sack. A meal at an inn could be had for 6d. and so could a whore.

Estimates for the period 1630-1643 indicate that the average annual income in England was £200 to £300 for gentry, £10 to £100 for beneficed clergy and £40 to £60 for a yeoman. A farm family's average weekly income in 1640 was 3s. 2d., including the earnings of the husbandman's wife. Wages paid to thatchers in the 1640s varied from 7s. 6d. a week in Essex to 6d. per day and meat in most other parts of the country, to 4d. and three meals a day in Yorkshire.

USURY

The first Usury Act of this period was passed in 1496 and made it illegal to lend or take money at interest. Merchants frequently ignored this law. So did monasteries, which made loans to gentlemen. In 1545 it became legal to charge interest up to 10 percent. This lasted until 1552. Under the Statute on Usury of 1572, the maximum interest rate was again set at 10 percent, but the lender had no redress under the law if the borrower refused to pay back more than the exact amount he'd borrowed. In 1624, interest was limited to 8 percent per annum.

England had no banks in the modern sense of the word, but many businessmen included currency exchange and loans among their services. The second earl of Southampton borrowed £500 from William Denham, a London goldsmith, in 1580. Dr. Fox, another well-known London moneylender, charged 6 to 7 percent interest on a loan of £500. A number of goldsmiths used money deposited with them for safekeeping to make loans. Brokers and scriveners placed out the money of others at interest, for a fee. Wealthy merchants loaned their own money.

One of the richest men in London, Sir John Spencer, who had made his fortune in overseas trade, was engaged in large-scale moneylending to needy gentlemen and peers by the 1590s. His estate was well over £300,000 at the time of his death in 1610. Another well-known money-lender was Juliana (Arthur) Penne. After her death in 1592, her son by her first marriage, Sir Baptist Hicks, carried on the business. Lawyers were also known to provide short-term loans to their clients, particu-larly in cases of land transfers. Sir Edward Stanhope and Sir Julius Caesar were prominent moneylending lawyers.

The English Crown borrowed from Antwerp at high rates of interest during the period from 1544 to 1574. James I took short-term loans from English merchants. In 1625–28 and 1638–42, Charles I also bor-rowed money in London.

At the other end of the scale, alehouse keepers made loans to their patrons. So did a peddler named Kit Miller. Miller had a thriving busi-ness at fairs, such as the one at Chelmsford, during the 1580s and 1590s. He sold counterfeit magistrates' seals (to seal travel permits and thus avoid arrest for vagrancy) and forged passports (a license to travel, which had to be signed by two justices of the shire). He also made loans to vagrants. They repaid him with interest "when they had gotten any cheat."

One way around the maximum interest rate was to offer a "com-modity" instead of part of the cash. This commodity was often worth far less than advertised and it was not uncommon for the lender to realize a profit as high as 100 percent.

IMPRISONMENT FOR DEBT

Going to prison for debt was common, and in some cases was by choice, since it kept a man's possessions safe for his heirs (death canceled debt). Some even went bankrupt deliberately, after investing the money they had borrowed. They were then unable to repay their loans but could live high in prison (with good food, comfortable furnishings, visitors, etc.) on the proceeds. London's Fleet, Ludgate and King's Bench prisons housed debtors.

When a firm went "bancquaroutta," everything was seized and sold. The fortunes of the Caves and Johnsons, merchants based at Calais until 1558, are studied in detail in Barbara Winchester's *Tudor Family Portrait* (London: Jonathan Cape, 1955). John Johnson was granted a year of grace before he was imprisoned in the Fleet for debt and was in and out all through the next two years, but his wife and children were on their own, dependent on relatives. Had Johnson been able to make a settlement, he could have gotten out of prison, but he would have been literally penniless.

SHOPPING MALLS

The Royal Exchange, Cornhill, was the Elizabethan equivalent of a shopping mall. Queen Elizabeth officially opened the Royal Exchange on January 23, 1571. Built by Sir Thomas Gresham (whose crest, the grasshopper, surmounted the bell tower in the center wing), it occupied a site between Cornhill and Threadneedle Street in London. It was designed by Henri van Paesschen, a Fleming, who took his inspiration from a similar structure in Antwerp.

The gateway from Cornhill gave access to a courtyard decorated with statues of the kings of England. Three brick wings (later stuccoed) rose four stories high and housed some 100 shops, including milliners, haberdashers, armorers, apothecaries, booksellers, goldsmiths and glass-sellers. In the evening, the shops were lit with candles. During the earthquake of 1580, shopkeepers fled the premises in a panic, but the building stood.

Covered walks supported by marble pillars were gathering places for merchants as well as shoppers. Space under this arcade served as a stock exchange and estate agency. The bells in the bell tower sounded twice a day, at noon and six in the evening. London's waits (town musicians) gave evening concerts at the Royal Exchange every Sunday and holiday from 1571 to 1642. The Royal Exchange was destroyed in the Great Fire of 1666.

In 1609, the New Exchange (officially called Britain's Burse, the name James I chose for it) opened on the Strand as a West End rival to the Royal Exchange. It followed a similar plan, with a long (201 feet) covered arcade facing the street. Inside, a ten-foot-wide corridor was flanked by rows of small booths (no more than 5½ feet deep) on either side. On the second level, reached by stairs at both ends, there were two corridors with more rows of shops. The shops, an even hundred in all, were to be leased for eleven years, but the rents were a bit high and only 27 shops were leased out when the place opened. Market regulations excluded ordinary perishable goods and encouraged shops like the "China houses" which sold oriental silks and porcelain. Hours were also regulated. The New Exchange was open from 6 A.M. to 8 P.M. in summer and 7 A.M. until 7 P.M. in winter. The New Exchange struggled along at first, but in the 1630s it enjoyed a new prosperity. In 1657, it was occupied by 109 shopkeepers, including 42 milliners and 32 sempsters.

SELECT BIBLIOGRAPHY

Bernard, G.W., ed. *The Tudor Nobility.* Manchester: Manchester University Press, 1992. Especially useful is the chapter "Henry VII and the English Nobility," by T.B. Pugh.

Challis, C.E. *The Tudor Coinage.* Manchester: Manchester University Press, 1978.

Fletcher, Anthony. *Tudor Rebellions.* London: Longman, 1968.

Stone, Lawrence. *Family and Fortune: Studies in Aristocratic Finance in the Sixteenth and Seventeenth Centuries.* Oxford: Clarendon Press, 1973.

CHAPTER ELEVEN

WAR AND PEACE

ngland spent less time at war during the period from 1500 to 1650 than in previous decades, which were filled with civil wars between Lancaster and York. It was not, however, an entirely peaceful era.

Peace treaties between nations were customarily sealed with a royal marriage. Henry VII attempted to rid England of enemies by negotiating such alliances. His daughter Margaret was married to King James IV of Scotland. His son Arthur wed Catherine of Aragon in 1501. And his daughter Mary was betrothed during his lifetime to the future Holy Roman Emperor Charles V. Unfortunately, Arthur died in 1502. The fact that Henry VIII married his brother's widow in 1509 was the basis for their divorce and the subsequent break with Rome some twenty-four years later. Margaret's husband was slain by English troops at Flodden. Mary's betrothal was set aside so that she could be married to the elderly French king, Louis XII, in 1514. He died a few months after the wedding.

Henry VIII, in between marriage alliances involving his sister and his daughter, periodically went to war with France and with Spain. England was at war with France in 1511–1514 (allied for part of that time with the Holy Roman Emperor and the Spanish king, and again in 1522–1525 and 1543–1545). That always meant war with Scotland, too, for every time the English were occupied in the south, the Scots attacked across her northern border. In 1528, Henry was at war with Charles V, but when Charles signed the Peace of Cambrais the next year with Francis I of France, Henry also abided by it.

Under Edward VI, another war was waged against France and Scotland, lasting from 1547 to 1550. Mary's marriage to Philip II of Spain brought England into the Spanish war against France in 1557. Under Elizabeth there was initially a period of peace, but enmity with Spain eventually brought on first a trade war and then a declared war. Connected to this was the war in the Low Countries. Private individuals were urged to finance armies to fight at the side of the rebels there. Under the Stuarts, foreign relations were mostly peaceful, although Elector Frederick of the Palatine (James I's son-in-law) did accept the crown of Bohemia in 1619, the start of what later became known as the Thirty Years' War.

EMBASSIES

The idea of a permanent resident agent at another court originated in Italy in the fifteenth century and became quite common throughout Europe in the sixteenth. Spain had an embassy in England from 1495 until 1584. France also sent an ambassador to England. There were English ambassadors at the courts of the Holy Roman Empire, the Netherlands, France and Venice until 1558, but by 1570 the only remaining English ambassador on the Continent was in France.

In 1557, the duke of Muskovea, the first ambassador to England from the tsar of Russia, arrived at court. In 1582, Ivan the Terrible suggested he might marry Queen Elizabeth's distant cousin, Lady Mary Hastings, but no one in England looked very favorably on the idea. For one thing, Ivan had recently married his seventh wife.

THE PALE OF CALAIS

This outpost in France was English until 1558. It extended nine miles inland at its deepest point and along eighteen miles of the English Channel from Gravelines to Cap Blanc Nez. With an area of about 120 square miles, mostly marshland, the English Pale had an approximate population of twelve thousand, including Picards and Flemings as well as English. From 1536 to 1543, Calais was represented in the English

Parliament. The normal military garrison at Calais (as at Berwick) was less than one thousand. A mile outside the walled town of Calais, on the road to Boulogne, was another small garrison at Newenhambridge, which controlled the sluices that regulated the flow of the Hammes River. This allowed the defenders of Calais to flood an extensive area to the west in case of enemy attack.

THE INVASION OF FRANCE IN WAR

In 1513, when Henry VIII brought his army to France, he took with him a portable wooden house, carried in twelve carts. It had two rooms, windows of "lantern horn" and a fireplace and chimney. The exterior was painted to resemble bricks. Henry also brought his own bed on campaign, and three more wagons transported a tent of cloth-of-gold and other tents and marquees, which connected to the prefabricated timber house to cover an area of some 4,000 square feet with additional "rooms," including one which held the royal close-stool.

The officers, including captains, lived in smaller tents. Henry's minstrels and players traveled with him. So did a corps of six hundred yeomen, fifty "King's Spears" (men of noble blood, each with an archer, light cavalryman and mounted attendant) and the garrison troops (some three thousand men normally scattered at over a hundred royal castles).

The army of thirty thousand was supported by a baggage train of between ten thousand and fifteen thousand wagons. A soldier's typical daily ration was a pound of biscuit, a pound of beef and eight pints of beer.

THE INVASION OF FRANCE IN PEACE—
THE FIELD OF CLOTH-OF-GOLD

The English made a peaceful "invasion" of France in 1520, to compete in tournaments and showmanship. In some ways it was not so different from 1513. Determined to compete with Francis I on a personal level, Henry VIII brought his entire court and then some. Not only did every courtier attend, but they were each entitled to a retinue, the numbers determined by rank. Every earl brought thirty-three servants, twenty horses, three chaplains and six gentlemen. Every knight was entitled to one chaplain, eleven servants and eight horses. Even an esquire

A swordfight, 1594
Similar sketches illustrate Giacomo di Grassi's His True Art of Defense, *a book used to teach swordsmanship.*

had a chaplain, six servants and eight horses. The ladies were similarly escorted. Each countess was allowed three gentlewomen, four menservants and eight horses. Each gentlewoman had a woman servant, two menservants and three horses. Even the chamberers were allowed one manservant and two horses each.

Including time at Calais, the English were in France from May 31 until July 18. They were in Henry's "temporary" palace at the site of the main events near Guines from June 7 to 20. The palace lodged approximately 820 people and had four towers at the corners and a gatehouse at the front. There was an inner court around which the four ranges of the building were grouped. There were three floors with a chapel on the ground floor. The choir was hung with cloth-of-gold and silk. The altars were covered with cloth-of-gold embellished with pearls. The gilded wooden roof had a frieze below it. On the high altar, under a rich canopy, were five pairs of candlesticks, a large crucifix and statues of all twelve apostles, each as large as a four-year-old child. The state apartments were on the first floor and the king and queen had oratories which looked down into the chapel. A separate banqueting house stood outside the castle wall. There was a large hall at the back of the structure, 328 feet long, reached by a broad staircase. Divided by two tapestries, its ceiling was of green sarcenet with gold roses.

For entertainment there were banquets, masques and dancing, but the main event was the tournament and its goal was to see who could break the most lances. The score on Saturday the sixteenth of June was Henry 18, Francis 14. In all, over the days of the event, 327 lances were broken.

THE ROYAL NAVY

Henry V made the first attempt to create a royal navy. Henry VII was the first English king to launch an active warship-building program. Henry VIII followed his father's lead and in the first half of the sixteenth century Portsmouth became a major naval base.

In the wars Henry VIII fought with France, his navy played an important role. On April 28, 1513, the English fleet engaged French galleys in Conquet Bay on the coast of Brittany. Sir Edward Howard was Lord Admiral. He had just boarded a captive vessel when a cable slipped (or was cut) and Howard found himself adrift on an enemy ship under the command of French admiral Prigent de Bidoux. Nearly fifty Englishmen, including the Lord Admiral, were dispatched with pike thrusts or thrown into the sea. A short time later, Bidoux returned Howard's embalmed body to the English, but he kept the heart, an act which provoked so much outrage in England that King Henry was able to muster popular support for his war and continue until he'd had his revenge.

In July 1545, when Henry VIII was again at war with the French, the French sent an armada against him greater than the Spanish force that would come in 1588. At least 225 ships left Le Havre carrying 30,000 troops. Henry had 60 English vessels gathered at Portsmouth. There was, however, no decisive sea battle. The French briefly took the Isle of Wight and there were a few exchanges of gunfire, but after several days the French simply sailed back across the Channel.

Under Edward VI and Mary I, Henry VIII's shipbuilding program was abandoned. Between 1547 and 1558, the number of ships in the royal navy decreased from over 80 to 26. As soon as Elizabeth succeeded her sister, however, she took up where her father had left off.

The most famous sea battle of the century was that fought against the Spanish Armada in 1588. There were 197 English ships gathered to defend English shores against 130 Spanish vessels. While it is true that the English repulsed the Spaniards, more damage was actually done to the Armada by rough weather during the retreat than by English guns.

After James I's treaty with Spain in 1604, the navy was once more allowed to decay. Under Charles I, the so-called Buckingham Wars in 1625 and 1627 were naval disasters, finally prompting Charles to begin to rebuild. Ironically, the effort came back to haunt him. When civil war broke out in 1642, the royal navy turned against him.

THE ENGLISH ARMY IN IRELAND

English monarchs traditionally appointed a Governor for Ireland, but in 1541, Henry VIII officially added King of Ireland to his titles. Crown lands were centered in the Pale, the area around Dublin, but the entire island was nominally under English rule. The Statutes of Kilkenny (1366) distinguished between "the king's Irish enemies" and "the king's English lieges" in Ireland. All were supposed to speak English and adopt English manners and customs. However, Ireland retained its own Parliament, Privy Council and law courts, and some English settlers had been there so long that they no longer thought of themselves as English.

From 1477 to 1534, Ireland was controlled for England by the earls of Kildare. In 1534, Gerald Fitzgerald, ninth earl, was recalled and lodged in the Tower, where he died on September 2. There was an attempt to wipe out the entire "Geraldine" faction, as the Fitzgeralds and their followers were called, but young Gerald, aged ten, was spirited away to be educated in Florence.

English-born Lord Lieutenants governed Ireland from that point onward. It was not a position one coveted, since the post was both dangerous and ruinously expensive to maintain. Treaties with Irish lords in the 1540s gave them new titles and this policy of "surrender and regrant" was repeated under Elizabeth in the 1560s. In spite of that, however, there were uprisings against English rule in Ireland in

1568 and 1579-83, in part over religious issues. A more serious revolt began in 1594 and continued through various ups and downs until 1603. In 1599 the English army in Ireland was destroyed at the Battle of Yellow Ford. Under the Stuarts, there was finally peace (though there was a rising of Irish Catholics in 1641), but there was also famine and increased Irish immigration into England and Wales. In 1628 enterprising ferrymen were charging three shillings each to carry passengers from Ireland to Wales across St. George's Channel.

HEADS OF STATE

England

Henry VII (1457–1509)
Henry VIII (1491–1547)
Edward VI (1537–1553)
Mary I (1516–1558)
Elizabeth I (1533–1603)
James I (1566–1625)
Charles I (1600–1649)

France

Louis XII (1462–1515)
Francis I (1494–1547)
Henri II (1519–1559)
Francis II (d. 1560)
Catherine de' Medici (1519–1589), Regent for Charles IX (1550–1574) and Henri III (1551–1589)
Henri IV (1553–1610)
Louis XIII (1601–1666)

The Holy Roman Empire of the German Nation
(The Low Countries, Eastern Burgundy, Savoy and much of Northern Italy)

Maximilian I (1459–1519)
Charles V (1500–1558) abdicated 1556
Ferdinand I (1503–1564)
Maximilian II (1527–1576)

Rudolf II (1552–1612)
Matthias (d. 1619)
Ferdinand II (d. 1637)
Ferdinand III (d. 1657)

Regents of the Netherlands or Low Countries
(Seventeen provinces ruled by the House of Burgundy and including Flanders, Holland, Utrecht, Brabant, Gelderland and Zeeland)

Margaret of Austria (1480–1530)
Mary of Hungary (1505–1558)
Margaret of Parma (1522–1586) replaced in 1567
Fernando Alvarez de Toledo, duke of Alva (1507–1582) recalled in 1573

Note: There was an ongoing war of liberation in the Low Countries from 1572 to 1610. William I, Prince of Orange, who led the rebels and the Union of Utrecht (1581), was assassinated in 1584. In 1648 the sovereignty of the Dutch Republic of the United Provinces was finally recognized, under the leadership of William II of Orange (1626–1650).

Portugal

Emmanuel I (d. 1521)
John III (d. 1557)
Sebastian (1534–1578)
Henry (d. 1580)
Philip II (Philip III of Spain)

Russia

Ivan III (1440–1505)
Basil III (1479–1533)
Ivan IV, the Terrible (1530–1584)
Fyodor I (1557–1598)
Boris Godunov (d. 1605)
Dmitry I (d. 1606)
Basil IV (d. 1612)
Michael Romanov (1596–1645)

Scotland

James IV (1473–1513)
James V (1513–1542)
Marie of Guise (1515–1560), Regent for Mary
Mary (1542–1587) abdicated 1567
James VI (1566–1625) (James I of England)

Spain

Ferdinand (1452–1516) and Isabella (d. 1504)
Charles V (1500–1558) abdicated 1556
Philip II (1527–1598)
Philip III (1578–1621)
Philip IV (1605–1665)

Popes

Alexander VI (1431–1503)
Julius II (1443–1513)
Leo X (1475–1521)
Clement VII (1478–1534)
Paul III (1468–1549)
Paul IV (1476–1559)
Pius IV (1499–1565)
Pius V (1502–1572)
Gregory XIII (1502–1585)
Clement VIII (1536–1605)
Paul V (1552–1621)

SIGNIFICANT EVENTS

April 28, 1513: Battle of Conquet Bay (France).

August 16, 1513: Battle of the Spurs (France).

September 9, 1513: Battle of Flodden (Scotland).

November 23, 1542: Battle of Solway Moss (Scotland).

September 10, 1547: Battle of Pinkie Cleugh (Scotland).

August 10, 1557: Battle of Saint-Quentin (France).

January 8, 1558: Fall of Calais.

1562: Treaty between Elizabeth and the Huguenot faction in France during the French Civil War.

1564: Anglo-French peace.

August 20, 1585: Treaty of Nonsuch promises five thousand foot soldiers and one thousand horse soldiers to the Dutch in return for possession of the towns of Flushing and Brill. This meant open war with Spain. The earl of Leicester led an expedition to the Low Countries in December.

1588: Spanish Armada defeated.

1596: The earl of Essex's attack on Cadiz.

1597: The Islands Voyage to the Azores.

August 14, 1599: Battle of Yellow Ford (Ireland).

1604: Peace of London signed with Spain.

SELECT BIBLIOGRAPHY

Cruickshank, C.G. *Elizabeth's Army*. Oxford: Clarendon Press, 1966.

Cruickshank, Charles. *Henry VIII and the Invasion of France*. New York: St. Martin's Press, 1990.

Ellis, Steven G. *Tudor Ireland: Crown, Community and Conflict of Cultures 1470–1603*. London and New York: Longman, 1985.

Quinn, David Beers. *The Elizabethans and the Irish*. Ithaca, New York: Cornell University Press, 1966.

Russell, Joycelyne G. *The Field of Cloth of Gold: Men and Manners in 1520*. New York: Barnes and Noble, 1969.

CHAPTER TWELVE

Y the end of the sixteenth century, around fifty thousand
Englishmen earned their living from the sea. English ships
had sailed all over the world. Along with contemporary accounts of such voyages, two twentieth-century projects have
yielded a detailed picture of shipboard life in the period from
1500 to 1650.

King Henry VIII's *Mary Rose* sank in the waters of the
Solent, between Portsmouth and the Isle of Wight, in 1545.
This vessel was recovered by underwater archaeologists in 1982. More
than 17,000 artifacts were found on board, everything from 2,500
arrows and 139 longbows to a barber-surgeon's chest containing sixty-
four items commonly used by sixteenth-century medical men.

The *Mayflower II*, docked at Plymouth, Massachusetts, is not a replica
of the original *Mayflower*, but she was modeled after an actual seventeenth-century merchantman, the *Adventure* of Ipswich. She was built
in England in 1957 and sailed across the Atlantic in fifty-three days, an
average seventeenth-century crossing time.

LIFE AT SEA

Food

Close to shore, crews might enjoy a great variety of foods. The salvaged
Mary Rose contained peas still in the pod, pits from wild cherries and

plums, hazelnut shells and the bones of fish, venison, beef and mutton. Her sailors ate from wooden plates and drank their beer from wooden drinking vessels. The officers used pewter.

On long sea voyages, however, the food was uniformly bad. Supplies often ran low, even with careful planning, and ship's biscuit had to be considered edible even when it was rotting and infested with weevils. Along with the dried biscuits, the basic rations on any voyage were beer, and beef or pork cured in brine. Other provisions might include oatmeal pottage, buttered peas, salted eggs, salted fish, bacon, neats' tongues in bran or meal (neats were oxen, bullocks or other cattle) and "bag pudding" made with raisins and currants.

The sea provided fresh fish to augment this diet. On a voyage in 1591, John Davys had his crew kill and salt penguins before starting through the Strait of Magellan. Porpoises were sometimes harpooned and hauled aboard to be butchered on deck. Porpoise liver, boiled and soused in vinegar, compared favorably to beef, but fried porpoise tasted like "rusty" bacon.

A ship might have a cook or the cooking chores might be rotated from man to man, but cooking could only be done when the seas were calm. Some ships used an open fire, insulated from the timbers by a bed of sand. Others had a brick fireplace in the forecastle, which had an opening in the roof to let smoke out. Cooking was also done on charcoal stoves in the tiller flat.

The statute of 1585, which fixed the wages of mariners on royal ships at 10s. per month (up from 6s. 8d.), also specified a daily ration of one gallon of beer, one pound of biscuit, and two pounds of pork and peas (or beef) four days a week. They ate fish the other three. This rate was in effect until 1625. Sailors on merchantmen, in addition to their keep, earned almost 20s. per month and those on privateers might hope to do even better by receiving a share of the profits. On a profitable voyage each might receive 40s. in addition to the normal pay.

Since perishable fruits and vegetables were difficult to keep aboard ship, scurvy was a constant problem. Most seafarers suffered from aching joints, painful gums and general lassitude. Some ships carried lemons as a cure for the most severe cases. On a passenger ship in the 1630s, a passenger's servant was whipped naked at the capstan with a cat-o'-nine-tails for filching nine lemons out of the surgeon's cabin and eating them rind and all.

Living Conditions

The ships were small by modern standards, since any ship a hundred feet long was considered fairly large in the sixteenth century. A typical main deck measured only 75' × 20'. The captain, or master, of the ship had a cabin, but the twenty to thirty crewmen aboard a ship of the *Mayflower*'s size slept in blankets on straw mattresses on the bare decks or in hammocks. Clearance between decks was barely six feet and every available inch would be filled with cargo or passengers. The hold and 'tween decks were dank, uncomfortable, foul-smelling and infested with rats and roaches. Latrine buckets added to the stench, since the beakhead, the area used as a seagoing "pissing place," was usually awash for most of a voyage.

Mariners were constantly wet. Cold water not only sloshed in the bilges with the constant rolling of the ship, it also dripped down through leaking decks and topsides. After storms, there were always more leaks. Repairs were made by stuffing cracks with clothing, bedding, animal hides and sail cloth. Bailing was augmented by pumps, which were worked by two men in much the same fashion as a hand car on a railroad. All too frequently bad stowage, misplaced ballast, or the use of inappropriate sails would swamp a ship.

COMMON SIZES OF ENGLISH VESSELS

type of ship	size in tons
pinnace	10, 20 or 30
bark	50 to 70
caravel	100 to 150
hulk	300 to 400
galleon; carrack	800 and up

Routine Aboard Ship

Ships of this period were steered by a helmsman using a whipstaff to work a rudder. He kept on course by watching a magnetic compass suspended on gimbals in a wooden case (illuminated by an oil lamp at night) and by listening to the reports called down from the mate on watch on the deck above. Each watch was four hours long.

Sailing necessitated using a zigzag pattern and storms frequently

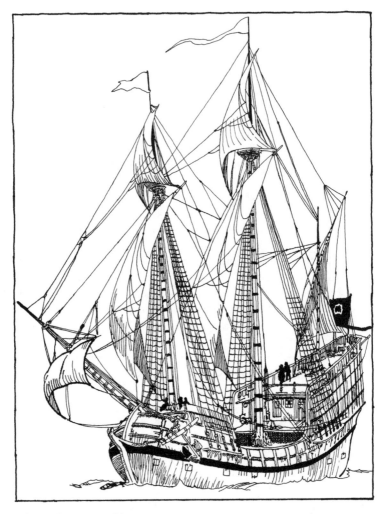

A sixteenth-century ship
This vessel was typical of the larger ships of the day. Its relative size may be seen by looking at the people on deck.

blew ships off course, but dead reckoning was still the favored method of getting somewhere. One established position in terms of distance, sailed along a known compass bearing and used a chip log to determine speed. This was a lead-weighted log on a knotted line which was tossed over the stern to measure a ship's speed. The length of the measured line paid out in a minute (a number in knots) and multiplied by sixty gave sailors the distance they'd sailed in one hour. The course and speed were recorded on a log-board and transferred to the log book every twenty-four hours.

SOME SAILING TIMES

From	To	Number of days at sea
Dartmouth	Isle of Wight	12
Weymouth	Barbados	40*
England	Sierra Leone	73
Plymouth	Cape Cod (summer)**	51
Plymouth	Cape Cod (autumn)**	66
Cape Verde	Brazil	54
Cape Florida	Scilly Isles	23
Penobscot Bay	the Azores	12
Coast of New England	Dartmouth	32

*This was excellent time. The trip usually lasted several months.
**This was by the southern route to the Canaries on northeast trade winds, then west using the southeast trade winds and the North Atlantic currents. The entire trip covered 5,420 nautical miles.

Although there were some specialized jobs, such as ship's carpenter, and a grommet (ship's boy) was responsible for turning the half-hour glass, most of the work involved handling the huge, square sails, which needed to be trimmed to match wind speed. As many as nine men at one time might be required to control a single sail, each on a separate line. In stormy weather all hands had to go aloft in order to take in the sails quickly enough. They got their orders from the boatswain, who used a whistle to signal such commands as "Pull harder" or "Let go!"

Whipping crewmen with the boatswain's rod was a regular Monday morning event aboard some vessels. Keel-raking (later called keelhauling) was reserved for those who committed the most heinous crimes, since the punishment, which involved being dragged down one side of the keel, under the ship and up the other, left few survivors.

MARINERS' SUPERSTITIONS

Storm-driven ships were believed to be bewitched and anyone suspected of being a witch might be thrown overboard. Evil could also be driven away by nailing two red-hot horseshoes to the main mast.

A frog could sense both the direction of land and the approach of a storm. If a frog was dropped into a barrel of water aboard a ship, it would swim toward land. If good weather was on the way, the frog swam near the top of the barrel. If a storm was coming, it swam at the bottom.

Among sailors it was often a point of honor not to learn to swim lest they be thought to lack faith in their ship's ability to return safely to port.

FLAGS

English ships flew the Cross of St. George, a red cross on a white ground, and the Lord Admiral, when in command of the fleet in 1588, also flew the royal standard (three lilies and three lions). James I's standard added a Scottish lion and an Irish harp and this was flown by the Lord Admiral in 1625. The "Union Jack," representing the union of England and Scotland, appeared after 1603. Ships from English ports hoisted the union flag on the maintop and flew St. George's cross at the foretop. Those from Scottish ports hoisted St. Andrew's flag. In 1634, Charles I restricted use of the union flag at sea to the Royal Navy.

Pirate ships in the sixteenth and seventeenth centuries never flew the Jolly Roger, a flag with white skull and crossbones on a black ground, but a few late seventeenth-century pirates did use a plain red flag. The color was supposed to symbolize the blood that would be spilled if the intended victim did not surrender.

MERCHANT SHIPS

Commercial vessels carried all kinds of cargoes. One booming industry was the East Coast collier traffic. Sea-coal mined above Newcastle was loaded onto barges to be taken to the mouth of the Tyne, then re-loaded into seagoing vessels below Newcastle Bridge. From there it was shipped to both English and foreign ports where it was in great demand because of a shortage of firewood.

With the Mediterranean and Baltic periodically closed off to English ships, the Muscovy Company was founded to establish trade with Russia as well as to look for a northeast passage to the Orient. The East India Company, which sent ships the long way around to the Far East, was granted the monopoly on the English spice trade in 1600. The Levant Company, founded to trade with Turkey, Syria and Egypt, braved the Mediterranean to reach Venice and Constantinople.

FISHING FLEETS

In 1563, Parliament declared that every Wednesday was an extra fish day, giving a huge boost to the fishing industry. In addition to regular fishing grounds closer to home, English fishing fleets also operated in the waters off Newfoundland, but Icelandic fishing grounds had been closed to England since the end of the fifteenth century.

PIRATES AND PRIVATEERS

By the end of the fifteenth century, piracy was a highly organized venture, especially in the areas around the Cinque Ports, the Scilly Isles and the south of Ireland. In the reign of Henry VII, an attempt was made to rid the English Channel of pirates, but the Navigation Act was only moderately successful. According to one estimate there were still four hundred pirates plying their trade in the Narrow Seas in 1558.

Pirate vs. Privateer
The practice of privateering predates the creation of all national navies. By the start of the sixteenth century, privateers were regularly

used to augment the English navy. The distinction between pirate and privateer often became blurred. In 1511, for example, Henry VIII gave orders for the capture of the Scots pirate, Barton. The Scots protested that Barton was a privateer. Ultimately, this disagreement, along with other differences, gave England and Scotland an excuse to declare war on each other. In 1544, Henry himself licensed privateers to attack French and Scots shipping. These English privateers also preyed on ships from Spain and the Netherlands and a prize taken ''by mistake'' was rarely returned.

By the Elizabethan era, Spain stopped bothering to distinguish between pirates and privateers and declared that all English "Sea Dogs" were *piratas*. In England, whether a particular English ship was a pirate or a privateer depended upon England's foreign policy at the time. During periods when no new letters of marque or commissions of reprisal were issued, English privateers suddenly became pirates, even though they did no more than continue to operate in exactly the same way they had been.

Under English law, piracy was illegal and punishable by death, but most homegrown pirates were never tried before the Admiralty Courts, let alone hung at the "pirates' gallows" at Wapping. Frequently, they were aided and abetted in their activities by the local gentry who financed the ventures and shared in the spoils.

Elizabethan Pirates

Organized bands of pirates operated out of havens along the coasts of Dorset, Cornwall, Wales and Ireland throughout the sixteenth century. In the area of Falmouth, taking ships was the primary business of one of Cornwall's leading families, the Killigrews, who held Pendennis Castle, at the entrance to Falmouth harbor, for the Crown. At the Killigrew family seat, Arwennack House, the women of the family received stolen goods and stored them until they could be sold for profit. Sir John Killigrew became Commissioner for Piracy in Cornwall in 1577, sworn to capture and prosecute pirates, but it was after that date that Lady Killigrew participated in at least two overt acts of piracy, on one occasion stealing bolts of cloth from a ship at anchor in Falmouth harbor and on another seizing two barrels containing Spanish pieces of eight.

One of the best known pirates of the Elizabethan era was also a woman, Grace, or Grania, O'Malley of Ireland. She was captured at least twice, and when she was tried in 1586 for plundering Aran Island, she was sentenced to hang. Sir John Perrot, Commissioner for Piracy in Pembrokeshire, secured a pardon for her from the queen.

Among English pirates, remarkably few fit the stereotype of the black-hearted villain. An exception was Stephen Heynes. When Heynes brought the *Salvator* of Danzig into Studland Bay as a prize and attempted to force her master to reveal where treasure was stowed away by sticking lighted matches under his fingernails, Heynes's own men went down on their knees and begged their captain to spare them having to witness such atrocities.

Finding Work as a Pirate

Before 1583, when two of the queen's ships raided the anchorage there and seized seventeen pirate ships, Studland Bay was the place to go to join a pirate crew. In the early years of the seventeenth century, would-be pirates could find a ship at Leamcon, on Roaring Water Bay in Ireland. Many sailors, however, broke into the business simply by getting together with a few other like-minded fellows and stealing a ship.

Piracy Under the Stuarts

Elizabeth I's ongoing war with Spain had brought about a temporary decline of piracy in English waters. Privateering in the West Indies had become phenomenally profitable, drawing potential pirates away, while at the same time the increased presence of royal ships gathered to defend England had cut pirates off from their former havens. When King James I came to the throne, he outlawed privateering by a proclamation of June 23, 1603. The number of cases of piracy immediately increased. By 1608 at least five hundred pirate ships were active at sea. As had been the case in Elizabeth's time, the very officials charged with capturing pirates were sometimes in league with them. Sir Richard Hawkins, appointed in 1603 as vice admiral of Devon, was tried, convicted and imprisoned in 1609 for receiving, aiding and comforting notorious pirates and taking bribes to free them.

Thames River Pirates

The Thames was navigable to merchant ships for sixty miles, all the way to London Bridge, which put it under the jurisdiction of the Admiralty. Between 1600 and 1640, fifty-one of eighty-six indictments for piracy committed on the English coast concerned crimes committed on the

Thames. Over seven hundred individuals were indicted for piracy not restricted to the coast.

Land Pirates

Land pirates were those who received stolen pirate goods or provided supplies to pirate ships. Until 1700 the statutes on punishments for pirates did not include accessories. From 1603 to 1640, only seventeen persons were indicted for harboring pirates or receiving stolen goods from them. Seven were women.

North Atlantic Pirates

Piracy in the North Atlantic was at its peak from 1608 to 1614 and operated out of bases in Morocco and Ireland. Many of these pirates practiced their trade for a few years and then surrendered under a general pardon and were allowed to keep all the loot they'd accumulated. Henry Mainwaring (1587–1643) was one of these, and he wrote a detailed account of pirate life after he was pardoned in 1616. He presented a copy of his book to James I in 1618. Mainwaring had taken a degree at Oxford and briefly studied law at the Inner Temple before he turned pirate in 1613. He was admiral of a pirate fleet before his surrender. Two years after his pardon, he was knighted, and by the end of his career, he had served as Lieutenant of Dover Castle, M.P. and Naval Commissioner.

Mediterranean Pirates

Another distinct group of pirates was based in the Mediterranean, primarily at Tunis, and enjoyed a heyday from 1592 to 1609. These English renegades were in league with "the Turk." To "turn Turk" was to convert to Islam in order to increase opportunities for advancement among the Barbary pirates, those operating from the western part of North Africa (the Barbary Coast). In the seventeenth century, they moved out into the Atlantic, raided in the English Channel and once even landed in Cornwall, attacking a church during services and taking sixty prisoners. A sallee-man or sallee rover was any pirate ship operating out of the port of Sallee on the Barbary Coast.

In the 1620s and 1630s, English piracy was in decline. Most of the raiders were Dunkirkers (French), Biscayners (Spanish) and Turkish rovers from Algiers and Sallee. Barbary pirates plagued English shipping throughout the reign of Charles I. Typical of their activities was the attack on the *Little David* in 1636. A London woolen draper had financed the ship to transport some fifty men and boys and seven women to Virginia as servants. Thirty-five miles off Land's End, the ship was taken by a sallee-man. The captured passengers were sold into slavery. The English women brought especially high prices.

The Sea Dogs

In 1569, Queen Elizabeth sent privateers to prey upon Dutch shipping in an effort to sever communication between the Netherlands and their Spanish allies. The spoils were sold openly at Dover, Plymouth and La Rochelle. Spain's practice of sending regular treasure fleets home from the Caribbean soon drew these "Sea Dogs" to that region. The combination of a violent annual hurricane season and powerful trade winds had forced the Spanish into a predictable schedule of sailing dates. All English privateers had to do was lie in wait and attack ships carrying gold and silver bullion, pearls, emeralds and other valuable commodities, including sugar. In 1591 a Spanish spy in London reported that because the privateers had been so successful, sugar was less expensive in England than it was in the Indies from which it had come.

By late in the sixteenth century, privateering had become a joint-stock business. Money was subscribed by individuals who received "bills of adventure" representing their stock. When the ship returned, each investor could claim a percentage of the profits. A number of London merchants formed syndicates to send out expeditions. Records list seventy-six English expeditions to the Caribbean, involving 235 vessels, between April 1585 and March 1603. One investor, Sir John Watts, later a founder of the East India Company, equipped squadrons of privateers to send to the West Indies in 1588, 1590, 1591, 1592, 1594 and 1597.

Not all voyages were successful, but enough of them produced spectacular returns to keep investors interested. The greatest prize of the century was taken off the Azores in 1592 by a fleet under the command of Sir John Burgh. "The Great Carrack" was Portuguese, the *Madre de Dios*, returning from the East Indies. Queen Elizabeth was one of the investors in this venture, which had been organized by Sir Walter Ralegh. She'd put up £3,000 and two ships. The earl of Cumberland invested £19,000 and Ralegh invested £34,000. The *Madre de Dios* carried everything from diamonds to Chinese silk. Even after heavy pilfering by crewmen before she was brought into port in Dartmouth, the cargo was valued at £150,000. The queen received £60,000, Cumberland was awarded £36,000 and Ralegh received the same amount, even though his investment had been much greater.

The English not only attacked treasure ships, they also plundered Spanish colonies. In 1595 a Spanish official wrote that "corsairs . . . lie in wait on all the sailing routes to the Indies, particularly the courses converging on this city of Santo Domingo. . . . If this continues, either this island will be depopulated or they will compel us to do business with them rather than with Spain."

In the seventeenth century, English privateers operated in the East as well as the West. They took ships off India, Java and Sumatra. One privateer, the *Sea Horse*, operating near Madagascar, was personally financed by King Charles.

PASSENGER SHIPS

Crossing the English Channel
In the sixteenth and seventeenth centuries, the English name for the English Channel was the Narrow Seas, although on maps it is usually labeled the British Sea (and the North Sea is usually the German Ocean). The French called the channel la Manche (the Sleeve). From its western entrance to the far side of the Strait of Dover is just under 350 nautical miles.

The time it took to cross from England to France depended upon point of origin and weather conditions and might amount to days, even weeks. In perfect conditions a ship could sail from Dover to Calais (a little over 20 miles) in two hours.

The "Great Migration"
Between 1630 and 1642, 377,600 persons left England to settle in the Caribbean, the Chesapeake Bay region and New England. To meet the demand for passenger vessels, all kinds of ships were pressed into service. Converted wine traders made the most desirable transports, since they had a sweeter smell and tight caulking. On any ship, however, passengers paid healthy fares (five pounds per person and three pounds per ton of goods) to endure primitive, cramped conditions during an eight- to twelve-week crossing.

Passenger ships leaving ports in the English Channel needed a constant east wind to take them out into the Atlantic. Prevailing winds in the Channel are from the southwest, which meant that failure to take advantage of the right combination of wind and tide could result in weeks of delay. Passengers stayed on board their ship while they waited, because anyone who went ashore risked being left behind if conditions changed abruptly. It made no difference who they were. Even one of Governor John Winthrop's sons "missed the boat" and was left behind in England when the Puritans set sail for Massachusetts Bay in 1630.

Ships carrying passengers to America brought back cargo and mail and almost always found return passengers waiting at the docks. A number of prominent colonists made several trips back and forth in order to settle land-claim disputes and recruit more colonists, but some English men and women decided that life in the New World was not all the promoters had promised. Neither the perils of the "downhill" voyage nor the outbreak of the English Civil War could dissuade these disillusioned souls from returning home.

DEFINITIONS

backstaff: This English quadrant, or sea-quadrant, alleged to have been invented by John Davys, was similar to the modern sextant (developed in 1730) and was used to fix a ship's latitude. One sighted with one's back to the sun.

buccaneer: A term which was not in use before the start of a "golden age of piracy" in 1690 which lasted until about 1725. In particular, buccaneers were pirates who used the island of Tortuga as a base of operations.

Cinque Ports: This term dates from the reign of Henry II and originally referred to five ports: Dover, Hastings, Hythe, Romney and Sandwich. Later, other nearby ports, in particular Winchelsea and Rye, were included in the Cinque Ports Confederacy, which enjoyed its greatest prosperity in the early fourteenth century. In the mid-thirteenth century, a Lord Warden of the Cinque Ports was appointed by the sovereign. By the beginning of the sixteenth century, most of these harbors were so filled in with silt that they could not be used for the newer, larger ships of the day. In 1565 there were sixty-four navigable creeks and landing places on the Essex coast. The most important were Harwich, Colchester and Maldon.

corsair: Originally a privateersman of the Mediterranean, especially the Barbary Coast, by 1590 the term was applied to any pirate or privateering ship.

East Indies: All land east of Africa.

Indies: The West Indies.

league: Although generally equated with a distance of 3 miles, contemporary manuals indicate that the Spanish marine league was 2.82 nautical miles. (One nautical mile equaled 1.15 land miles.) There was general agreement that 60 nautical miles equaled one degree of latitude and that seven leagues was a respectable day's sail.

letters of marque: Naval commissions or authorizations to carry on naval warfare issued by a belligerent nation to the owners of a privately owned armed vessel (a privateer). Pirates carried on naval warfare without benefit of letters of marque and sailed against all flags rather than in service of their sovereign.

Lord High Admiral: Head of the royal navy and a member of the Privy Council. The office became a permanent post in 1406 and paid two hundred pounds per annum, but the Lord Admiral was also entitled to claim all captured pirate booty.

mariner: Any person employed on a ship, but most commonly an able-bodied seaman. At any given time in the sixteenth century, there were only about five thousand experienced mariners in England. No experience at sea was necessary to become an ordinary seaman. The term sailor was used for any member of a ship's company below the rank of an officer.

on the account: When a man said he'd been "on the account," he meant he had been engaging in piracy.

Spanish Main: Coastal regions of Spanish America in the Caribbean from the Lesser Antilles to the Yucatan. This area was the chief theater of operations for the Elizabethan privateers.

SIGNIFICANT SEAFARING EVENTS

1496   First dry dock in England built at Portsmouth.
1497   John Cabot claims North America for England.
1533   Triangulation first used in mapmaking.

1536	Punishments for pirates established by statute.
1536	Lighthouse near Newcastle financed by charging passing ships a fee of 2d. for English vessels and 4d. for foreigners (the earliest lighthouse seems to have been at Winchelsea in 1261).
1555	Muscovy Company chartered.
1569	Gerhardus Mercator publishes the first accurate chart to enable mariners to adjust distances at sea.
1580	Sir Francis Drake circumnavigates the globe.
1588	Spanish Armada defeated.
1589	Publication of Richard Hakluyt's *The Principal Navigations, Voyages and Discoveries of the English Nation.*
1594	Four hundred Spaniards land in Cornwall to burn two towns.
1608	Binoculars (a Dutch invention) first used at sea.
1620	Private lighthouses banned until 1640.

SELECT BIBLIOGRAPHY

Cressy, David. *Coming Over: Migration and Communication between England and New England in the Seventeenth Century.* Cambridge: Cambridge University Press, 1987.

Miller, Helen Hill. *Captains from Devon: The Great Elizabethan Seafarers who won the Oceans for England.* Chapel Hill, North Carolina: Algonquin Books, 1985.

Senior, C.H. *A Nation of Pirates: English Piracy in its Heyday* (1603–1640). New York: Crane, 1976.

Williams, Neville. *The Sea Dogs: Privateers, Plunder and Piracy in the Elizabethan Age.* London: Weidenfeld and Nicolson, 1975.

bis. deburgo fr̄i septēm frater hurag. bartolo
ater hurag. bartolomeus. de pariolis. deburgo fr̄i
bis. deburgo fr̄i septēm frater hurag. bartolo
ater hurag. bartolomeus. de pariolis. deburgo fr̄i
bis. deburgo fr̄i septēm frater hurag. bartolo
ater hurag. bartolomeus. de pariolis. deburgo fr̄i
bis. deburgo fr̄i septēm frater hurag. bartolo
ater hurag. bartolomeus. de pariolis. deburgo fr̄i
bis. deburgo fr̄i septēm frater hurag. bartolo
ater hurag. bartolomeus. de pariolis. deburgo fr̄i
bis. deburgo fr̄i septēm frater hurag. bartolo
ater hurag. bartolomeus. de pariolis. deburgo fr̄i
bis. deburgo fr̄i septēm frater hurag. bartolo
ater hurag. bartolomeus. de pariolis. deburgo fr̄i
bis. deburgo fr̄i septēm frater hurag. bartolo
ater hurag. bartolomeus. de pariolis. deburgo fr̄i
bis. deburgo fr̄i septēm frater hurag. bartolo

PART THREE

Renaissance Society

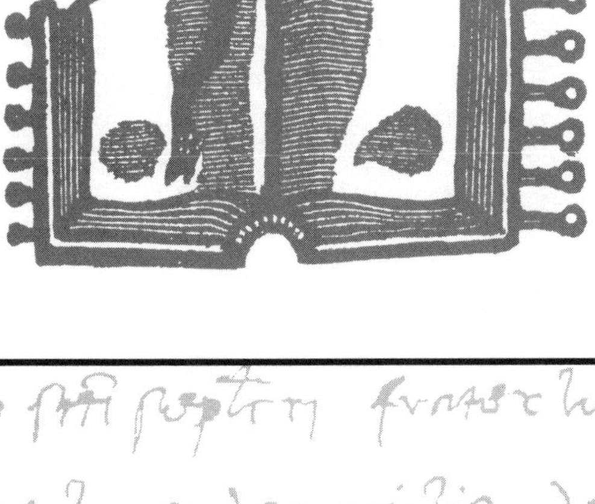

CHAPTER THIRTEEN

EDUCATION: SECULAR AND RELIGIOUS

A t age five a gentleman's son began to learn to read with the aid of a hornbook, a wooden tablet with a handle. Pasted onto the wood and covered with a thin sheet of transparent horn was a printed sheet containing the alphabet and the Lord's Prayer in English. In the early seventeenth century, Sir Hugh Platt invented alphabet blocks to aid in teaching letters.

Children used the catechism, psalters and the Bible as textbooks at an early stage in their education. Other, nonreligious reading material included translations of Aesop and books retelling the Robin Hood and King Arthur stories. In addition, there was an oral tradition of nursery rhymes and fairy tales, many of which now began to be written down. "Tom Thumb" was an old favorite by the time it was first published in 1621 and there were medieval versions of "Jack and the Beanstalk" and "Cinderella."

Reading was taught before writing, and although it has been estimated that only 30 percent of all men and only 10 percent of all women could write their own names at the outbreak of the Civil War, many more than that could read. Girls were often taught to read (along with sewing and housewifery) but not to write.

LITERACY

Much of the population did not have an opportunity to go to school. The children of laborers and small farmers had no time. City dwellers were more likely to attend school than those who lived in the country, but even there large numbers of the poor remained illiterate.

In 1536, Sir Ralph Eure took pride in the fact that he could write nothing but his own name, since he was able in that way to refute charges that he'd penned a treasonous note. He seems to have been an exception, however. Most noblemen and gentlemen were literate by the mid-sixteenth century. Many had valued learning for genera-tions. John Howard, first duke of Norfolk, took books with him on his campaign against the Scots in 1481.

One group that tended to be well educated were "upper" servants such as the chaplain, steward, secretary and waiting gentlewoman, all of whom might be called upon to handle accounts or write letters for their employers. Merchants, vintners and grocers were generally liter-ate by the 1580s. One study, of Tudor York, suggests that the overall literacy rate there may have been as high as 50 percent by 1603. Under the Stuarts, however, there seems to have been a decline in the level of literacy in the general population.

PENMANSHIP

The common English cursive script known as "Secretary" was widely used by scriveners. Pietro Carmeliano, one of Henry VII's chaplains, used the "Italian" style, a cursive script developed from the Roman hand which was easier to read but also easier to forge, and it was this that was taught to Henry VIII's children. Pencils were being made of graphite in England by 1584, but the preferred writing implement was the third or fourth feather of the wing of a goose. A handful of quill pens could be purchased for 1d. In 1585, half a ream of paper and half a pound of sealing wax cost 2s. Letters were folded into an oblong shape and sealed with sealing wax imprinted with a signet ring. Ink was kept in inkhorns, small lead bottles or pewter inkwells. The best quality ink was made from Italian oak apples (galls) and green vitriol. One ink recipe calls for two ounces of gum, two ounces of copperas and four ounces of galls. Invisible inks were made from orange juice, onion juice, milk and urine.

SCHOOLS

Petty Schools

Canterbury had as many as ten petty schools in the early 1600s. These were small groups, often meeting in the teacher's house or in a church. Sometimes boys and girls met together, sometimes separately. The basics of reading and writing were taught. Educators of the time seem to have expected elementary education to last only to about age seven, after which time Latin became the most important subject in the curriculum.

Grammar Schools

The grammar school provided what we would think of as secondary education and emphasized classical learning. Those who were admitted already knew how to read and write in English. Among the subjects taught in grammar schools were ciphering (elementary arithmetic), composition (the models were Cicero for prose and Ovid and Virgil for verse), geography (which included a mix of fact and fiction and delved into astronomy and anthropology as well as natural philosophy, astrology and navigation), history, mathematics, map drawing, Greek and Latin. Latin in particular was important as it was still the universal language of clergy, scholars and the law. A Latin grammar book composed by William Lily became the required text by royal proclamation in 1540. Greek and Latin books were customarily chained to desks.

Modern languages were considered less crucial, although their usefulness in the area of foreign diplomacy became more evident as the sixteenth century progressed. Sir Richard Morrison, ambassador to Emperor Charles V from 1500 to 1553, knew Latin and German (actually Dutch) but not French. He studied Greek in his spare time and read Machiavelli in order to learn Italian. Lord Lisle, assigned to Calais, was fluent in French. Lady Lisle never bothered to learn any language but English and, although she could read, she had someone else write her letters.

Schools maintained by abbeys, such as that at Durham, which had eighteen scholars, had to be refounded after the monasteries were closed. Best known of the early grammar schools were Winchester (founded 1387), Eton (founded 1441), the Royal Grammar School in Lancaster, the New School at St. Paul's in London (founded c. 1509), and the Westminster School (founded anew in 1540), where the boys

176

were nicknamed "Anthony's pigs" to distinguish them from "Paul's pigeons" at nearby St. Paul's. In 1561 the Merchant Taylor's School was founded in London.

Manchester Grammar School was a free school which opened in 1516. It was modeled on the school in Banbury, Oxfordshire, and endowed through the lease of several cornmills. Anyone in Lancashire could attend and there was no age limit. In 1548, Edmund Pendilton, who had a degree of Bachelor of Grammar, was schoolmaster, but although the endowment provided funds to pay the master £10 per annum and the usher (assistant master) £5, Pendilton received only £4 1s. 9d. School began at 7 A.M. in winter and 6 A.M. in summer.

Cheltenham Grammar School (founded 1585) paid its schoolmaster £16 per annum and its usher £4. Each local boy was charged a 4d. entrance fee. Here the days ran from 6 A.M. to 6 P.M.. There was no summer holiday.

Between 1558 and 1603, 136 new grammar schools were founded, bringing the total to approximately 360 in that year. Another 83 were founded between 1603 and 1625, and 59 between 1625 and 1642.

Private Schools

At the turn of the century, private secondary schools were a growing trend. Some grammar schools had taken in boarders, but most concentrated on day boys who were either on scholarship or paid fees. The typical private school added French, German and fencing to Latin and Greek. A 1599 census of Ealing, Middlesex, near London, includes the household of Master Peter Hayward and his son, Thomas. With them lived eighteen boys, ages six to seventeen, a mixture of sons of gentlemen, sons of merchants and sons of yeomen.

Home Schooling and Schooling for Girls

In 1512 the earl of Northumberland's household included a Master of Grammar who was paid 100 marks per quarter to maintain a schoolhouse at the earl's castle at Leckinfield. In addition to the earl's three sons, young gentlemen being fostered in his household would have been included in lessons.

Early in the sixteenth century, London was a gathering place for those interested in developing a wider and more liberal curriculum for schools and universities. Among the leaders were Desiderius Erasmus, Juan Luis Vives, John Colet, Thomas Linacre, William Grocyn and Sir Thomas More. When Henry VIII's daughter Mary was seven, a curriculum of study was designed for her by Juan Luis Vives. A number of peers and gentlemen thereafter began to educate their daughters as well as their sons.

Girls were not permitted to attend grammar schools, and in 1543 an "Act for the Advancement of True Religion" forbade women (along with artificers, apprentices, journeymen, servingmen, husbandmen and laborers) to read the Bible in English. Apparently they were beginning to interpret it for themselves. In many private homes, however, the resident tutor-chaplain continued to teach both girls and boys, and by 1581 it was becoming more common for girls to learn to read and write. Indeed, there was a higher degree of literacy among women at this period than at any other time until the latter nineteenth century.

In the seventeenth century, however, scholarship for women once more began to be discouraged. Girls who were taught at home learned from their mothers, with the occasional master brought in to instruct them in language, music, dance and writing. A copy of Sir Philip Sidney's *Arcadia* was considered an appropriate gift for a young girl in 1637, but most of the acceptable books were religious in nature. The only secular volume a Puritan lady was likely to own was her herbal. At the same time, a few girl's schools began to open. Mrs. Salmon ran one at Hackney. In 1617 there was a "Ladies' Hall" at Deptford, and Mrs. Friend's school at Stepney charged scholars an annual fee of £21 in 1628.

HIGHER EDUCATION

The Universities

Statistics on sixteenth-century admissions to Oxford and Cambridge indicate that some scholars started there as young as eleven or twelve (there was even one nine-year-old admitted to Cambridge), but most began their university studies between the ages of fifteen and eighteen. Twenty-two was old to begin and yet Cambridge did have one scholar start at thirty-eight and Oxford one at forty-eight.

Six-year scholarships were available, paying 1s. for each week of residence at a college (£2 13s. for a year, which provided for up to four weeks annual leave). Students paid for meals at the buttery.

In 1608, nineteen of the ninety justices in Kent had attended both a university (which awarded the degree Bachelor of Civil and Canon

A family receiving religious instruction, 1563
The original of this woodcut is found in John Day's The Whole Psalmes in
foure partes. *Prayers were led by the head of the household or by a family
chaplain and often were held both morning and night. Here the father expounds
upon some point while his family listens.*

Law) and one of the Inns of Court. By 1636, over half had. In Lincolnshire in the same year, two-thirds of the county magistrates had attended either a university or one of the inns or both.

Women were excluded from Cambridge, Oxford and the inns but
several women founded colleges. Frances Sidney Radcliffe, countess
of Sussex, left £5,000 in her will to found Sidney-Sussex College at
Cambridge.

The Grand Tour

The idea of a grand tour to finish off a young gentleman's education
did not become fashionable until early Stuart times, but there had
been individuals who traveled in Europe before that. Some had gone
abroad to study at universities on the Continent. Others had been in
exile during the reign of Mary I. About eight hundred Protestant men,
women and children, the "Marian Exiles," settled in Emden, Wesel,

Zurich, Strasbourg, Frankfort, Basle, Geneva and Aurau from 1554 to 1558. Another group of exiles spent part or all of Mary's reign traveling in France and Italy.

Foreign travel increased after England made peace with Spain in 1604. The Grand Tour of William Cecil, Lord Cranborne, lasted from 1608 to 1610, with a brief return to England to marry. He was accompanied by a tutor, a doctor, a brewer and several footmen. The total cost of this two-year jaunt was over £8,500.

EDUCATION OF ROYALTY

John Skelton was Henry VIII's first tutor until he was removed for writing satire and bawdy songs. Educated with Henry from the time he was seven were the "children of honor," chosen for both their high birth and their handsomeness in appearance and manner. Henry's two sisters were taught Latin, French, composition, music, dancing and embroidery. In 1498 a Flemish girl, Jane Popincourt, was brought to court to teach the two princesses to speak French by conversing with them in that language.

Both of Henry VIII's daughters were well educated. Elizabeth numbered Roger Ascham and John Aylmer among her tutors (Aylmer also tutored Lady Jane Grey). Ascham wrote *The Scholemaster*, published posthumously in 1570, which set out Elizabeth's schedule of study for 1548 and included Greek every morning and Latin every afternoon. She continued to translate works from Greek into Latin and back again as an educational exercise throughout her life. Her brother, Edward VI, was tutored by John Cheke and John Belmain and had at least fourteen youths in his "school."

A typical day for King James at the age of eight included prayers, Latin, composition, arithmetic, cosmography (geography and astronomy) and either dialectics or rhetoric. His son, the future Charles I, was sickly as a child but with the affectionate care of his governess, Lady Carey, he eventually learned to walk and talk. He studied Latin, Greek, French, Italian, Spanish, mathematics, music and theology and doubtless visited the model farm constructed at Combe to teach his sister Elizabeth about birds and beasts. In addition to chickens and cows this farm was stocked with parrots and monkeys.

RELIGIOUS EDUCATION

Education in religious beliefs and morality were inseparable from education in general in the sixteenth and seventeenth centuries. Church and state were one, in the person of the monarch. Even before the break with Rome, the king was "Defender of the Faith" and in a position to enforce piety.

The Dissolution of the Monasteries

The Dissolution of the Monasteries was the closing of 655 monasteries, 90 colleges, and 2,374 chantries and free chapels by Henry VIII, beginning in 1536. The Chantries Act specifically closed those small monastic institutions which had been established to say prayers for their founders. Since many chantries included schools, these were closed down, too, as were the schools supported by churches and cathedrals.

The public was told that monasteries were dens of iniquity and illiteracy (some were, but not all) and that if the abbeys went to the king there would be no more need for taxes (a total fabrication). Eight cathedrals and 6 abbeys were exempted, but even they were looted. St. Cuthbert's shrine in Durham was destroyed in 1537 and his body reburied in a plain tomb in 1542. In September 1538, the shrine of St. Thomas à Becket at Canterbury was demolished.

In 1500 there had been ten thousand monks and two thousand nuns in 825 religious houses. For women, the religious life had offered opportunities for advancement unavailable elsewhere. Some houses also provided education. There were approximately 138 nunneries in England, about half of them Benedictine. Twenty-one were abbeys, where the community was governed by an abbess, and the remainder priories, governed by a prioress (a prioress was an abbess's deputy). The richest were at Syon and Shaftesbury. In England the Franciscan nuns were called Minoresses and their house in London was also a prosperous one. Most nunneries, however, were small and poor, with fewer than thirty inmates. In these, little learning went on because there were few books. By the close of the thirteenth century, English nuns were no longer literate in Latin. Knowledge of French among them had all but disappeared by the fifteenth century.

The nunnery of Wallingwells, near Worksop in Nottinghamshire, attempted to escape dissolution by paying more than an entire year's income for exemption under the 1536 act. In June 1537, the prioress reached a private agreement with a wealthy layman to lease the nunnery for twenty-one years in return for use of the convent buildings. In spite of this attempt at survival, the nunnery was dissolved in December 1539. Another group of nuns, from the Bridgettine house at Syon Abbey in Middlesex, quietly moved to Lyford Grange, near Wantage, Berkshire, and survived there as a community until 1581.

Religion and Education after the Reformation

Edward VI's *Book of Common Prayer* in English came into use on Whitsunday 1549. It set forth the liturgy (order of worship) while the "Forty-two Articles" embodied the theological doctrine of the new church. Under a 1550 statute, all Catholic service books were to be destroyed and possession of one was punishable by a fine and imprisonment. In 1551, all altars were supposed to be replaced by communion tables. Although, under Queen Mary, England briefly returned to the Catholic fold, the "Elizabethan Settlement" of 1559 permanently established the Anglican Church as the church of England. A modified version of the 1552 Prayer Book and the "Thirty-nine Articles" followed.

Church services after the Reformation were not all that different from Catholic services, except that now the sermon was in English. Vestiges of Catholic ritual remained. The sign of the cross was still used during baptisms. The surplice was still worn. And women were still "churched" after childbirth. Sunday services began with prayers at 7 A.M. (5 A.M. in cathedrals and schools). Psalms were read, followed by lessons from both Old and New Testaments, a Litany, Communion if any were present to receive it, and the Decalogue, Epistle and Gospel (with a reading of the Nicene Creed). Another psalm, a sermon or homily and yet another psalm were followed by baptism at the font, if there were any who desired it. Children were usually baptized within the first month of life. Afternoon services began at 2 P.M. and included psalms, lessons and a sermon. Those between the ages of six and twenty were also catechized for an hour. At fourteen the rite of confirmation was performed. All those over fourteen were required to receive Communion at Easter and twice more during the year and attend the parish church.

Local Clergy

Parish priests included curates (posts generally held temporarily by newly ordained priests), vicars and rectors. The lower clergy included chantry priests and chaplains. Some chapels had lay readers. None of these were necessarily well educated. In 1551, John Hooper, bishop of Gloucester, reported that of the 311 clergymen in his bishopric, 168 could not repeat the Ten Commandments. The Elizabethan and Jacobean clergy, however, slowly began to reverse this trend. In 1642, 90 percent of the clergy in Leicestershire had university degrees.

The Royal Injunctions of 1547 forbade religious processions to invoke divine aid, thus banning local Plough Monday processions and church ales. Instead of local saints' days, the first Sunday of October was made a holiday (see chapter fifteen for more details on festivals). Rogation (a yearly confirmation of parish boundaries by walking them off) survived only as a municipal function. More injunctions, in 1559, specified that no bills or banners could be carried for Rogation and only the curate and the leading property owners of the parish could participate.

Up until 1600, many areas in the north of England did not have literate clergy or regular sermons. Because of their usefulness as preachers, James I did not take severe measures against Puritan ministers in Lancashire. Endowing lecturers to preach in remote areas was also a common practice, especially among those who made their fortune in London after leaving home. Lectureships were already popular in London, where 43 percent of 129 parishes had a lecturer in the 1580s. These preachers were supposed to be licensed by the bishops (who also licensed schoolmasters, schoolmistresses, surgeons, midwives and chaplains in private homes).

Sectarianism outside the established church was relatively uncommon until archbishop of Canterbury William Laud alienated those working for reform from within the church by making "Arminian" innovations. Parliament also objected to the changes Archbishop Laud wanted. In 1642, all the bishops were expelled from the House of Lords.

There was a proliferation of lay preaching by both men and women in the 1640s. In 1645 this was forbidden by Parliament. By the beginning of the Civil War, approximately 6 percent of the population were participating in organized dissent.

RELIGIOUS "PARTIES"

Anglicans: Members of the state church of England.

Arminians: Followers of the Dutch theologian Arminius, they rejected the concept of predestination and upheld the Catholic doctrine of free will.

Covenanters: Scottish Protestants opposed to Archbishop Laud's policies.

Jesuits: Members of the Society of Jesus, known for their missionary zeal. They went to England to convert the English to Catholicism and willingly became martyrs. For more details see page 99.

Levellers: This group within the Parliamentary army, while not a religious sect, did want the House of Commons to be supreme over the king and the House of Lords and thus over the Church of England. They tried to define and limit the powers of Commons but did not, as is often charged, advocate abolition of private property or redistribution of wealth.

Lollards: Followers of John Wycliffe (d. 1384), they were persecuted until the 1530s, then absorbed into the reformed religion.

Presbyterians: Activist Puritans who were also followers of John Knox, they disputed the supreme authority of the Crown and sought a church governed by assemblies of clergy and lay elders rather than bishops. They also wanted to replace the Anglican prayer book with the Directory (order of worship) used in Geneva.

Puritans: A term originally coined by Catholics for their enemies, primarily the followers of John Calvin who based their beliefs on the doctrine of predestination, its meaning remained ambiguous throughout this period. Puritans were never a separate sect but worked within the Church of England. Anglican and Puritan within that church are roughly parallel to liberal and conservative within any present-day American political party. In a political sense, Puritan generally meant anyone who advocated an anti-Spanish foreign policy.

Quakers: Founded by George Fox in 1647, the Quakers rejected ordained clergy.

Ranters: The Ranters rejected all conventional morality by meeting in alehouses and allowing divorce.

Recusants: Also called Papists, recusants were Catholics remaining in England after 1562, when the Council of Trent declared that Catholics could not be present at a heretic service. There were 30 recusant women in gaol in York between 1579 and 1594 for refusing to attend church. Eleven of them died there. In 1590, 700 of the 941 recusants presented in Lancashire were indicted. In 1604 the bishop of Chester estimated he still had 2,400 recusants in his diocese, the majority of them women. One recusant, Grace Babthorpe, after spending five years in prison, went to Louvain in 1617 and joined the community of English nuns there. One of her sons was a Jesuit. Although some two hundred priests were executed between 1571 and 1603, it is estimated that there were still 60,000 Catholics in England in 1650. Another estimate gives the number of priests at about six hundred in 1642. In the 1640s the percentage of the population that was still Catholic was probably only about 1 or 2 percent.

Separatists: Puritans who rejected the idea of reform from within. In 1593 they were given a choice between conformity and exile and many chose exile in the Low Countries, including those Pilgrims who founded the Plymouth Colony.

SELECT BIBLIOGRAPHY

Byrne, M. St. Clare. *Elizabethan Life in Town and Country*. New York: Barnes and Noble, 1961.

Collinson, Patrick. *The Elizabethan Puritan Movement*. Berkeley: University of California Press, 1967.

Scarisbrick, J.J. *The Reformation and the English People*. Oxford: Blackwell, 1985.

CHAPTER FOURTEEN

EMPLOYMENT

I n many cases, a person's clothing revealed his occupation. Hooded, ankle-length, woolen gowns and square caps distinguished the academician, from university don to student to schoolmaster. At Cambridge, scholars were to wear their hair "polled, knotted or rounded" and dress in gowns of "black, puke, London brown or other sad color." Protestant clergymen were advised to wear "a comely black surplice with sleeves." Physicians usually wore long, fur-sleeved, black gowns with a cap of white linen beneath a close-fitting black velvet cap. Civic officials such as mayors, sheriffs and aldermen wore different gowns for different occasions, in particular, in London, scarlet trimmed with sable, or violet (really indigo) trimmed with bear fur. Headgear was a black silk cocked hat with a steel chain ornament. Wigs and black gowns for lawyers and judges came later. Counsel below the rank of serjeant wore no headgear and robes of "sad" color. Serjeants at law wore a headdress of white taffeta called "the coif" with a black velvet or silk skullcap over it. Their robes might be any color or combination of colors. Judges' robes were lined with silk or miniver and varied in color from scarlet to violet.

In some parts of Europe, clothing was also used to distinguish persons who were considered inferior. Lepers wore gray coats and red hats, prostitutes wore either yellow dresses or scarlet skirts, and Jews wore a huge yellow circle on the breast. This practice does not seem to have been followed in Renaissance England. The only color consistently used to denote any one group is blue, which symbolized constancy and was therefore associated with serving men and apprentices.

DOMESTIC SERVANTS

Service in a household began in the early teens. Most servants were between the ages of fifteen and twenty-nine. Household servants received wages, board, lodging and an allowance of clothing. In most households they were regarded as chattels (but then, so were wives and children) and their time was wholly their master's. A box on the ear or a whipping with a horsewhip was acceptable punishment for a servant. Severe beatings, however, were cause for the justices to release a servant from his or her commitment.

In London, St. Paul's functioned as an employment bureau, while fairs served the same purpose in rural areas. Those who sought jobs indicated they were available by signs or symbols. For example, a cook wore a red ribbon and carried a beating spoon, a housemaid wore a blue ribbon and carried a broom and a milkmaid carried a pail.

Great households had numerous servants, ruled over by a steward,

---

A LORD SHERIFF'S SERVANTS

Thomas Cullum was one of 250 drapers in London in 1634. He had a shop in Gracechurch Street, purchased cloth from factors and employed dyers in the finishing process. His expenses ran between £550 and £850 a year. In 1644 he bought six houses for £800, four in the Minories and two on Tower Hill and received rents the next year totaling £82. In 1645–6 he served as sheriff. By that time he was a widower and his children were grown, so for his year in office, which carried social responsibilities, he hired a cook, an undercook, cook's laborers, a steward, butler, porter, two underporters, a yeoman of the wine cellar, a running porter, a scouring woman and maid and a coachman and footman. Their combined wages came to £134. His expenses that year totaled some £2,394 more than those of a normal year.

---

sometimes called a house-steward but never butler or majordomo. The butler was only in charge of the buttery. Provisions were obtained by an acater. One list of servants in the late Elizabethan and early Stuart eras includes positions as varied as mole catcher, bargekeeper and spaniel keeper. Some servants are listed by their post rather than their surname, as in "Richard Horsekeeper." Also on the list is a nameless "blackamore" who received clothing but no wages. Women servants included the housekeeper, laundresses and maids and, when the family included women and children, waiting gentlewomen, nursemaids and governesses. Most cooks in gentlemen's and noblemen's households were men.

Lord Marney's household in 1523 numbered 32. Among the earls, Henry Bourchier, earl of Essex, had a household of 50 in 1533. The thirteenth earl of Oxford had several hundred people in his household. The earl of Rutland's household in 1539 numbered 135 and in 1612 had increased to 194. The earls of Northumberland always had large retinues. The seventh earl, who used his poverty as one reason to rebel against the queen in 1569, had a household that numbered 120 in 1568, while the ninth earl, even during his imprisonment in the Tower (1605–1621), had enough servants, including a "reader," to require that some of them live in a rented house on Tower Hill. The custom of using pages, traditionally the first post assigned to young gentlemen sent into a noble household to be trained, was dying out by the middle of the seventeenth century, but Northumberland still kept "riders" who wore his livery and were used to send messages.

Livery

Meant to deter noblemen from keeping private armies, the Tudor law of "livery and maintenance" required those who kept liveried retainers in addition to regular attendants and household officers to obtain a license from the Crown. Though illegal private armies might wear livery, there was neither an army nor a navy uniform at this time.

All noblemen and many gentlemen put their household servants in livery. In its simplest form, livery consisted of loose, hanging shoulder-sleeves embroidered with the master's arms. Blue and gray were the most common colors for livery, though tawny livery was often worn by the servants of churchmen.

Certain posts customarily called for the wearing of a particular color or style. Yeomen, keepers and those who managed hunting-dogs

A huntsman with his hound, 1575

Keeper of the Hounds was a position of some importance in royal and noble households. The clothing shown here probably represents the livery that went with this position. Coursing hares with hounds was a popular country sport and was one of the competitions included in the Cotswold Games.

usually wore Kendal green. Yeomen warders at the Tower of London still wear scarlet livery of early Tudor design. At one point in the reign of Henry VIII, court pages wore gold brocade and crimson satin in chequers while male attendants were in gray, white and scarlet kersey, but there was no one pattern for the entire period.

THE STATUTE OF LABORERS AND ARTIFICERS

This 1563 statute regulated hired labor, provided for periodic wage assessments to be made by justices of the peace and regulated apprenticeship. Every unmarried person between twelve and sixty, and every married person under thirty who had an annual income of less than forty shillings, was bound by law to hire out as a servant for a term of one year at a time. Not only were the wages fixed by statute, so were the hours of work, from 5 A.M. to 7 or 8 P.M. from March to September and from dawn to dusk September to March. Two hours were allowed for meals but a penny was deducted from wages for each additional hour of work missed. From May through August, workers were allowed an extra half hour for a nap.

Servants were forbidden to leave their employment and they could not be dismissed before the year was up without a hearing before two justices. A master who broke this law was fined forty shillings and a servant "unduly departing" was imprisoned until he or she undertook to finish out the year. Anyone who took on an uncertified worker could be fined five pounds.

The term of apprenticeship was officially set at seven years for "every craft, mystery, or occupation." Employers were supposed to be charged with breaking the law if they did not comply with compulsory apprenticeship. Enforcement, however, was inconsistent and in some areas almost nonexistent. In 1616, when London distributors of dairy products complained that they were being harassed because of the terms of this statute, the Privy Council stepped in to stop prosecutions and declare that, although the regulations were "good," they would in this case stop a necessary trade if they were strictly adhered to.

GUILDS

The Twelve Great Livery Companies of London in order of precedence were the Mercers, the Grocers (formerly called the Pepperers), the

Drapers, the Fishmongers, the Goldsmiths, the Skinners, the Merchant Tailors (originally called the Linen Armourers), the Haberdashers (originally part of the Mercers), the Salters (first incorporated by Queen Elizabeth), the Ironmongers, the Vintners and the Dyers (who were responsible for the swans on the Thames). When the Weavers Guild combined with fullers (from the Drapers) and shearmen (from the Tailors) to form the Clothworkers Guild, they supplanted the Dyers as one of the twelve. The Dyers became the first of the lesser companies.

At York, the terms mercer, grocer and chapman were at times synonymous. In general, however, mercers dealt in cloth, lace, pins, thread, ribbons and buttons, while grocers sold dried fruits, spices, sugar and so forth. To confuse matters, however, the haberdashers had two branches. One sold smallwares, everything from sewing cottons and silks to buttons, pins, needles, gloves, daggers, glass, pens, lanterns and mousetraps. The other sold hats.

A list of London crafts from 1422 includes 111 occupations. Turners were seventy-fifth on the list. To be admitted to this guild, a turner completed his apprenticeship and made a stool with turned legs as his "proof piece." Master craftsmen could produce remarkable pieces. An organ-clock, built by Thomas Dallam, organmaker, and Randolph Bell, clockmaker, played a sequence of madrigals to mark the hours. Queen Elizabeth sent it as a gift to Mehmed III, Sultan of Turkey, in 1598.

The same guilds existed on a local level throughout England. What varied was which one dominated the community. In York, Bristol and Exeter the mercers were the largest guild. In Northampton, shoemakers (also called cordwainers) had greater numbers than any other guild. In Chester the shoemakers and glovers predominated. Butchers had the greatest numbers in Leicester, weavers in Worcester and Norwich and butchers and cappers in Coventry. In every major town, mercers, tailors, shoemakers, butchers, bakers and tanners were always included in any list of twelve largest guilds.

In Bristol in the seventeenth century, the sopers also flourished. They used olive oil imported from Spain to make "Castile" soap. Soap was often homemade and it was also imported. It came as liquid (imported in barrels from Flanders) and in solid tablet form, which cost more. Soap was manufactured in London as early as 1524. Two pounds of sweet soap, made into balls, cost nine pence in 1612. Laundry soap was made from boiling tallow and wood ash.

WOMEN IN TRADES

A guild of professional laundresses existed in London from early in the fifteenth century, but in most cases clothes were not washed as frequently as they are today. Once or twice a year was the norm and sometimes they were simply brushed and beaten with wooden bats to get the lice out. A scene of a public washing grounds in 1582 shows water being heated in large copper cauldrons for the purpose, but clothes were also washed directly in rivers and streams. Wet clothes were hung to dry on lines and over convenient bushes. Spots and stains were removed by dampening and rubbing with a ball made of bull's gall, white of egg, burnt alum, salt, orris powder and soap. Bluing for bleaching was introduced to England from Holland around 1500, but for badly discolored tablecloths, napkins and sheets, cleaning and sun bleaching was a ten-day process that involved long soakings in summer sheep's dung and the application of a paste made of dog's mercury (also used to make a bright yellow dye), mallow and wormwood. This paste was spread over a buck sheet and doused with boiling lye to achieve results.

In 1511 the Worsted Weavers of Norwich were forbidden to use women to weave worsteds because women were not strong enough to do it correctly. On the other hand, a widow was often allowed to take over the business of her late husband, running it until she remarried or until one of her sons was old enough to replace her. A list of smiths from Chester in 1574 includes thirty-five men and five widows. The lists of the Stationers Company from 1553–1640 show about 10 percent were women. Some had their own apprentices. In some cases a woman was regarded as her husband's partner and was confirmed in the possession of his business on his death. There was a woman shoemaker in York in 1589 and there are records of women tanners, pewterers, tailors and glovers. In Manchester a single woman could be a member of a merchant guild, although she could not be a burgess. Women were liable for duty as churchwardens if they owned or occupied tenements.

A 1630 list from Salisbury indicates that fifteen of forty-three alehouse keepers were women. So were four cooks and three innkeepers. Some women got licenses to sell on their own after working for a shopkeeper. There are also early-seventeenth-century accounts of women working as coal bearers, petty chapmen and carriers.

Silkwomen had no guild, but this employment, concentrated in

London, was generally done by women married to men of wealthy merchant families. Raw silk was only imported in small quantities until the middle of the sixteenth century (11,904 tons in 1560), but by 1621 (with 117,740 tons) it was England's largest raw material import.

APPRENTICES

Training in crafts, trades, and sometimes even professions such as the law was primarily done through apprenticeship, which usually began at fourteen and lasted seven years, at which time the apprentice was tested by the guild to determine if he should become a journeyman. During the apprenticeship, the apprentice received food, clothing, lodging and education, in particular an education in the "mystery" of the master's trade. During these years the apprentice was forbidden to contract a marriage (or fornicate), frequent alehouses or taverns, or engage in games of chance with cards and dice. At the end of the apprenticeship, the apprentice received two suits of clothing, a sum of money, and/or a set of tools.

Under Elizabeth, younger sons of gentlemen began to be apprenticed in craft guilds, a career choice which would have been frowned upon in an earlier era. About 10 percent of those apprenticed by their parents were girls. The percentage was higher (25 to 30 percent) among pauper children apprenticed by their parish under the terms of the Statute of Laborers and Artificers (1563).

The usual "uniform" of an apprentice was of russet cloth, often in a dark blue but seldom black. The doublet was tight-fitting, longer in the skirt than that of a gentleman, with tight sleeves of a different color, and buttons of polished pewter. It was worn with loose upper hose, gray stockings and shoes, and a leather belt and pouch. Apprentices also wore "sheep's color" and the fabrics fustian, canvas, sackcloth and wool. They wore blue cloaks in summer and blue gowns in winter, with breeches and stockings of white broadcloth. Their points were of leather or thread. They were forbidden to carry any weapon but a knife.

The round woolen "flat cap" (it had a low, flat crown) is particularly associated with London apprentices. In an attempt to regulate commerce, a series of sumptuary laws had been passed to force people to wear English woolen caps. In 1511 no one below the degree of knight was to wear a foreign cap or hat. In 1529 the upper classes were forbidden to spend more than 2 shillings on an imported cap or bonnet. A

1572 Act of Parliament declared that every person above the age of six years, except women and certain specified officials, was henceforth on Sundays and holy days to wear a woolen cap manufactured in England. These laws were largely ignored. The 1572 act was repealed in 1597.

WORKERS WITHOUT GUILDS

Goods were sold on a small scale by unorganized workers variously called chapmen, higglers, hucksters, badgers, hawkers and pedlars. On a larger scale, "factors" were paid on a commission basis to sell wares. Those who called themselves "clothiers" were generally the middlemen in the sale of cloth. They bought wool from chapmen and fellmongers, put it out to combers, spinners, weavers and fullers, then sent the finished product to market. Woolens were England's leading export.

In the Jacobean period, one needed stock worth £70 to set up as a merchant and stock worth £30 to set up as a tradesman. Samuell Gorton, a yeoman's son from the Manchester area, did well enough as a factor for a cloth merchant to marry the daughter of a prosperous London haberdasher, set himself up as a clothier, and style himself a gentleman. He went on to emigrate to New England and found the settlement which later became Warwick, Rhode Island.

Spinning, lacemaking, buttonmaking and knitting were occupations associated with the poor. Workers were paid by the piece and were never guild-organized. Spinning and knitting were done by both men and women. Even without a knitting frame (invented in 1590), a part-time knitter could complete two pairs of worsted stockings a week. Stockings were always in demand, even though the average person only wore out two pairs a year.

THE TOBACCO TRADE

The most lucrative trades in London in 1614 were alehouse-keeper, tobacco-seller and proprietor of a brothel. Tobacco was cultivated commercially in Virginia from 1614 on and, although the date of its introduction into England by John Hawkins in 1565 has been questioned, there is no doubt that by 1590 "drinking tobacco" was "commonly known" in London. Londoners were reportedly "constantly smoking" by 1598. By 1613, Englishmen spent £200,000 or more a year on tobacco, most of that in London. By 1615 tobacco shops were as common there as alehouses. The sale of tobacco frequently provided a front for an unlicensed tippling house or bawdy house as well. The boldest brothel-keepers displayed tobacco pipes on their signs.

In 1618, Virginia tobacco cost between 3s. 9d. and 4s. 9d. a pound wholesale. An attempt was made to grow tobacco in Gloucestershire. One entrepreneur was said to have made £20,000 in just a few years. As early as 1619, however, growing tobacco in England was prohibited. No real attempt was made to suppress the crop before 1627 and even then the effort was not particularly successful. In 1638 local tobacco sold for 3s. 4d. a pound while "outlandish" tobacco cost as much as 5s. Imports rose from a worth of £55,143 in 1620 to £230,840 by 1640 and the price slowly came down. A great deal more tobacco was smuggled in, in spite of King James's well-known dislike of the habit (he wrote *Counterblaste to Tobacco*, first published in 1604). After the London monopoly on tobacco importation was broken in 1639, Bristol and other ports began to import it legally and also began to manufacture tobacco pipes.

MINING

Lead and tin were England's major exports after cloth. Lead was the most profitable (it was used in roofing) and England was its leading European producer. Steel was successfully manufactured in Sussex by 1565. Zinc and copper mining began in England in the sixteenth century.

The Weald (a tract of land covering parts of Surrey, Sussex and Kent) was a source of iron ore even before the Romans mined there. Iron was refined close to the mines. The first blast furnace was in operation at Newbridge, Sussex, in 1496, and by the 1570s, there were at least sixty-seven of them, mostly in the Weald. In 1650 there was a total of eighty-six blast furnaces operating in England. The process for producing wrought iron used charcoal for fuel and, as a result, the area was soon stripped of most of its oak and beech. At the Rievaulx ironworks in the 1620s, the labor force of eighty included thirty wood-cutters, eight general laborers on day wages, twelve miners for ore, nine carriers of ore and charcoal, six carriers of wood and six colliers. The output was nearly all in crude bar iron.

Coal mining was the most important of the small scale operations. In 1563-4 some thirty-three thousand tons of coal were carried from

Newcastle to London by ship. By the 1630s, some six thousand workers depended on the local coal industry there. Nearly half of them worked underground.

MANUFACTURING

Technological advances in the late sixteenth century led to the use of coal to fire furnaces for the production of glass as well as bricks. There was a glasshouse in London as early as 1549 and two glasshouses were built at Fernfold in Sussex in 1567. In the last quarter of the century, glasshouses were built in Rosedale in Yorkshire. Both bottle and window glass were produced. English delftware was being made by 1567, but stoneware had to be imported from Germany until around 1626.

Coal-fired furnaces were also used to produce table salt by boiling sea water in large iron salt pans. At Droitwich in Worcestershire, at Nantwich, Middlewich, and at Northwich in Cheshire, salt came from the crystallization of naturally occurring brine. Salt was also imported from the Mediterranean and the Bay of Biscay.

Production of guns and cannons was another new industry. Guns were cast in iron at Buxted, Kent, from about 1543. Manufacture of gunpowder, however, depended upon saltpeter, which continued to be imported from the Continent until the 1560s. After that, artificial saltpeter was manufactured in England. One factory near Fleet Prison in London blew up during a fire in 1588. The area along the Thames between Woodford and Bow Bridge became a center for the production of gunpowder. London gun foundries were located in Houndsditch and at the corner of Water Street and Thames Street.

Starchworks also proliferated. The practice of clear-starching had been introduced from the Netherlands in 1560 by the wife of William Boonen, Queen Elizabeth's Dutch coachman. By 1564, Mistress Dinghen Vanderplasse began to give instruction in starch making for 20s. and taught the art of starching ruffs for £5. Blue pother starch was more costly than white. Although Queen Elizabeth attempted to ban "the use of blue starch in making up linen" in 1595 and 1596, her edicts were apparently ignored. Early in the next century, yellow starch, colored with saffron and other dyes (most dyes were imported), came into fashion. By 1614 the starchworks at Stratford, Essex, had thoroughly polluted the air.

UNEMPLOYMENT

Although some occupations expanded rapidly during this period (there were two hundred chimney sweeps in London by 1618), there was also widespread unemployment. London counted about one thousand beggars in 1517; by 1594 there were more than twelve thousand. Many people ended up on the Tudor equivalent of welfare, too poor and uneducated to break out of the pattern. The "meaner husbandman" and the laborers who worked for a daily or yearly wage (as hedgers, ditchers, reapers, shepherds, herdsmen and the like) were already at subsistence level, and in bad times they either starved to death or turned to crime in order to survive.

Legislation to deal with the poor was passed in 1531, 1547 (including unenforceable measures against vagrancy), 1563, 1572, 1576 and 1597. The 1572 statute mandated that beggars fifteen years of age and older be whipped and burnt on the ear unless "some honest person" would take the offender into service for a year. "Rogues, vagabonds, and sturdy beggars" included the unemployed, the petty chapmen, counterfeit scholars, tinkers, minstrels, players, jugglers, fortune-tellers, and seafaring men pretending to have lost their ships. Under the law of 1597, offenders, male or female, were stripped to the waist and whipped until they were bloody, then sent from parish to parish until they were back in the parish in which they had been born.

Vagrancy was a crime, but most vagrants were not the petty criminals and con-men portrayed in the popular pamphlets of Robert Greene (whose mistress was the sister of the famous cutpurse "Cutting" Bull). One estimate indicates that unmarried men made up 51 percent of vagrants, single or separated women approximately 25 percent, married couples 13 percent, and children under fifteen 10 percent. It was rare they could travel more than forty miles without being caught.

The Poor Relief Act of 1601 made each parish responsible for its own poor. The poor were classified as deserving (those who were ill, disabled, or too young or old to work) and undeserving, a category which unfairly included those who were willing to work but unable to find jobs and those who had large families.

In 1637 a royal proclamation required all tradesmen and artificers within three miles of the capitol who had served a regular seven-year apprenticeship to incorporate. It prohibited those not belonging to any company from practicing their trade after November 1 of that year.

ORGANIZED CRIME

There were some bands of outlaws and highwaymen operating during this period, but the most widespread organized crime was smuggling. Called "free trade" by those who engaged in it, smuggling could involve everything from bribing officials and making false declarations at the Customs House to running goods ashore and loading vessels under cover of darkness. Customers (the officials in charge of customs for a port) also engaged in this illegal trade.

Organized Prostitution

Some twenty thousand to thirty thousand unmarried apprentices provided a steady clientele for prostitutes in the area around London. A young man looking for a good time could buy company for 6d. in the Liberty of the Clink in Southwark. Although Henry VIII had tried to ban the "stews" there in 1546, they continued to thrive. Between eighteen and twenty-two licensed brothels were in operation at any given time during Elizabeth's reign. They were painted white or whitewashed and had tradesmen's signs such as The Cardinal's Hat, chosen for its resemblance in color and shape to the tip of the penis. The Crane operated as a brothel from 1503 to 1633, when it was converted into a soap factory. It was owned by the Tallow Chandlers' Company for that entire period. The "Single Women's Churchyard" in Southwark was a burial ground for whores.

Elizabeth Holland was convicted of illegal brothel-keeping in 1597 and sentenced to be "carted." This meant she was put into a cart at Newgate, probably wearing only her shift, possibly with her head shaved, but definitely wearing a piece of paper stuck to her forehead on which the name of her offense was written; the cart carried her to Smithfield, Cornhill and the Standard in Cheapside. At each place crowds would gather to witness her public humiliation. The cart went on to Bridewell, where she was probably whipped, and finally back to Newgate, where she remained until she paid a fine of forty pounds. All along the way, people threw fish and other garbage and "basons" were rung before her. For "basons" read basins, literally pots and pans. In the country the community turned out to shame those who violated community standards of decency and made this "rough music" to accompany the carting or "riding" of a whore. In London, barbers hired out their basins for cartings.

Rough music also accompanied the placarding (wearing of a sign detailing her shortcomings) or ducking (forcible immersion in the nearest body of water, sometimes on a ducking or cucking stool) of a scold, although in the Northeast a scold (a nagging woman) might be put into a metal head-and-mouth clamp called a brake instead. Related traditions are the hanging of antlers or horns over a cuckold's door and the charivari or skimmington, used to ridicule husbands who were ruled by their wives. A "skimmington ride" could vary in significance from youthful highjinks directed against a stuffy neighbor all the way to the excuse for a violent riot.

Rural Prostitutes

Most rural prostitution was amateur, as in the case of a married village woman who charged 4d. to fornicate in the fields. In Norton by Crannock, Staffordshire, however, Ellen Smith, enterprising wife of an alehouse-keeper, employed five or six servant women to make "a solemn night's dancing" to "recreate" the customers. Studies of Somersetshire records indicate that the Swan in Wellington and the Bear in Wells were notorious brothels and that Glastonbury was overrun with whores. Ann Morgan of Wells apparently had a sliding scale of fees. Soldiers were charged 2s. 6d., double the going rate.

Keeping a house of bawdry was a common-law offense, but a "bawd" was any person of either sex who procured or pandered to immorality. That definition included a man who got a woman pregnant and then paid someone else to marry her. Such behavior fell within the province of the church courts. In 1604 a revision of canon law required churchwardens to report all persons who committed adultery, whoredom, incest or "other uncleanness or wickedness of life."

SELECT BIBLIOGRAPHY

Burford, E.J. *Bawds and Lodgings: A History of the London Bankside Brothels c. 100–1675.* London: Peter Owen, 1976. This book contains errors in historical fact and should be used with caution.

Charles, Lindsey and Lorna Duffin, eds. *Women and Work in Pre-Industrial England.* London: Croom Helm, 1985.

Clark, Alice. *The Working Life of Women in the Seventeenth Century.* New York: Augustus Kelley, 1968. A reprint of the "classic" 1920 study.

McMullan, John L. *The Canting Crew: London's Criminal Underworld*

1550–1700. New Brunswick, New Jersey: Rutgers University Press, 1984.

Quaife, G.R. *Wanton Wenches and Wayward Wives: Peasants and Illicit Sex in Early Seventeenth Century England.* New Brunswick, New Jersey: Rutgers University Press, 1979. While largely a statistical study, this does give details of some of the cases heard by the Somerset Quarter Sessions and the Consistory Court of the Diocese of Bath and Wells during the years 1600–1660.

Salgado, Gamini. *The Elizabethan Underworld.* New York: St. Martin's Press, 1977.

Spufford, Margaret. *The Great Reclothing of Rural England: Petty Chapmen and Their Wares in the Seventeenth Century.* Cambridge: Cambridge University Press, 1984.

Williams, Neville. *Contraband Cargoes: Seven Centuries of Smuggling.* London: Longman, 1959.

CHAPTER FIFTEEN

ENTERTAINMENT

1541 statute designed to promote archery practice for national defense attempted to suppress unlawful games in alehouses and elsewhere. Artificers, laborers and servants were not to play tables (backgammon), tennis, dice, cards or slide-groat (also called shovel-board) and none but noblemen were supposed to play at bowls. Since the size of the fines levied against country gentlemen for this "crime" was only four- to eightpence for each offense, it seems likely these were regarded more as a bowling tax than as a punishment. In general, legislation concerning entertainment was cheerfully ignored.

King James felt the Puritans of Lancashire were too severe in limiting Sunday activities, and in 1617 he issued a list of sports that might lawfully be played after church, including on it archery, leaping (jumping contests, including leapfrog), May-games (any activities used to celebrate May Day), Morris dancing and piping (playing the bagpipes). The *Book of Sports (The Kings Majesties Declaration to his Subjects Concerning lawfull Sports to be used)* was issued for the entire country in May 1618. King Charles reissued it in 1633. By 1642, however, with Puritans in control of Parliament, almost every recreation was prohibited, at least on Sundays.

FAIRS

Frost Fairs

In addition to water festivals, pageants, and firework displays on the Thames, there were also ice carnivals or frost fairs whenever the river froze solid enough to support booths and traffic. This happened a dozen times at London Bridge between 1550 and 1700. Particularly hard freezes occurred in 1517, 1537, 1564–5 (when there are records of archery and dancing on the Thames), 1595, 1607, 1608 and 1620.

Trade Fairs

The Cloth Fair of St. Bartholomew in Smithfield was one of the biggest trade fairs in England. On St. Bartholomew's Day (August 25), the aldermen met the Lord Mayor and Sheriff of London at the Guildhall Chapel. After a prayer they rode to Newgate, where a proclamation was read. The procession then went through the fair, back through the churchyard to Aldersgate, and ended at the Lord Mayor's house. Roast pork was traditional fare at this gathering.

Smaller trade fairs were held at Stratford on Holy Rood Day (September 14) and in Bristol on St. James's Day (July 25). The Temple Fair was always held on St. Paul's Day (January 25). St. Luke's Day (October 18) was marked by the village of Charlton, near Greenwich in Kent, with the Horn-Fair, an event put on by women. Many fairs were held on Sundays.

FESTIVALS

Before the Reformation, there were ninety-five feast days and thirty saints' eves. Afterward there were twenty-seven holidays. London celebrations were less spectacular than those in cities in Catholic Europe and shops stayed open except on Christmas and Easter. Bell ringing was associated with many celebrations. Traditionally bells had been rung to mark the canonical hours (actually more than an hour in length) and as a call to arms.

The major festivals, religious and secular, were:

New Year's Day (January 1): Gifts were given to the monarch.

Twelfth Night (Epiphany, January 6): The final festivity of the Christmas season, often celebrated with mummings.

Plough Monday (first Monday after Epiphany): In the North, sword dancers performed and "Plough Stots" toured the villages asking for alms. The money they collected was used to keep "Plough Lights" in the church until the Reformation, after which it went to provide ale for the ploughmen. The ban on burning candles in church after the Reformation also ended celebrations of Candlemas (February 2).

St. Valentine's Day (February 14): At the court of Henry VIII, valentines were chosen by lot. The man then had to give a suitable gift to the lady who selected him. In the seventeenth century, it was believed that birds chose their nesting mates on this day.

Shrove Tuesday: In a final fling before Lent (forty weekdays from Ash Wednesday to Easter Eve, during which eating meat was forbidden), Englishmen staged feasts, masques and cockfights. Traditions included both eating and tossing pancakes, football matches and cockthrowing, a sport in which a cock was tied to a fixed point and cudgels or broomsticks were thrown at it until it was killed. The dead bird went to the person who killed it. In some areas it was also traditional to attack brothels (and, in London, the playhouses). Twenty-four Shrove Tuesday riots are documented in London between 1603 and 1642.

Easter (date varied): Celebrated by playing sports of all kinds and sometimes by holding church ales (ale was brewed and sold to raise funds).

All Fool's Day (April 1): April Fool jokes were not played.

Whitsunday (Pentecost, fifty days after Easter): Church ales continued to be held on this day even after the Reformation.

St. George's Day (April 23): It was proper to wear blue on this day, on which twenty-eight towns held fairs. The Knights of the Garter were granted special permission to continue to observe their saint's day after the Reformation and usually did so with tournaments.

May Day (May 1): After spending the previous night outdoors, revelers decorated a maypole and then danced around it. London's maypole was traditionally set up in the Strand.

Midsummer (June 24): On Midsummer Eve, fires were lit all over the country, at least until the mid-sixteenth century. Divination was practiced by sowing hemp seed. Similar to the Lord of Misrule (a mock king), a Summer Lord presided over these festivities, which might include processions and pageants. Houses were decorated with St. John's wort (this was also the Eve of St. John the Baptist), fennel and green birch.

First Sunday in October: After the Reformation, this was the day set aside to honor local patron saints.

All Hallows's Eve (October 31): Celebrated with seed cakes, ducking for apples, dancing around the fire and bell ringing. London had the Lord Mayor's Show, a water pageant.

All Soul's Day (November 2): In Lancashire special soul-cakes were baked and given to children.

Gunpowder Treason Day (November 5): Marked by bells, bonfires, church services and suspension of everyday activities, this was a day of reflection prompted by the discovery of the Gunpowder Plot in 1605. The burning of Guy Fawkes in effigy was not added to the celebration until the nineteenth century, but people did dance around fires.

Accession Day (November 17): After about 1572, Elizabeth's "crownation day" was celebrated nationwide with spontaneous bonfires, bell ringing, feasts and sermons. At court there were annual tilts, usually at Whitehall, from 1570 to 1619. Bonfires and bell ringing on November 17 (as well as on the Stuart crownation days of March 24 and March 27) continued well into the seventeenth century.

Christmas (December 25): In some areas a yule log was an ash faggot. A King of the Bean or a Lord of Misrule presided over the entire Christmas season, which was from Christmas Eve until Twelfth Night.

PROFESSIONAL ENTERTAINMENT

fools: Court jesters or fools were kept by English monarchs and occasionally by others. Sir Peter Legh, whose father had maintained a band of musicians and a troupe of players under Elizabeth, kept both a jester and a piper in Jacobean times.

masques: Originating at court under Henry VIII as an outgrowth of dancing and mumming, the masque reached its peak in the reigns of James and Charles, when Inigo Jones and Ben Jonson pooled their talents to create a new art form. Amateur actors, both men and women, performed in court masques but the costumes, scenery, music and script were all done by professionals.

minstrels: Wandering minstrels were still popular prior to the seventeenth century, although after 1572 they had to have a passport to travel. Town musicians or "waits," originally employed to play night and morning for the watch, also gave public concerts and hired themselves out to play at playhouses and for weddings. They wore livery and silver chains and badges. The most popular instruments bought for waits by towns were the shawm and sackbut, but lone waits often played the bagpipe. At this time the bagpipe had only two drones.

mummings: Popular on Christmas and May Day. By the sixteenth century, mummings had developed into little plays. The roles of women were usually taken by men.

mystery plays: A mystery was a trade or skill, and each trade guild in a town was responsible for mounting a play on a pageant wagon to portray a story from the Bible. This medieval tradition continued into the sixteenth century.

plays: Miracle plays, morality plays and interludes were performed long before any permanent playhouse was built. The common players of medieval England occasionally included women in their companies. There is, however, only one record to indicate that any woman ever performed on the public stage prior to the Restoration, and that was in a play acted at Blackfriars in 1629 by a French company. Women's roles were customarily taken by men.

Early in Elizabeth's reign, the Privy Council issued a proclamation declaring that plays must not deal with any matter of religion or of state, and that none could be performed without permission of the mayor of a town or the Lord Lieutenant of the shire or two justices of the peace for the locality. A new play had to be licensed (at a fee of seven shillings) and when one offended, as was the case of *The Isle of Dogs* in 1597, Edmund Tilney, official censor for stage plays, had the power to ban all plays in retaliation and arrest those directly responsible on charges of sedition.

Companies of players (this term was more common than actor) sought patrons among the nobility and wore their livery. They performed primarily in guild halls and in innyards, setting up portable

stages to act upon. There were boys' companies as well as adult companies. The first building constructed exclusively for the performance of
plays was the Theatre in Shoreditch, built in 1576. The average play
there ran three hours. The company consisted of ten players, ten hire-
lings, a number of musicians, stagehands and feegatherers and five
boys in training. They gave performances every afternoon except
Sunday and were closed during Lent and in plague time. During
plague time, players went on tour, taking a smaller company of only
ten to twenty men.

A 1578 sermon at Paul's Cross by John Stockwood launched the
Puritan attack on plays and players. Most objections to plays, however,
were because of the rowdy crowds dispersing after dark. Where plays
used to begin at four, in the 1590s they had to start by two and be
done between four and five. In 1600, between eighteen thousand and
twenty-four thousand Londoners paid their penny and went to see a
play every week. After Charles I was removed from power in 1642, the
theaters were shut down by decree, although some players did continue to perform in short farces called drolls and in variety acts.

Shakespeare was not the only "playmaker" of this era, and was not
even the most popular. Robert Greene (who could command a fee of
twenty nobles for a play), Christopher Marlowe, Ben Jonson and John
Webster were also writing during this period and Elizabeth Tanfield,
Lady Carew, wrote the first original play in verse in English by a woman
(*The Tragedie of Miriam, the Faire Queene of Jewry*) which was published
in 1614. It is Shakespeare, however, about whom the majority of books
on English drama are written. Even some of those that are highly spec-
ulative are good sources of information on the times.

puppet shows: Accused of being obscene and sacrilegious, puppeteers
were treated as vagabonds and sometimes paid not to perform. Puppet
shows were also called "motions."

tumblers: Like puppeteers, tumblers were sometimes accused of being
obscene or sacrilegious, treated as vagabonds and paid not to perform.

wonders: A wonder was any oddity shown for money. Animal wonders
ranged from dancing dogs and horses to the royal lions in the Tower
of London. These lions had an exercise ground in the moat and were
fed mutton and live chickens. King James tried, unsuccessfully, to
create a new sport by having the royal lions fight bears, but the lions

refused to cooperate. Other sights at the Tower included crocodiles, red deer, antelope from India, a flying squirrel from Virginia, a wolf and a porcupine. At Paris Garden one could see lynx and tigers, and at St. James's Park were five camels and the elephant sent to James I by Philip III of Spain.

The *Golden Hind*, the first English ship to circumnavigate the world, was put in drydock at Deptford in 1581 as a monument. Souvenir-hunters took bits of it home with them.

A "nine day's wonder" was comedian William Kempe's Morris-dance from London to Norwich in 1600. The trip actually took a month. In the 1630s, adult Siamese twins toured England. Native Americans were looked upon as wonders, whether they were captives on display or visiting dignitaries; Manteo and Wanchese drew huge crowds in 1584. In 1605, George Weymouth, while searching for a suitable place to found a Catholic colony in the New World, kidnapped five Indians from an island off the Maine coast. Sir Ferdinando Gorges commandeered all five upon Weymouth's return to England, then sent two of them to Sir John Popham, Lord Chief Justice. The five, including a woman known only as Mme. Penobscot (after her tribe), were taught English and English habits, including an appreciation of beer, and then sent out to make speeches to raise money for colonization. Pocahontas, who by then had been baptized Rebecca and was married to John Rolfe, arrived in London in 1616 with her husband to raise funds for the Virginia colony. The climate and unhealthy sanitary conditions of the "civilized" world proved fatal. She died, probably of tuberculosis, in 1617.

READING AS ENTERTAINMENT

Early in the sixteenth century, few people owned books, although listening to stories being read aloud was always a popular pastime. Cheap, popular almanacs were available from 1567 onward. Joke books were also published in large numbers, since riddles were popular, and earthy humor always sold well. Broadsides, chapbooks, pamphlets, travel books, books of poetry and books of plays were also published, although the latter were not generally printed until a play (the exclusive property of its company of players) was no longer being performed.

ballads: London alone had some three hundred ballad sellers in 1641. Two sheets of broadside ballad cost one shilling. About three thousand ballads were licensed between 1500 and 1700. One estimate puts nine thousand more in circulation.

newspapers: The earliest newspapers printed in English originated in Amsterdam because printing the news was illegal in England. The law was changed in 1621 to allow foreign news to be printed, and the "Coranto" appeared in that year. Newspapers were banned again in 1632. Early newspapers were a single sheet printed on one side and came out weekly. The first daily newspaper appeared in 1702.

poetry: Early poets, though they were not necessarily published in their own lifetimes, included William Dunbar, John Skelton, Sir Thomas Wyatt, and Henry Howard, earl of Surrey. Under Elizabeth, Sir Philip Sidney and Edmund Spenser were writing. Late in the period came John Donne, Robert Herrick and John Milton.

popular fiction: Balladeer Thomas Deloney also wrote longer works (early novels, although neither the term nor the genre had been clearly defined at this stage in literary history) such as *Jack of Newbury* (1597). Abridged editions of this tale enjoyed even greater popularity than the original. Chapbooks were the mass-market paperbacks of the Renaissance. They were action-adventure tales which frequently had a romantic subplot thrown in. Chapbook versions of tales of chivalry (such "romances" as *Bevis of Hampton* and *Guy of Warwick*) were enormously popular with the public and so were any stories dealing with Robin Hood or St. George. Among the most popular heroines, "Long Meg" was a rarity, a strong woman who succeeded in life on her own. Most stories about women dealt with the tragic consequences that came of falling in love with a man of a higher station in life. *Patient Griselda* was essentially a tale of a woman's virtue and fidelity in spite of having an abusive, aristocratic husband.

songbooks: Though not strictly speaking a type of reading, songbooks were immensely popular books. Between 1580 and 1630, some eighty vocal collections were published. The madrigal became extremely popular during the 1560s, as did the ayre, a song performed to lute accompaniment. John Dowland was a master of that genre. Composers whose music is still performed include Thomas Tallis, William Byrd and Orlando Gibbons.

SPORTS AND RECREATIONS

archery: Shooting at butts was done with both longbow and crossbow.

ballon or wind ball: A type of handball played with an inflated bladder, the game may also have had some similarities to football.

billiards: A popular game, played outdoors in the seventeenth century.

bowling or bowls: Played on both village greens and private grounds by both men and women. The third earl of Southampton liked to play every Tuesday and Thursday in the company of thirty or forty knights and gentlemen.

bull-baiting and bear-baiting: An established pastime in London by 1174. Most towns had a bull-ring by 1500. Henry VIII had a Master of the Royal Game of Bears, Bulls and Mastiff Dogs. English mastiffs included Lyme mastiffs, dogs of immense size and pale lemon color, with large heads like bloodhounds, black ears and muzzles and soft brown eyes. In 1526, Paris Garden opened in Southwark, charging an entrance fee of one penny and an extra penny for the best places in the galleries. At its height, it had three bulls, twenty bears and seventy mastiffs. Puritan preachers denounced this pastime, primarily because the most important matches took place on Sundays. In 1592, however, the Privy Council forbade theaters to open on Thursdays . . . in order to increase public attendance at bear-baitings on that day.

card games: A pack was a deck, a bunch, or a "pair of cards"; a trump was a tumbler and a knave was a jack. The Worshipfull Company of Makers of Playing Cards was chartered in 1628, after which the importation of foreign-made playing cards was forbidden. Popular games were primero (fashionable c. 1530–1640; three cards were dealt to each player, each card having three times its usual value), one-and-thirty, noddy, gleek and Pope July. A new game in the Elizabethan era was triumph (whist). Bassett, lanterloo (loo) and cribbage debuted in the seventeenth century. Picket (piquet), also called cent, had been played since around 1550 but suddenly caught on under the Stuarts.

checkers: Also called draughts in England. The earl of Leicester had checkers made of crystal inlaid with silver and garnished with his heraldic device, the bear and ragged staff.

A card game in a tavern, 1525
This scene takes place in a tavern, but card games were also a popular form of
entertainment in private homes. As can be seen here, cards in the Renaissance
were not much different from those we use today.

chess: The earl of Leicester had an ebony chess board, with chessmen
made of crystal and precious stones. Chess was one of the few games
not played for money.

cockfighting or cocking: Although well established during the Middle
Ages, the first regular cockpit was constructed by Henry VIII. James I
had a "cockmaster" responsible for breeding, feeding and training
gamecocks for fights in the royal cockpit. Cocks were bred chiefly in
Norfolk in the seventeenth century. Cockfighting was suspended in
plague time but was not prohibited by law until 1654.

Cotswold Games: Developed around 1612 from a local celebration
into a nationally known competition by a Norwich-born lawyer, Robert
Dover (1582–1652), the games were held in rural Gloucestershire

every Thursday and Friday after Whitsunday. Competitions included singlestick fighting, wrestling, leaping, pitching the bar, throwing the hammer, tumbling, running races, horse-racing, handling the pike, leapfrog, shin-kicking, hunting and coursing at the hare, dancing and, in tents, card games and chess. Music included bagpipes and, to add a classical element, a man dressed as Homer who played the harp. The games were stopped after 1643 but revived with the Restoration.

cricket: A new game played by schoolboys in Kent and Sussex late in the sixteenth century.

dancing: Popular everywhere, country dances included the roundel, hay, trenchmore, jig, and dump (a slow, mournful dance). Court dances were the cinquepace (galliard), the pavane, the brawl (bransle) and the volte. Morris dancing was usually done only by men. The name may be a corruption of Moorish, hinting at a medieval Spanish origin. In London, "dancing houses" (dancing schools) were outlawed from 1553 (they were suspected of being fronts for less respectable activities) but by 1574, legislators gave up trying to close them down and regulated them instead.

dice games: Dice were made of gold, silver, ivory, wood and bone. Popular dice games were hazard and pass-dice, a game that involved each of two players throwing dice until they came up "doublets" (the same number on both dice). If the number was over ten, the caster won. Tables (backgammon) was also played by two people, using a hinged board (divided into four "tables"), two dice boxes and fifteen men each. There were fourteen different kinds of false dice. The fine for making or selling them was 3s. 4d. for each offense.

fencing and dueling: Henry VIII was a patron of the new Italian school of fighting with rapier and dagger rather than sword-and-buckler, though some men looked down on "this poking fight" of foreign invention. There were fencing schools in London from 1569 on, the first taught by Rocco Bonetti. He was still the most popular instructor in London in 1599. The duel of honor was a concept unknown in England until the late sixteenth century, but it had become a cause of official concern by the Jacobean era. A 1613 law made it murder to cause a death during a duel.

fishing: Fishing and angling were popular among both men and women.

football: Played with an inflated bladder in a leather casing between rival teams. The playing field might be all the ground between two villages, or a street in London. It was a rough sport usually accompanied by broken bones and bloodshed and had been banned as early as 1349. Although football was again prohibited in 1541, it continued to be played and enjoyed new popularity in the early seventeenth century when it was called campball or "camping" ("knappan" in Pembrokeshire). Another attempt to ban football was made in 1617 and again ignored. A variant of football played in Leicestershire went by the name bottle-kicking.

golf: Played in Scotland by the fifteenth century and known there as "the Royal Game." James I brought golf to England.

horse racing: Langanby, Cumberland, had a racecourse by 1585 and Kingmoor and Doncaster did by 1595. Bells were given as prizes. James I built the racetrack at Newmarket and introduced Arabian blood into English horse breeding. Under Charles I races were held at Hyde Park.

hunting: Killing game in a royal forest was punishable by a large fine or a year and a day in gaol. Those Englishmen (and women) who could hunt legally used both crossbows and longbows and were aided by hawks, falcons and dogs. Game dogs included land spaniels, water spaniels and hounds. The latter included harriers, terriers, blood-hounds and greyhounds. In the late sixteenth century, the occupants of the Royal Kennels were divided into hart hounds, buckhounds and otter hounds. Harriers hunted hare, fox, badger and otter but were usually trained specifically for one. Terriers were used to go into earths and holes after rabbits, foxes and badgers. Bloodhounds were used to hunt and also to track down cattle stealers on the borders with Scotland. The English greyhound was prized abroad for boar hunting.

pall-mall: An early form of croquet, this involved hitting a boxwood ball through an iron ring suspended above the ground. It was played by both men and women in the early seventeenth century.

shovel-board: A gambling game, also called shove ha'penny and slide-groat. In sixteenth-century shovel-board, a coin or some other disk was driven by a blow of the hand along a highly polished floor or along a long table marked with transverse lines. A "shovel-board shilling" was often used. The term shovel-board also referred to the shovel-board court. In 1601, the Petre family had a shovel-board fourteen feet long in their gallery at Ingatestone Hall.

sliding: Neither the term skating nor the iron skate reached England from Holland until the late 1600s, but from the 1100s, the shinbone of an animal was bound to the shoe with leather thongs and a iron-shod pole was used to stay upright on the ice.

stoolball: A team sport similar to cricket and played in Bedfordshire, Hertfordshire and Norfolk in the sixteenth century. Variants involved striking the ball with a paddle, the hand or a wooden staff similar to a baseball bat.

swimming: Those who swam in England's rivers usually used bladders to stay afloat. Sea bathing was not yet in fashion. During Elizabeth's reign, courtiers proposed holding a swimming race from Westminster to London Bridge but the queen forbade it as being too dangerous.

tennis: Played on a covered court with balls stuffed with hair. Henry VIII was an avid player but the game did not really catch on until the reign of Charles I, when there were fourteen licensed tennis courts in London alone.

tournaments: Even though their primary purpose was no longer training for war, tournaments continued to be held for the spectacle. At Whitehall the tilt-yard ran from the Holbein Gate at the north to the inner gate at the south. In Elizabethan times the public was admitted for twelvepence each and the queen watched from a window in her gallery.

wrestling: Although the rules varied from county to county, wrestling was popular everywhere. Matches often took place in cockpits. Women engaged in wrestling matches on at least one occasion in the early seventeenth century.

SELECT BIBLIOGRAPHY

Bentley, Gerald Eades. *The Profession of Dramatist and Player in Shakespeare's Time, 1590–1642.* Princeton: Princeton University Press, 1971.

Cressy, David. *Bonfires and Bells: National Memory and the Protestant*

Calendar in Elizabethan and Stuart England. Berkeley: University of California Press, 1989.

Hotson, Leslie. *Mr. W. H.* New York: Knopf, 1964. Hotson argues that Black Luce, a whore, was the Dark Lady of Shakespeare's sonnets.

Ogburn, Charlton and Dorothy. *This Star of England.* New York: Coward-McCann, 1952. This book was written to prove that Edward de Vere, seventeenth earl of Oxford, actually wrote Shakespeare's plays.

Reay, Barry, ed. *Popular Culture in Seventeenth-Century England.* New York: St. Martin's Press, 1985.

Rowse, A.L. *Sex and Society in Shakespeare's Age.* New York: Charles Scribner's Sons, 1974. Rowse proposes Emilia Bassano Lanier as the Dark Lady of Shakespeare's sonnets. He claims she was the mistress of Lord Hunsdon, patron of the Lord Chamberlain's Men, and also the author of a long poem published in 1611.

Vale, Marcia. *The Gentleman's Recreations: Accomplishments and Pastimes of the English Gentleman 1580–1630.* Totowa, New Jersey: Rowman & Littlefield, 1977.

CHAPTER SIXTEEN

LANGUAGE

There was a tremendous richness of language during the Renaissance. New words were coined and borrowed from other languages at a great rate. Some we still use. Others have either changed their meaning drastically or become archaic. As for spelling, although a dictionary was published in 1604 (Robert Cawdrey's *A Table Alphabeticall*), there was no real standard, which resulted in considerable creativity.

Most larger libraries contain the twenty-volume *Oxford English Dictionary (OED)*, whose entries list the earliest printed occurrence of each word in an English book. Keep in mind that the word may have been used for years, even decades, before it first appeared in print. On the other hand, an item mentioned as a novelty in London in a certain year might not come into general use in remote rural areas until much later. For example, the *OED* cites the first use of the word *tea* in an English book in 1599, shortly after the drink was introduced in Portugal. At least another fifty years passed before anyone brewed and drank a cup of tea (or called any beverage that) in England. A regular tea time was much longer in coming.

LANGUAGES OF ENGLAND

A scholar writing in 1635 asserted that twelve languages were spoken in the British Isles, including Walloon, Dutch and French, which continued to be the language of diplomacy. Under Henry VII, Thomas Howard (later second duke of Norfolk) commissioned one Alexander Barclay to write a book called *Introductory to Write and Pronounce French*. At that time, two dialects of French were in use, Norman French and Francian (that of Paris). The latter became the official language of France in 1539.

Latin was still used in legal and ecclesiastical work, even after the Reformation. The Cornish language continued to be used in Cornwall and Devonshire. One reason the Cornish objected to Edward VI's *Book of Common Prayer* was that, as it was in English, they could not read it.

Sir Edward Stradling of St. Donats, patron of bards and harpists, also collected books and manuscripts relating to Wales. In 1592 he funded the publication of a Welsh grammar. The print run was 1,250 copies.

Computer analysis of Shakespeare's works shows that he used 31,534 different words and suggests that he knew many more. New uses were given to terms drawn from the military, government, seafaring, agriculture and the legal system. In addition, loanwords came into English from other countries around the world.

LOANWORDS

Spanish	armada, cargo
Italian	madrigal, miniature, trio
High German	carouse
Low German	luck, frolic, rant, wagon
Arabic	alcohol, cipher, elixir
Romany	pal, cosh

Standardization of grammar and usage was influenced by the publication of the King James Bible (1611) because it soon found its way into so many homes and was then used as a teaching tool. It was, however, behind the times compared to common speech, especially in its use of *thee* and *thou*. The *th-* forms of second person singular were rare in upper-class speech by the sixteenth century. Contemporary grammar books also existed. *A Bref Grammar for English* appeared in print in

A printing press, 1568
Based on a woodcut in A Book of Trades, *this sketch shows various stages of printing. The man on the left is applying ink to the type.*

1586, and in 1633, Charles Butler's *English Grammar* contained an "Index of Words Like and Unlike."

THE FLAVOR OF THE LANGUAGE

By 1611 the speech of London and its environs was evolving into a standard, modern English, although even upper-class English still sounded quite different than it does today. For example, some consonants which are now silent, such as the *k* in *knight*, were sometimes still pronounced (although Shakespeare makes a pun of *knight/night*). There also continued to be distinctive regional speech patterns, which gave away both a person's geographical origin and his place in society. In some cases local dialects were almost incomprehensible to outsiders.

One of the easiest ways to give the flavor of the times to dialogue is to avoid three contractions which were very rare in the sixteenth century and did not appear in print until much later: *it's, don't* and *doesn't*. Write them out, or in the case of *it is* substitute *'tis*. *'Twas, 'twere* and *'twill* follow the same pattern. Only in the seventeenth century did *'tis* begin to be replaced by *it's*.

In the sixteenth century *do* was used as a verbal auxiliary ("I do wonder") and double constructions (*more fitter, most unkindest*) were common. An Elizabethan would be grievous sick or find a sight wondrous strange or passing (surpassingly) fair because the *-ly* suffix was not yet required for adverbs. Other frequently found constructions and combinations of words include "I doubt not," "forbid them not" and "methinks." The possessive *thy* continued to be used and followed the same pattern we use today with *my*. *Thine* and *mine* ("mine uncle") were used before a vowel or an *h*. Also still in use were *doth* and *hath*.

There were many popular catch-phrases in use, even at the upper levels of society. Lady Russell, in speaking to Anthony Bacon, reportedly said, "By my faith, nephew, if thy tale be true, then Topnam (an English town) has turned French."

Epistolary style was often overblown. This letter was written by the countess of Essex to Sir Robert Cecil in 1599. Her husband was under house arrest, and Cecil had arranged a conjugal visit.

> Simple thanks is a slender recompense for so honorable a kindness as you have done me, in procuring me her Majesty's gracious consent for my infinitely wished access

to my weak lord; yet, when they come from a mind truly desirous to deserve it, and from a person that only wants ability to requite it, I doubt not but the same virtue that led you to so charitable a work, will likewise move you to accept in good part so beggardly a tribute. Believe, Sir, I pray you, that as pity only and no merit of mine was the true motive of your honorable mediation on my behalf: so no time or fortune shall ever extinguish in my lord and me a thankful memory and due acknowledgment of so undeserved a benefit, from him whom this friendly favor assures me will never be proved my lord's malicious enemy; the respect of your manifold business makes me forbear to trouble you longer with my scribled lines, but in thankfulest manner to rest your exceedingly beholden friend, Frances Essex.

GIVEN NAMES

Naming a child after the reigning monarch or his or her spouse was good politics. After the publication of the Geneva Bible (1560), many children were given biblical names. Popular, too, especially among Puritans, were names of virtues, such as Prudence, Temperance and Honor. One single family in late Elizabethan times included children named No-Strength, More-Gift, Mercy, Sure-Trust, Stand-Well and Comfort. In some areas local saints' names, such as Frideswide, Ursula and Werburga, were given to children in Catholic families.

Until middle names were popularized by the Stuart kings in the early seventeenth century, most children were given only one name. There were exceptions, such as Henry Algernon Percy, fifth earl of Northumberland, and Sir Thomas Posthumous Hoby, but few middle names are found in the genealogies of the sixteenth century.

Some of the more unusual given names gleaned from family trees are Ambrosia, Anastasia, Clementine, Damascin, Dousabella, Grisold or Grizel, Nazaret, Philadelphia and Sabine for women, and for men, Cuthbert, Endymion, Peregrine and Polydore. The name Frances was first used as a female name in 1517, when the former Queen of France, Henry VIII's sister Mary, named her daughter after Francis I of France, who had helped her make a second marriage, a love match, with Charles Brandon, duke of Suffolk.

Nicknames (an ekename or also-name) were used among intimate friends and family members. Queen Elizabeth called many of her closest associates by pet names, such as Pygmy and Crow. The earl of Shrewsbury addressed his wife, Bess of Hardwick, as "None" in his letters.

Some of the commonest nicknames in use in Renaissance England include Sander (Alexander), Robin (Robert), Kit (Christopher), Hal or Harry (Henry), Will (William) and Noll (Oliver) for men, and Bess (Elizabeth), Franke (Frances), Kate or Kat (Katherine), Moll (Mary) and Nelly (Eleanor) for women. Nicknames such as Bob, Liz, Hank, Billy and Kathy were *not* in use.

FORMS OF ADDRESS

kings and queens: In Tudor times "Your Majesty" came into fashion to supplement the use of "Your Grace" ("if Your Majesty pleases," etc.), but in less formal situations, courtiers addressed a queen as "ma'am" and a king as "sir." The king's wife was called the queen even if she had not had a coronation, but marriage to a reigning queen did not automatically make her husband king.

princes and princesses: Princess Mary (later Mary I) was called "the Lady Mary" during periods when her father, Henry VIII, had declared her illegitimate. Her half-sister Elizabeth was likewise bounced back and forth between being "Princess Elizabeth" and "the Lady Elizabeth." In direct address, "Your Grace" was used.

dukes: In narrative a duke would be called "His Grace" or "the duke of Norfolk," never "Lord Norfolk," and in dialogue he would be addressed as "Your Grace." His wife was "Her Grace" or the "duchess of Norfolk" and "Your Grace" in dialogue. A close friend might call the duke "Norfolk." The duke's heir usually went by one of his father's lesser titles. The third duke of Norfolk's eldest son was Henry Howard, earl of Surrey. Daughters and younger sons of dukes used "Lady" or "Lord" before their given names and the family surname. Norfolk's younger children were Lady Mary Howard and Lord Thomas Howard. The wife of a younger son, unless he had been granted a title of his own, went by *his* given name, as in Lady Thomas Howard.

marquesses, earls and viscounts: All three followed the same form using, for example, "His Lordship" or "the earl of Leicester" or

"Lord Leicester" in narrative and "my lord" in dialogue. Wives were marchioness, countess or viscountess, respectively, and addressed following the same pattern as their husbands. The children of a marquess were styled in the same way as children of a duke, as were the heir and daughters of an earl, but the younger sons of an earl did *not* have "Lord" before their names nor did any of a viscount's children.

Honorable: Nowadays the younger children of lesser peers use "Honorable" before their names, but in Tudor and Stuart times, the children of peers were generally called by their first name with the prefix "Lady" or "Lord."

barons: William Cecil, Baron Burghley, was called Lord Burghley, rarely Baron Burghley. His wife, Mildred, was Lady Burghley (*not* Lady Mildred).

baronets: This was a new title introduced by James I in 1611. A baronet was not a peer but was superior to a mere knight. Baronets used "Sir" before their given names. Sir George Brown would be called Sir George, not Sir Brown, but his wife would be Lady Brown.

other "Lords": The Lord Mayor of London was addressed as "my lord," but he would never be called Lord London. London's mayors usually received a knighthood upon assuming the mayoralty. Judges of the courts of King's Bench and Common Pleas were also addressed as "my lord," and so were those who occupied the position of lord of a manor under the old feudal system, even those who were actually plain, untitled gentlemen. "Your worship" was the proper form of address for a justice of the peace.

knights: A knight was addressed in the same way as a baronet. By the sixteenth century, "Dame" was rarely used for the wife of a knight, although in earlier times use of that title had distinguished her from the wife of a peer.

others addressed as "Sir": Certain offices conferred the style of a knight, if not an actual knighthood. "Sir" was used as a courtesy title with the names of clerics, in particular with household chaplains.

esquires and gentlemen: They were entitled to use the word "Master" (Mr.) before their surnames and might also be addressed as "your worship" by inferiors. "Reverend" was not used before a clergyman's name, so he was likewise addressed as Master So-and-So. Doctors were also more likely to be addressed as Master than Doctor.

gentlewomen: "Mistress" (Mrs.) was used for maidens, wives and widows of gentle birth. "Dame" sometimes served as a courtesy title for a schoolmistress.

Goodman and Goodwife: These terms were used more in Colonial New England than in Old England, but a merchant might be addressed as Goodman Jones and his wife called Goody Jones. In the language of the times the terms farmer and peasant were rarely used. Substantial farmers were called yeomen. Subsistence farmers were husbandmen. Agricultural workers were laborers. Other wage earners were designated by their craft or trade (tiler, brickmaker, thatcher, etc.).

titles and women: Women who inherited titles in their own right or had courtesy titles because of their father's title, kept these titles if they married beneath them, rather than assuming their husband's style of address. Marriage to a peeress in her own right did not confer the same rank on the husband. Children (even those of a royal princess) took their style of address from their father.

The fourth and fifth earls of Derby died within a year of each other. The fourth earl's widow, Margaret, was the dowager countess of Derby, while her daughter-in-law Alice, the fifth earl's widow, continued to be called the countess of Derby. Her sister-in-law, the sixth earl's wife, Elizabeth, was also countess of Derby. First names help distinguish them, but in the documents of the times these were frequently left out.

In 1606, in the course of a Star Chamber case, Charles Howard, earl of Nottingham (1536–1624), informed Lady Russell (1528–1609) that "by the law of arms you are no Lady Dowager," because her husband, John, Lord Russell (heir to the second earl of Bedford) had died during his father's lifetime. She replied that the law was "otherwise" before he was born. On letters, Lady Russell signed herself simply "Elizabeth Russell, Dowager," but she had already consulted one of the heralds on the subject of titles. Since she'd come so close to becoming a countess, she felt she was entitled to be buried with all the honors due a viscountess.

The case of Ann Stanhope (1497–1587) is an extreme example of how forms of address changed with changes in the family fortunes. The daughter of a knight, Ann was Mistress Stanhope early in life. Had she married Edward Seymour before he was knighted, she would have become Mistress Seymour. As it happened, she moved directly to Lady Seymour, and would have remained Lady Seymour had he been made Baron Seymour of Sudeley. He wasn't. That title went to his brother. Sir Edward became Viscount Beauchamp and his wife was Lady Beauchamp. When Beauchamp was elevated to earl of Hertford, she became Lady Hertford and their eldest son took the courtesy title Lord Beauchamp. Hertford's career peaked at duke of Somerset, during his tenure as Lord Protector to Edward VI, his nephew. Ann was thus duchess of Somerset, and (to her enemies, as she was a somewhat forceful woman) the Lady Protector. Somerset was later attainted and executed as a traitor and his title was forfeited. Confined in the Tower of London herself, Ann was now plain Mistress Seymour, but once Queen Elizabeth succeeded to the throne in 1558, Ann's son was "restored in blood" to become earl of Hertford and she thereafter used the title Dowager Duchess of Somerset. She continued to be called this even after she married a commoner. He, however, remained plain Master Francis Newdigate.

COMMON SLANG TERMS

Abraham man: Real or bogus ex-inmate of Bedlam; madman.

apple-squire: Servant in a brothel.

beak: A magistrate.

bellman: Watchman.

bit: Money.

black art: Picking locks.

blackjack: Leather beer-jug coated with tar on the outside.

blue-coats: Servants.

cant: Criminal language; beggar's language.

cheat: Thing.

cheats: Gallows.

cony: Dupe, victim (literally "rabbit").

cony-catching: Trickery, especially at cards.

cozen: Cheat.

cup-shotten: Intoxicated.

darkmans: Night.

familiar: A spirit in animal form that assisted witches.

knight of the post: Hired witness (perjurer).

maltworm: A tippler.

pettifoggers: Petty legal practitioners.

pottle: Tankard containing two quarts.

pudding-prick: Skewer.

roaring boy: Swaggering bully.

sign of the smock: A brothel.

stews: Brothels.

COLOR NAMES OF THE RENAISSANCE

blue: Bice (pale blue), milk-and-water (bluish-white), plunket (light blue or sky blue), popinjay, violet (indigo), watchet (pale greenish blue), whey (pale whitish blue).

brown: Abraham, beasar (the color of a bezoar stone), heare (hare) color, fig, horseflesh color (a brownish pink or bronze), puke (dirty brown), russet (dark brown—not to be confused with the fabric russet, which can be gray).

flesh, neutral or tan: Carnation, claie-color (deep cream), Dead Spaniard, hair (bright tan), lady blush, maidenhair (bright tan), peach-color (a deep pink), sheep's color.

gray: Ash, dove, rat's color (dull gray).

green: Kendal, Lincoln, pease-porridge tawny (brownish green), popinjay, sea-green (bluish or yellowish green), virli (vivid green), willow (light green).

orange: Blecche, lion-tawny (ochre-orange), marigold (orange-yellow), orange-tawny (orange-brown), roy (a bright tawny), tawny (a dusky brown-orange).

parti-colored: Marble, medley.

red: Brassel (brownish red), Bristol, flame, gingerline (reddish violet), incarnate, lusty gallant (light red), maiden's blush, murrey (purplish red), pear (russet red), sanguine (blood red), scarlet (vivid red containing yellow), stammel.

yellow: Cane-color, goose-turd (yellowish green), isabelle (light buff), marigold, peach (yellow flushed with pink), primrose (pale yellow), straw (light yellow).

SELECT BIBLIOGRAPHY

McCrum, Robert, William Cran, and Robert MacNeil. *The Story of English*. New York: Viking Penguin, 1986. Chapter Three, "A Muse of Fire," is dedicated to the Tudor and Stuart eras.

Partridge, Eric. *Shakespeare's Bawdy*. London: Routledge and Kegan Paul, 1955. This is the "classic" study of language in this era.

CHAPTER SEVENTEEN

LIFE IN LONDON AND OTHER CITIES

L ondon's government was administered by a Lord Mayor, aldermen, common councilmen and two sheriffs, each of whom had sixteen sergeants, each with a yeoman and six clerks. The city was divided into twenty-five wards (twenty-six after 1550) and further splintered into precincts. Beadles were employed to keep the peace, supervise trade and oversee matters of sanitation on a local level.

In 1500, the population of London (one square mile north of the Thames and enclosed by a wall) was 40,000. In 1631 a census of that same area counted 130,000. It is "greater London," however, including Southwark and other out-parishes, to which population figures usually refer.

About 8 percent of the population were transients, and women outnumbered men by thirteen to ten. By 1640, London was the largest city in Europe and twenty times the size of any other English city.

A MISCELLANY OF LONDON

London Bridge
A stone bridge completed in 1209, this was the only bridge across the Thames at London. The wooden drawbridge at the Southwark end was

APPROXIMATE POPULATION OF GREATER LONDON	
1550	120,000
1600	200,000–250,000
1634	230,000–339,824
1640	375,000–400,000

raised for high-masted ships for the last time in 1500. A new gate was built at that end of the bridge in Tudor times. Its tower was three stories high with a covered way below. On the battlements above this stone gateway were a series of poles which displayed the severed heads of executed traitors. These were parboiled and dipped in tar to make them last longer and customarily left in place until they rotted. The head of the earl of Essex, executed in 1601, was still displayed in 1612.

On the north side of the drawbridge stood Nonsuch House, a huge, square wooden building, four stories high with cupolas at each corner. Prefabricated, it was erected in 1577 and straddled the bridge so that pedestrian traffic had to pass through an arched tunnel in the middle of the building.

All along both sides of the length of the bridge were merchants' houses and shops, some rising as high as seven stories. The thoroughfare in the middle was at places as narrow as nine feet. After a fire in 1632, only twenty-five of approximately two hundred buildings were still standing.

The Tower of London

Begun by William the Conqueror in 1067, in Tudor and Stuart times the Tower was used as a prison (see page 129) and as a menagerie (see page 206). Monarchs traditionally spent the night before their coronation in the royal apartments there, but otherwise it was not much used as a royal residence.

St. Paul's

A public thoroughfare known as Paul's Walk went right through the cathedral and was so heavily used that in 1554 carrying beer casks or baskets of bread, fish, flesh or fruit through the Cathedral had to be forbidden. It was also forbidden to lead mules or horses through.

Street scene at the Southwark end of London Bridge, 1616
Note the child with the hoop, the coach, and the heads rotting above the gatehouse, all typical urban sights.

In 1561, lightning struck the spire. The resulting fire melted some of the bells and the roof of the steeple fell in. The roof was rebuilt but the steeple was not replaced. For a penny, people could climb to the top. Many of them carved their names before they went back down.

Churches

Under Henry VIII, there were 120 little churches with chantries and graveyards in London. After the dissolution, there were still almost as many parishes (any area having its own church and priest), but in the churches that remained there were no candles or incense. Painted walls had been whitewashed, altars had been stripped and saints removed from their niches. On a list made in 1638, there are 101 London parishes and their incumbents. Out-parishes, such as St. Botolph's without Aldgate, were located beyond the city walls but still considered part of greater London.

All these churches had bells, rung to mark the canonical hours before the Reformation. "Bow Bells," the bells of St. Mary-Le-Bow, Cheapside, were famous throughout London. They rang every night at nine and, after 1520, sounded a regular "retreat from work" as well.

Waterworks and Conduits

As it flows through London, the Thames varies between eight hundred and fifteen hundred feet in width. It is still a tidal river at London, and at flood tides this made it nearly impossible to pass safely beneath London Bridge, where the piers of the arches were protected by timber frameworks called starlings and the waterway between arches was very narrow at any time. Prudent travelers landed on one side and walked to the other to reembark rather than take a risk and "shoot the bridge." Waterworks, built in the 1580s on two arches of London Bridge, used the river currents to drive a series of waterwheels, which worked a pump to raise water to a cistern on a tower high enough to supply piped water to much of London.

At the west end of Cheapside was the little (or pissing) conduit. At the east end, adjacent to the Poultry, was the Great Conduit. Water was supplied to the Great Conduit by lead pipes from Paddington and was also piped to some houses. It was brought to others by paid water carriers who used great wooden "cans" which looked like milk churns. The poor fetched water for themselves from conduits, fountains, wells and direct from the Thames. There were more than twenty-five conduits, wells and pumps in Elizabethan London.

In Plymouth, Sir Francis Drake had been responsible for supplying water to the city from the River Meavy, a project completed in 1591. Mills set up along the watercourse paid Drake back for his efforts. This became the model for bringing the "New River" to London early in the seventeenth century. Between 1609 and 1613, the River Lea was diverted along a new cut which carried water to Islington and fed into great conduits there to supply the city's needs.

Although people generally avoided drinking water if they had other choices, most did not quite grasp the concept that raw sewage contaminated rivers and streams. Neither was the idea of boiling water to purify it understood.

Streets

Side streets were narrow and tortuous, with room for only a single horseman to pass through. Cheapside was both the main shopping street and the broadest of all London streets. It had room for various structures at its center. Opposite Wood Street was the Eleanor Cross, dating from the reign of Edward I. Gilded and adorned with statues, it was a place from which proclamations were made—until it was destroyed in 1643 in a burst of Puritan frenzy. Opposite Mill Street stood the Standard, a square pillar with a conduit and statues and an image of Fame above. It was often used as a site for executions.

THE HOUSING BOOM

In 1585 Our Lady's Row in York was described as including nine separate housing units, six tenements and three cottages. Urban tenements in most cities were rebuilt in the sixteenth century to reflect a new taste for privacy. In medieval houses, only the hall had been heated. Now chimneys were a stack of brick instead of wattle and daub and one could serve six apartments or more. By the end of the sixteenth century, glass had also become inexpensive enough to be used in most new houses in the city.

Most London houses were two or three stories high (about thirty feet) with about two hundred square feet of space on the ground floor. Frontages on the street ran between sixteen and twenty feet. The house opposite would be about fifteen feet away but because of the structure of the houses, each floor overhanging the one below, people could reach out of their attic windows and shake hands with the residents of the house across the street.

Built of wood or of wood and Flemish wall (lath and plaster or other filling), these houses had rooms at the back and front on each upper floor and a cellar, shop and kitchen on the ground floor. There might be a garret in the gable where the servants slept. A narrow alleyway might run along one side of the house to a small, long (five to ten feet deep) garden or court at the back.

In the seventeenth century, merchants' houses got taller, rising to five or six stories with a narrow front. Some merchants merged three houses into one, using all three fronts. At the other extreme, tenements were created by subdividing existing buildings. In 1603 a law was passed stating that no new houses could be built within three miles of the city and forbidding existing tenements to be further subdivided. This law was poorly enforced, with the result that in 1612 a chandler in Clerkenwell made one tenement into fifteen.

Half-timbered Tudor houses surviving into the twentieth century in Chester, Exeter and Shrewsbury show that they were built to a unit-house plan. Each house has a shop on the ground floor at the front, with the kitchen behind. The first floor contains a hall running back from the street. On the upper floors are bedrooms. Records show that a wealthy Exeter merchant might have as many as fifteen rooms in his house while a tradesman could have four or five.

Thatch as a roofing material was banned in Norwich in 1570, Bristol in 1574, and Oxford in 1582, as well as in many other towns, because of the danger of fires. Slate and tile were to be used instead, and only stone or brick for chimneys and flues.

URBAN PROBLEMS

Sanitation

In towns, "Rose Alley" was the euphemism for any spot popular as a urinal and the act itself was called "plucking a rose." London's public latrines overhung the River Fleet. Any river that ran through a heavily populated area got to be little better than a sewer, with dead animals floating in it to add to the ambiance. The Fleet, however, was one of the worst. It had once had several docks and been wide enough for shipping. Prisoners had been admitted into Fleet Prison by a water gate. By 1502, however, the channel was all but impassable, filled in with the "filth of the tanners" and other noxious substances. It was cleaned that year and again in 1606, when the Council ordered the cleansing of all town ditches and sewers as a means of controlling the danger of plague, but by 1652 it was once more impassable by boat.

If they didn't empty directly into the nearest river, privies had to be cleaned periodically. This was usually done at night by a bucket brigade which carried the waste to a laystall or laystow (the common dung heap). In 1612 it cost one shilling to have a privy cleaned. Although it was forbidden to throw the contents of chamber pots out of windows and into the street, most people did so anyway.

Garbage was deposited in kennels in front of one's door. Drainage gutters carried raw sewage down the middle of cobbled streets, but unpaved streets had no drains at all. Even when kites (the red kite, which is now nearly extinct) and ravens did their part to clean up the filth, the stench remained.

Air Pollution

By 1604, Londoners were complaining about "smutty air," the result of burning so much coal in fireplaces and in small, tiled stoves of glazed earthenware. In 1652, smoke pollution was so bad that one could no longer see the Tower from the roof of St. Paul's.

Stray Animals

Cats, swine, rabbits and pigeons were thought to be dangerous in times of plague, although the rat was rarely a suspect. Dogs were also persecuted. In 1543, loose dogs were to be banished or killed and buried out of the city of London at the common laystalls. Hounds, spaniels and mastiffs might remain in the city if they were kept indoors. In 1563 this order was amended so that a dog might go out on a leash. Those who disobeyed were fined 3s. 4d. or lost their dog. A mayoral proclamation that same year ordered the slaughter of loose cats and dogs. Many London parishes had their own dogkillers. In 1578, citizens had to be forbidden to throw out of doors "any dead dogs, cats, whelps, or kitlings, or suffer them there to lie in such careless order as at this present they do."

A SAMPLING OF URBAN CENTERS

Brighton: The largest of Sussex's eighteen market towns, Brighton was a major fishing port even though it had no proper harbor. In 1514 it was burnt by French raiders. In the early seventeenth century, the Brighton fishing fleet regularly fished for herring in the North Sea. In the 1520s, Brighton had fewer than 1,000 inhabitants, but by the 1670s the population had more than doubled.

Bristol: A separate county (from the fourteenth century) as well as a city and the seat of a bishopric, Bristol was a major urban center from about 1550 onward and the distribution center for southern Wales. A population of 12,000 in 1600 made it the third largest English city. An international port, second only to London in importance, it also had a virtual monopoly on the supply of cod. In the sixteenth century it had a reputation for being cleaner than most cities.

Canterbury: The largest town in Kent, with a population of 6,000 by 1650, it remained an ecclesiastical center even after the destruction of the tomb of Saint Thomas à Becket and the subsequent decrease in its tourist trade. The archbishop of Canterbury, highest prelate in the reformed church, had his seat there.

Chester: County town of Cheshire, a port on the river Dee, which monopolized trade with Ireland and was distribution center for northern Wales. It was also the administrative headquarters of the County Palatine and Earldom of Chester (a feudal honor held by the heir-apparent). In 1541, Chester became the seat of a bishopric. It was damaged by fire in 1564. The population was 7,600 in the 1660s.

Colchester: The only major town in Essex, it was a port with a population of 9,000 in the mid-seventeenth century.

Coventry: A medieval cloth-manufacturing center in decline during the sixteenth century; after the loss of its cathedral and its cycle of mystery plays, the population of this Warwickshire market town was around 6,000 in 1600. In the seventeenth century, Coventry was famous for ribbon making and tanning leather.

Dublin: With a population of about 8,000 in 1540, Dublin was the sixth largest city in the British Isles and the center of English government in Ireland. It had a cathedral and, after 1592, a university. Dublin was a major port, but by 1600 it was in decline and the population had dropped to about 5,500.

Edinburgh: A much more provincial capital than London, Edinburgh was the center of Scots government. Its population in Shakespeare's time was approximately 9,000 (though some claims have been made for a population as high as 30,000), while Glasgow had about 4,500 and Aberdeen about 2,900. All of Scotland had a population of only 500,000 to 600,000.

Exeter: A provincial capital and cathedral city in Devonshire, Exeter became a county borough in 1538. Its population was 8,000 in 1520 and 9,000 in 1603. Plagues ravaged the city in 1570, 1590 and 1625.

Gloucester: Although generally in decline during the sixteenth century, Gloucester gained a cathedral in 1549 and became a separate county in 1605. It had fourteen churches. The population in 1563 was above 4,000 and, in spite of epidemics in the 1590s and 1630s, had reached 5,500 by 1672.

Ipswich: A port city in Suffolk (in East Anglia), Ipswich had a population of about 5,000 in 1600, by which time glass-fronted shops were replacing wooden pentices (hinged shop fronts on which goods were offered for sale) there.

Leicester: This Leicestershire market town was the center of the leather trade and regional headquarters for the Duchy of Lancaster. It had a population of 3,000 in 1509, when it was said to be in a "sad and derelict state," and 3,500 in 1603. Plagues caused great loss of life in 1564, 1579, 1583, 1593, 1604, 1606–7, 1610–11 (when 700 died), 1625–6, 1636 and 1638–9. By the mid-seventeenth century, Leicester was renowned for hand-knitted stockings.

Manchester: Not a city but a township, Manchester had a population of 2,000 in Elizabethan times. Called "the London of the North," this Lancashire trade center relied on the new "cottons" for its wealth. It was already a center of the woolen industry by 1540, and by 1566 cloths of mixed wool and linen were being produced there. Much of the flax and linen was imported from Ireland via nearby Liverpool.

Newcastle-upon-Tyne: Coal-related jobs (35,000 tons per year were shipped in the 1560s and 500,000 tons per year in the 1650s) brought the population up to about 12,550 in the 1660s. Newcastle was also a provincial capital. In the sixteenth century, its location in Northumberland had made it a key supply center for troops based on the border with Scotland. A major outbreak of plague occurred in 1636.

Norwich: The second largest English city, with a population of 12,000 in 1520, 15,000 in 1603 and 20,000 by 1620. About 12,000 of the 20,000 were Englishmen while the rest were "strangers" from the Low Countries. Freemen in this Norfolk city nominated and elected sixty common councilmen, one of two sheriffs and all twenty-four aldermen and nominated two candidates for mayor. The mayor was paid £100 in 1600 (raised to £140 in 1616). The sheriff had an annual salary of £30 before 1545 and £80 after 1545. Out of this income he was required to pay for an elaborate feast to celebrate his election and purchase the violet robe he wore on ceremonial occasions. Norwich was a provincial capital, a diocesan center and a leading cloth-making city. It suffered from epidemics in the early 1580s and from 1589–92.

Portsmouth: A dockyard under Henry VII and a major naval base under Henry VIII, this Hampshire city continued to grow during the sixteenth and seventeenth centuries while nearby Southampton declined. Southampton's population had dropped to about 4,200 in 1596. Portsmouth had 1,000 inhabitants by 1600.

Shrewsbury: Although not the seat of a bishopric or an administrative center, Shrewsbury (population 4,000+) was the shire town for Shropshire and had social, political and trade importance for both Shropshire and Wales. The Severn was navigable to thirty miles higher than Shrewsbury, making the city a convenient regional supply depot for goods coming from Bristol.

Westminster: Although it had always been independent of London, and was briefly a city with its own bishop from 1540 to 1550, Westminster officially became a separate municipality by Act of Parliament in 1585. Its boundaries extended from Temple Bar to Kensington and from the Thames to Marylebone. Among other things, that same act restricted the number of common alehouses to 120 along the Strand (the highway between Westminster proper and London), 20 around St. Martin's and 60 in the Parish of St. Margaret's (the area near Westminster Abbey). Because the court was often at Whitehall Palace and because Parliament and the central courts met in Westminster Hall, the population of Westminster varied greatly. One figure for 1513 sets it at a little over 3,000.

Winchester: A Hampshire city, it had a population of 3,000 in 1603. Mayors received £10 at the time of election and another £10 following their term of office (after an audit of the city accounts). If a newly elected mayor failed to entertain the retiring mayor, bailiffs and other officials with dinner at his own expense, £5 was deducted out of the first payment. Mary I wed Philip of Spain in Winchester Cathedral in 1554. The city also had a college.

Worcester: A regional center, cathedral city and cloth town, Worcester was not incorporated until 1555. It became a separate mayorality with county status in 1621 but remained the county town of Worcestershire. The population was 4,250 in 1563 and 8,300 in 1646. More burial ground was needed by the early seventeenth century. Plagues accounted for large numbers of deaths in 1558, 1593–4, 1603, 1609, 1618, 1637 and 1644–5.

York: The ecclesiastical and provincial capital and chief administrative center for northern England, York had (in 1639) 1,786 houses within its walls (enclosing 260 acres) and 370 without. The 1548 population was 8,000. It had increased to 11,000 by 1603 and 12,000 by 1630. Entering the city from the London road at Micklegate Bar, one came first to a wide street running downhill to the Ouse Bridge (rebuilt in 1566). Beyond the bridge the center of town was crowded and narrow and still unpaved in 1571. City government consisted of a mayor, aldermen, two sheriffs, a recorder and a town clerk. The city held two annual fairs, at Whitsun and at the Feast of Saints Peter and Paul (June 29). The Archbishop held a Lammas Fair for two days beginning in the afternoon of the thirty-first day of July. This city was remarkably free of epidemics for the entire period from 1552–1603.

SELECT BIBLIOGRAPHY

Atkinson, Tom. *Elizabethan Winchester.* London: Faber and Faber, 1963.
Beier, A.L. and Roger Finlay, eds. *London 1500–1700: The Making of a Metropolis.* London and New York: Longman, 1986.
Dyer, A.D. *The City of Worcester in the Sixteenth Century.* Leicester: Leicester University Press, 1973.
Evans, John T. *Seventeenth Century Norwich: Politics, Religion and Government 1620–1690.* Oxford: Clarendon Press, 1979.
Holmes, Martin. *Elizabethan London.* New York: F.A. Praeger, 1969.
Palliser, D.M. *Tudor York.* Oxford: Oxford University Press, 1979.
Robertson, A.G. *Tudor London.* London: MacDonald, 1968.

Stow, John. *A Survey of London.* London: Alan Sutton, 1995. This is a new edition of the 1598 text with an introduction by Antonia Fraser.

Willen, T.S. *Elizabethan Manchester.* Manchester: Cheltham Society, 1980.

Wilson, F.P. *The Plague in Shakespeare's London.* Oxford: Clarendon Press, 1927.

CHAPTER EIGHTEEN

RURAL LIFE

U nder Henry VIII, marsh and fenland in the eastern counties were still in their native state and used for fishing, wild fowling and raising stock. When stubble was burned in the autumn it looked as if the marshes were on fire. The bodies of fresh water known as the Norfolk Broads were already in existence, having been formed by flooding and by extensive peat cutting in the late fifteenth century. Forests of oak, scrub and timber covered much of the Weald of Kent and Sussex. Windsor Forest stretched from Wokingham to Windsor. When Catherine of Aragon journeyed from Exeter to London upon her arrival in England, she saw more fat sheep grazing on the hills than she'd have seen anywhere else in Europe. Fields in this area were laid out in strips with very few hedges, and there were many windmills.

A 1590 report lists three general types of land: forests and wooded tracts; areas of waste, swamps and fens; and cultivated open fields. Some nine hundred forests, chases and parks were still wild enough that people feared getting lost in them. By 1614, however, many forests were in danger of disappearing. In addition to the overuse of wood in manufacturing, both James I and Charles I sold off trees to raise money.

On the more positive side, there were several projects for draining the fenlands under the Stuarts. In 1634, Parliament brought in a Dutch engineer, Cornelius Vermuyden, to supervise one such undertaking, which eventually increased the number of acres of cultivated land by 400,000. Rowland Vaughan had devised a system of irrigation in Hereford in the 1580s. As for champion (open-field) farming, except in

Devon, Cornwall and Kent, where there had been extensive enclosures, this was still the norm in the early seventeenth century.

In 1649, in *The English Improver or a New Survey of Husbandry,* Walter Blith listed six improvements landowners should make: floating and watering of land; draining of fens, bogs and marshland; ploughing of old pasture and enclosure without depopulation; careful use of manures; planting of woods; and "the more modest improvement of lands presenting special problems."

The weather had an impact on crops and rural life. It was bad throughout western Europe in the 1590s. The worst period of famine in England was from 1593 to 1598. In a study of statistics on all grains from 1546 to 1603, 1555–7 and 1596–7 were years of dearth, while 1549–50, 1551–2, 1554–5, 1573–4, 1585–6, 1590–1 and 1594–6 were "deficient" and 1550–1, 1586–7, 1597–8 and 1600–1 were "bad." In general, there were dry, mild winters, even though this time was part of what has been called the Little Ice Age (which lasted from the fourteenth until the mid-nineteenth centuries). One of the worst winters was in 1607, when five cold weeks began just before Christmas. Also in 1607, floods inundated Somersetshire, Norfolk, Bedfordshire, Kent, Lincolnshire and Huntingdonshire. Summers were usually wet, cool and cloudy, especially in the late sixteenth century.

CROPS

Corn was the contemporary name for any cereal crop. Of the "corn" crops, wheat required the best ground and brought the best prices. Barley, oats and rye were also major cereal crops. In the highlands, where there was relatively little sunshine, only oats would grow. What we call corn (Indian maize) was not known in Europe until the late 1600s.

The entire year was full of hard work in the country. In January and February, farmers ploughed, harrowed and spread manure. Fertilizers were used more and more as the period went on. Marl was considered to be better fertilizer than dung, muck or lime and was said to last twenty years if used properly. Winter was also the time to set trees and

Haymaking, early seventeenth century
In addition to showing a country scene, this woodcut also illustrates the humor
of the time. Puns were extremely popular.

hedges; prune fruit trees; lop timber; sow peas, barley and oats; gather browse for cattle; and fill up holes in the pasture. Threshing was done at Candlemas (February 2), when tillage began and there was an end to free grazing on the previous year's stubble.

In March it was time to sow flax and hemp, sow white peas and sow barley and pease after sowing wheat. Plowing, sowing and harrowing continued until Easter. Land for wheat and rye was "stirred" and barley sown on "light" land as late as possible. Barley was "drink-corn" as was a barley and oats mixture. Vetches, oats and some wheat were also sown. In April and May, gardens were planted, hop vines trailed to their poles, ditches scoured and coppices cleaned. June meant liming, marling and manuring fields and summer ploughing. Hay was mowed after Midsummer Day.

Lammas Day (August 1) marked the start of grain harvest. Some threshing was done, trees and hedges were pruned, rosebushes and bulbous roots were planted and the land was prepared for spring crops. In early September rye was sown (rye and wheat were the "bread-corn" of the country, but rye was slower to ripen than wheat and therefore sown earlier than winter wheat). Red wheat was sown in the Cotswold

Hills. The end of harvest was usually celebrated with sports and fairs, and Michaelmas (September 29) marked the end of one farming year and the beginning of the next.

Throughout the autumn ("fall" is an American term), grapes were harvested, crab apples were gathered to make verjuice used in cooking, cider and perry were made, woodcutting was done, turf and peat were dug for fuel, and rushes were collected, peeled and dipped in oxen or mutton fat to make rushlights. In November, after all new sowing was complete, strawberry and asparagus beds were covered and barley was threshed for malt. Plough land was prepared for beans in December and the women did the winnowing. Women, in fact, did much the same work on farms as men did, only for less pay. In addition, country-women were responsible for the animal tending, cheese making, cleaning, cooking, foraging, gardening, haymaking, sewing, spinning, weaving and weeding.

ENCLOSURE

The forced enclosures of the eighteenth century have given enclosure (enclosing land with fences, hedges or walls) a bad name. In the sixteenth century, the process often helped the local economy, making the land more productive. Enclosures were first made early in the thirteenth century and expanded gradually. After 1550, enclosure was mainly done to create more efficient, arable farmland, although fences and hedges did also keep cattle from straying and gave shade in the summer.

Better land management improved productivity. One estimate places about 50 percent of the farmland in England under enclosure by 1600. Enclosed land was usually farmed "severally" or "in several," and plowing enclosed land actually increased the need for laborers. A furlong was the distance a pair of oxen could plough a furrow without tiring. On an average, this measured 220 yards. Plowed strips were twenty to thirty feet wide and were divided by grassy pathways called balks. In 1593, Parliament established the statute mile at eight furlongs (1,760 yards), but the length of a mile continued to vary from county to county, ranging from 1,925 to 2,728 yards.

Because of the profits from wool, some landowners turned arable land into pasture, which produced a corn shortage and a labor surplus. When public outcries called excesses in enclosures to national attention, legislation was passed to control such practices. Disrupting lawful enclosure, however, was also illegal. In 1553, ten men found guilty of tearing down enclosures were sentenced to rebuild them.

In Kent, there were extensive enclosures by 1549. Weald fields were enclosed by shaws of oak, beech or ash. Post and rail fences were used in Romney Marsh. Hedges were used elsewhere, and quicksets could be raised from berries of whitethorn. In Northamptonshire, whitethorn and hazel trees, crab apples and holly were used for hedging. Plashing was the job of thinning hedges, then bending the remaining branches and intertwining them so that in the spring the growth would be twice as thick as before.

Many yeomen farmers raised both crops and sheep, and in some areas corn-sheep husbandry was combined with apple orchards. When Sir Bassingbourne Gawdry of Norfolk died in 1606 he had over 240 acres of "standing corn" and flocks totaling over 5,000 sheep.

LIVESTOCK

One Berkshire yeoman paid twenty pounds for one hundred sheep in 1586. Sheep had value in the fleece, skin (writing material as well as leather), milk (six ewes gave the yield of one cow) and manure, and although they were used for meat, it was not the most important by-product. Lambing took place in late February or March and sheep were weaned in May. They were washed and sheared before Midsummer Day (June 24) and the fleeces taken to market. In some areas, spring sheepshearing was followed by a festival with special tarts, cakes and pastries. After shearing, wool was wound, cleaned and packed into great canvas bags that held about one thousand pounds apiece. Sheep were counted in August and marked with reddle (red ochre) to keep them separate in a combined flock.

Bullocks were also counted every August, and in the autumn, when the larger fairs were held, the butcher sent an agent to reach an agreement for the delivery of cattle. Cattle from the north and west were moved in herds by drovers, using their own tracks across the landscape, to be sold for meat. Most livestock was slaughtered for the winter supply of meat and because it was expensive to keep animals over the winter, but a cow or two was usually kept for milk. Smaller than the modern animal, one cow might give 120 to 150 gallons a year. Cows were fed on grass, mistletoe and ivy.

Goats were kept, though seldom in the lowlands. More common were pigs, which were lanky with longer legs and snouts than modern breeds. In some areas they ran free in the woods all summer. A hogs-herd earned 1s. 5d. per quarter in the mid-sixteenth century. In other areas pigs had a ring in the nose and were yoked in pairs to keep them from wandering. In some boroughs and cities a swineherd collected the pigs and took them into the countryside each morning. Each sow farrowed twice a year and litters ran anywhere from seven to nineteen piglets. Pigs were kept for bacon and were slaughtered at Michaelmas, after they'd been fattened up on fallen acorns, beechnuts, crab apples, hazelnuts and leaves. If they were kept over the winter they were fed on whey.

Bees were kept, as honey was a common sweetener. Wicker hives coated with clay and thatched with straw were used. Church towers were also sometimes used for hives.

Doves were raised in dovecotes, some with as many as six hundred holes. Poultry included swans and geese as well as chickens. Swans were fattened in coops on oats and peas. Geese produced five goslings a year.

Domestic animals included not only dogs and cats, but weasels, which were trained to kill rats and mice. When there were no cats or weasels available, arsenic was used to kill rodents.

MANORS AND FARMS

By Tudor times, the English peasant had evolved into the yeoman and the feudal lord was simply a landlord. No longer was the villein bound to the land. The concept of knight service still existed in some cases, but applied more to the landowner and his relationship with the Crown. There were several types of tenants. Freeholders made fixed payments for life. Leaseholders had a fixed rental for a set number of years. The customary tenant (or copyholder) paid rent but owed no services to the landlord. These tenants could be forced out by raising rents. Laborers worked on lands rented by others for wages and usually cultivated two or three acres of their own in the common fields. In many areas, farmers supplemented their income by doing piecework in the cloth trade.

A manor was a unit of estate management. Most feudal manors included one or more hamlets and a larger village. Since a knight or peer might well own more than one manor, on those where he did not actually live, a steward (or sometimes a bailiff, reporting to a steward responsible for more than one manor) was the actual overseer, managing the farm, buying grain and cattle, and supervising workers. One holdover from the feudal period was the requirement that corn be ground at the lord's mill, which could be expensive.

Accounts were presented on Lady Day and at Michaelmas. In the 1620s, a new method of accounting was introduced. The old way was on parchment with Roman numerals. The new used paper and Arabic numerals. A typical large manor might require three large volumes, one for income and two for expenditures.

TOWNS AND VILLAGES

The terms parish and town were used interchangeably in the seventeenth century although technically they were not always the same. The parish (an ecclesiastical division) gained prominence as parish officials (churchwardens and petty constables) gradually took over functions previously performed by officials of a manor. In 1555, surveyors of the highway, appointed by the churchwardens, were added to the list of parish officials, and in 1597 the Poor Law stipulated that each parish have two to four overseers of the poor.

Large villages were common in the south and east, small villages and hamlets more prevalent in the north and west. Even in small villages, a large proportion of the population worked for the rest. In Ealing, which had 404 inhabitants in 1599, 109 were servants, living in 34 percent of the households. Seventy-eight percent of the males and 58 percent of the females were between the ages of twenty and twenty-four. The average village population was under 200.

In each village, even the smaller ones, there were usually a number of men engaged in specialized work, commonly a baker, a carpenter, fullers, millers and smiths. If there was no tanner, villagers did their own tanning. Itinerant labor also supplemented work that was done in each household. Specialists came in with dung carts at mowing time and branded animals and gelded suckling pigs. There were also slaters, thatchers, tilers and tinkers. A trip to the nearest town gave access to chandlers, coopers, glaziers, saddlers, shoemakers and tailors.

The average town had 400 to 900 people. A 1588 estimate indicates that there were more than 590 market towns. Another estimate, for

1603, puts the number of market and shire towns at about 641. In 1612, Dorset and Sussex each had 18 market towns, Westmorland only 4, but equally rural Lancashire had 15.

By the seventeenth century, the larger market towns had begun to specialize. Bewdley was known for caps, Lanport for eels, and so forth. Most towns also had schools, at least a petty school and frequently an endowed grammar school. Some market towns were also county towns, that is, the focus of trade routes and the location of medieval fortifications. Most county towns had town walls. In general they also had craft guilds.

DEER PARKS AND ROYAL FORESTS

Although there were nowhere near the number of woodlands of an earlier age, there were some preserves left. In Nottinghamshire, Sherwood Forest took up a quarter of the county. In Oxfordshire, the royal forest of Wychwood still covered two-thirds of the shire in 1603.

The dukes of Norfolk had hunting rights in Framlingham deer park. In a normal year 100 to 200 deer were given to local gentry and others as regular presents. There seems to have been a good-sized herd. Even the hard winter of 1510, which killed 1,307 of Framlingham's deer, did not decimate it.

In the Forest of Dean in Gloucestershire, which was Crown property, natural resources included game, timber, iron and coal. Foresters, keepers and underkeepers oversaw the land on a day-to-day basis, charged with keeping out those who did not belong there. The forest had its own system of justice, consisting of four separate courts. The minelaw was probate court, trial court and parliament all in one for miners. The court of attachments, held every six weeks, was run by verderers to deal with offences against the king's timber and game. The swanimote met three times a year and was composed of freeholders of the forest. The justice seat was supposed to meet every three years in a site outside the forest, but the only recorded meeting in the fifteenth or sixteenth centuries in Gloucester was in July 1634. Most of the cases dealt with the theft of timber from the Forest of Dean.

ANTIQUITIES

Hadrian's Wall in Cumberland was known during the Renaissance as the Picts' Wall. Stonehenge in Wiltshire was believed to have been built by Aurelius Ambrosius (d. 506). In Somerset, thermal springs had prompted the Romans to build baths which were in more or less continuous use afterward. In 1612, Bath had five open-air baths for people and one (outside the city wall) for horses.

GYPSIES

Gypsies, whose origins were obscure (they were called "offspring of Ptolemy" and "Moon men"), were in France early in the fifteenth century and had reached England, possibly through Scotland, by 1500. The first statutes against them date from the 1530s, and from 1537, efforts were made to deport all gypsies. Some were sent to Norway. The number of recorded cases of "problems" with gypsies throughout the rest of the century, including an accusation of high treason in 1577, indicates how little success this policy had. In 1602, two Englishwomen were tried and convicted of consorting with gypsies. One was hanged; the other was reprieved due to pregnancy.

SELECT BIBLIOGRAPHY

Campbell, Mildred. *The English Yeoman Under Elizabeth and the Early Stuarts.* London: Merlin Press, 1983. This is a reprint of the "classic" 1942 reference.

Fussell, G.E. *The English Countrywoman: A Farmhouse Social History, A.D. 1500–1900.* London: A. Melrose, 1953.

Mingay, G.E. *A Social History of the English Countryside.* London and New York: Routledge, 1990.

Schmidt, Albert J. *The Yeoman in Tudor and Stuart England.* Washington: Folger Shakespeare Library, 1961.

Speed, John. *The Counties of Britain: A Tudor Atlas.* London: Pavilion Books Ltd., 1988. Speed's atlas dates from 1612. Detailed commentary on each county shown on a map is by Alasdair Hawkyard.

Wrightson, Keith and David Levine. *Poverty and Piety in an English Village: Terling 1525–1700.* New York: Academic Press, 1979.

CHAPTER NINETEEN

TRAVEL AND TRAVELERS

Less than 20 percent of the population ever traveled far from home. Most did, however, at least visit the nearest market town on a regular basis. In Elizabethan times the average distance traveled by customers to open market was seven miles. The most common way to travel was on foot, and by walking one might cover three or four miles an hour under optimal conditions during daylight. Very few people traveled at night and no one traveled purely for pleasure. Not only were road conditions terrible, but roads were ill-marked, making getting lost a danger. Highwaymen were also plentiful.

TRAVEL BY LAND

Anyone who could afford to hire a horse or a mule rode. Estimates seem to run around 20 to 30 miles a day as an average that a man could cover on horseback. Keep in mind that it took extra time to ford streams and be ferried across rivers. Bridges were few and far between. Only four crossed the Thames, at Kingston, Chertsey, Staines and Southwark. The 120-mile journey from Stratford to London took three days on horseback. English gentlemen, who thought it unmanly to ride in any vehicle or on a mare, preferred geldings to high-strung stallions

THE WRITER'S GUIDE TO EVERYDAY LIFE IN RENAISSANCE ENGLAND

who might throw their riders. They rated a horse by its color, bay being best, especially if it had a white star on its forehead.

Sidesaddles

Women also rode on horseback. If they rode astride they used a man's saddle. Riding apillion involved the use of a pillion, a leather or padded cushion on a wooden frame which was strapped to the horse's back behind the saddle. A footboard hung from the offside and the woman clung to the man in front of her. This design may have led to the development of the sidesaddle, or it may have developed concurrently with it. There are records of Empress Matilda in the twelfth century riding "sideways in her saddle." Some sources credit the introduction of the sidesaddle into England in 1382 to Anne of Bohemia. However early it was developed, it did not become generally popular until after 1533 when Catherine de' Medici set the fashion by bringing one with her to France from Italy. The pillion continued to be used throughout the Renaissance.

Hired Horses

Horses could be hired at the same stages (approximately every ten miles) used by the royal post, although until 1635 this was limited to the four main roads of the kingdom. The cost of posting increased, as did everything else in this period. Official riders on public business paid 1d., 1½d. (1584), then 2½d. per mile. Private travelers paid 2d. until 1609 when the rate sent up to 3d. a mile. A guide was paid 4d. (the guide's groat) at each stage and employing one was compulsory, since he brought back the hired horses from stage to stage. He was also willing to carry up to fourteen pounds of the traveler's belongings.

Some gentlemen who did not own horses could hire one for the entire journey at a rate of 12d. for the first day and 8d. per day thereafter. Another alternative was to buy a horse for the journey and sell it at journey's end.

Horses in England by the sixteenth century included the Turkey horse, the Barbarian or Barb (small and swift), the Sardinian, the Neapolitan (with a long, slender head), the Spanish Jennet, the Hungarian, the High Almaine or German, the Friesland, the Flanders (used as a draught horse), the Sweacian or Sweathland (Swedish—of a mean stature and strength, pied with white legs and body of another color), the Irish hobbym and the Galloway nag. The Great Horse re-

ferred to the English war-horse. The best horses (in order of importance and cost) were war-horses, palfreys (riding horses for the upper
class), rounceys (ridden by men-at-arms), hackneys and carthorses.

Pack Trains

Pack trains used mules rather than horses on long hauls and carried
goods in wicker panniers called dorsers or in cloth packs slung over
crude, padded saddles. They could cover 15 to 20 miles a day but they
were usually slower because of poor road conditions or mountainous
terrain. By early in the fifteenth century, scheduled pack trains ran
from Kendal to Southampton, taking one month for the round trip.
They carried letters as well as goods and when they went to areas where
they could take carts, they also took passengers. The usual charge was
from 2d. to 4d. per hundredweight of goods (during Elizabethan
times). A woman was charged at the same rate as half a pack. A woman
traveling from Oswestry to London (120 miles) paid 4s. 6d. and bought
or brought her own food. As this was not only less comfortable but also
less dignified than riding a horse, young gentlemen usually chose to
hire a "padd-nag" at 6d. per day rather than ride in a wagon.

Mr. Pickford of Lancashire and Yorkshire was a goods carrier in the
early Stuart era. His pack-horse trains consisted of thirty to forty horses
carrying up to 350 pounds each in single file across the Pennines. Since
Pickford took the precaution of hiring armed guards (the law made
him responsible for any losses by robbery), long-distance travelers often
joined the pack trains for safety. Carts were rarely used for pack trains
in remote areas such as Scotland, Cornwall, Devonshire and Northumberland. As late as 1760 there was no road suitable for wheeled
vehicles between Manchester and Liverpool in Lancashire.

A variety of two-wheeled and four-wheeled wagons and carts were
also used to transport goods and people. In hilly districts, sledges were
sometimes substituted. An attempt in 1605 to restrict heavy vehicles
with iron rims on their wheels (in order to save the roads) and a royal
proclamation in 1621 that forbade the use of four-wheeled wagons
were both largely ignored. After 1632 owners of overloaded vehicles
were fined 50s.

In 1637 *The Carrier's Cosmographer* listed regular wagon departures
from various London inns at stated times, a practice begun in late
Elizabethan days. Carriers left for Yorkshire from the Belle Sauvage
Inn on Mondays, but the majority seem to have left on Fridays and

Saturdays. Every important town had carriers who traveled to and from London at fixed intervals. Some made the trip as often as three times a week.

Road Conditions and Routes

Some wide (up to sixty-four feet), paved roads survived from Roman times, but other "highways" were never more than narrow horse paths. A main highway, of which there were no more than twenty even by 1600, was probably only thirty feet wide.

There were few signposts on these roads, though there may have been milestones. Maps existed but were expensive and not always accurate. Hiring a local guide was essential. No one traveled alone if he could help it. The gentry and nobility often took a large retinue, even though that meant they'd be lucky to cover fifteen miles in a day. Their baggage, often including furniture moved from one house to another with its owners, was carried in carts. Traveling chests, for clothing and other personal belongings, were made of leather soaked in oil to make them waterproof and reinforced with iron fittings. A curved top also ensured that rain ran off. These chests were lined with linen to protect the contents from dust and were fastened with locks.

In 1577, William Harrison's *Description of England* included a list of all the major thoroughfares in England and gave distances between the principal towns. All roads had their hub at London. There were four old Roman roads still being heavily used at the end of the medieval period. Watling Street went north to Chester and south to Dover. Ermine Street went to York. The Icknield Way went into East Anglia. The Fosse Way led to Lincoln.

Specialized roads included saltways (for the distribution of salt from Cheshire and Worcestershire) and drove-roads (for cattle). These avoided both regular roads and towns. Causeways were common in the Fenlands. Three of them, built in the eleventh and twelfth centuries, linked Ely to firmer ground. Other causeways were at York and in a section of the highway between London and Banbury. Another linked Nottingham with the bridge across the Trent.

Both weather and road conditions made travel times unpredictable. In mid-sixteenth-century England the journey between London and Northamptonshire (eighty miles or so) could take anywhere from two days to a week. During the winter months, some country houses in the Midlands and north were completely cut off from civilization for weeks at a time. In 1555, Parliament passed an Act requiring every parish to elect two surveyors to keep the highways in repair by forced labor. Over the next hundred years, however, little was done beyond spot repair of the worst holes. London to Durham was still reckoned a four- to five-day journey; London to York, four days; and London to Newcastle, two days.

The Coach

In the Middle Ages, women often rode in four-wheeled covered wagons drawn by three or four horses in tandem. These "chariots" were large, lumbering vehicles made of wood and iron. The interior was padded with cushions and a small stepladder was used to get in and out.

The closed, four-wheeled vehicle with seats inside for passengers and one seat outside for the driver (but as yet with no springs or window glass) first appeared in Hungary sometime after 1470, a development from the design of the carriages used to transport artillery. The word *coach* may have been derived from Kocs, a small village between Vienna and Budapest. The first coach was imported into England from the Netherlands in 1555 for the earl of Rutland. Mary I had one by 1556. Queen Elizabeth ordered one from Holland in 1560. The first coach arrived in Scotland from France with Mary, Queen of Scots in 1561.

Coaches might be drawn by two or more horses or by mules. The duke of Buckingham was the first to use a six-horse team in London, but more horses were common in the country, where they were needed to pull the coaches out of the muck and mire. There is one record of a lady in Kent whose coach was drawn by six oxen.

Once introduced to the British Isles, coaches quickly caught on. The earliest models were quite primitive, although they were upholstered and elaborately carved and painted. The first vehicles to resemble our modern concept of a coach were not seen until 1580.

By 1599, Londoners were complaining about traffic jams. In 1601 a bill was introduced in the House of Lords to restrain excessive use of coaches but it did not pass. *A Discourse on Leather* (1629) claimed the twin cities of London and Westminster contained between them as many as five thousand coaches and carouches (the calash and the carouche were names for smaller four-wheeled coaches designed for in-town use). In 1636, *Coach and Sedan Pleasantly Disputing for Place and Precedence* included a code of conduct for vehicles.

In 1641 a new coach cost the earl of Bedford more than £30 but

A mid-seventeenth-century hackney coach
Shown here is a coach for hire with driver and footmen. The curtains at the sides of the coach could be closed for privacy.

the old one could be traded in at a value of £5. Six new coach horses added another £150 to the price. The most popular coach horses were dappled Flanders mares and a pair cost £47 pounds in 1608.

Hackney Coaches

Coaches could be hired for special journeys as early as 1595, when John Dee sent his wife and family from Mortlake to Coventry in a coach drawn by two horses. The cost was 10s. per day. The first coaches for hire in the way we use taxicabs were nicknamed Hackney Hell Carts. The word came from the French *haquenee*, an ambling nag. These coaches were able to carry two passengers and were drawn by two horses, one ridden by the driver. They were already being blamed for congestion in London in 1619. By 1625 there were twenty of them operating in London.

The first regular coach stand was across from Bedford House on the Strand. There a retired sea captain named Bailey began to hire out four coaches and coachmen in livery in 1633, an improvement over going to a stable to find a coach for hire. By 1635, hackney coaches had become so numerous, based at inns all over the city, that King Charles limited their numbers and also regulated their fares. The cost of a coach for an entire day in London was 8s. 6d.

Weekly service between Aldersgate and St. Albans was available by 1637. The journey from London to Salisbury took two days by stagecoach and cost anywhere from 20s. to 30s. The trip from London to Chester took four days, as did that from London to Exeter. From London to Newcastle was a six-day journey. The average distance covered in a day was thirty to forty miles.

Litters and Sedan Chairs

Horse litters had been used since the Middle Ages. These were suspended between two horses and carried ladies and the infirm. Padded with cushions and sometimes mattresses, they were more comfortable than coaches or chariots for long journeys. In the mid-seventeenth century, Ann Clifford, countess of Dorset, Pembroke and Montgomery, traveled between residences in northern England in a horse litter, her ladies in waiting and other female servants following in coaches and her menservants on horseback, with a train of baggage wagons bringing up to the rear. A litter carried by men rather than horses was used by Queen Elizabeth.

The sedan chair, a seat enclosed in a box and carried on poles by two men, had been invented by 1581, but it was more common in France and was rarely seen in England before the reign of Charles I. In 1634 a proposal was made to use sedan chairs as an alternative to the hired coach in order to relieve traffic congestion. The idea caught on but did little to decrease the number of coaches. Rather, it cut into the watermen's business.

TRAVEL BY WATER

The Thames

London had some 2,000 watermen licensed to take passengers across the Thames. About one-third of the householders in the Liberty of the Clink earned their living that way, charging 1d. for each crossing. For one man to hire a boat for a trip to Westminster from London cost 6d. with the tide and more against. To Chiswick it was 2s. 6d. for a round-trip fare.

Wherries were upholstered, with embroidered cushions for seats, and held two to five passengers. Public barges and tilt-boats (tilts were canopies) competed for passengers on the route from Windsor to Gravesend and back. Each could carry around twenty-five people. Barges charged 4s. a boat load. Tilt-boats cost 10s. to 15s. for the boat-load. "Light horsemen" and tide-boats also provided passenger service on the Thames.

The Thames was a major delivery route for dairy products from Essex and Suffolk; fruits, vegetables and hops from Kent; cattle and sheep fattened in East Anglia, the midlands and home counties; and coal from Newcastle, which was transferred from lighters to barges to travel to Reading, Henley or Abingdon and be exchanged for a cargo of corn or malt. London also shipped out foreign luxuries like wine, sugar and prunes and bulky native commodities like chalk and fuller's earth. In general, water transport was cheaper than land transport. Freight that cost 1d. per mile by water would cost anywhere from 4d. to 12d. per mile overland.

River boats were all sailing vessels but some also had rowers and a steersman. If sails, oars or poles weren't enough, the vessels could be pulled by men or horses along tow paths. Large barges were used to carry goods. Eight men could handle one large enough to carry more than forty five-horsed wagons. Some wealthy men owned their own barges, and had bargemen in livery. The earl of Bedford's barge men wore broadcloth lined with orange baize to correspond with the gowns of the porters at Woburn Abbey.

Other Waterways

Some waterways no longer navigable today were still used during this period. In 1600 the Thames went to Reading and to within two miles of Oxford. The Trent reached beyond Nottingham. The Avon was navigable to within four miles of Warwick and reached Stratford. The Cam reached Cambridge. The Dee went to Chester, the Lea to Hertford and the Medway to five miles above Maidstone. The Humber-Ouse waterway was important between Hull and York because the main road had to keep to the better-drained land to the west. The Great Ouse went to Bedford, the Little Ouse to Thetford, and the Yorkshire Ouse to York. On the Severn, most cargoes went downstream from Worcester to Bristol; the principal upstream terminus was Bewdley. Small, sea-going vessels could get as far as Tewkesbury. Shrewsbury could also be reached by river. On the Exe, seagoing ships reached Topsham.

The first canal in England was built from Exeter to Topsham in 1564–8 and was three miles long. The upper reaches of the Thames, especially above Burcott, were regulated by inefficient single locks and weirs (dams), usually erected in connection with mills. In 1578, seven weirs, twenty-three locks, sixteen floodgates and more than twenty mills existed on the Thames between Maidenhead and Oxford. In 1580, citizens of Abingdon listed twenty-five weirs, locks and mills as hampering movement between their town and Maidenhead. The first double-gated locks (called turnpikes) appeared on the Thames circa 1606.

Downstream travel was swift, but moving upstream required the use of sails, oars or poles, or that the craft be hauled upstream by oxen or horses walking a towpath. Thames barges going upriver from London took four days to reach Henley, a distance of some forty miles. Towpaths also had high tolls.

POSTAL SERVICE

A "common carrier" was used by most towns to provide a regular service to London by around 1400. The first postal system was established in 1482, covering the 335 miles from Berwick to London in relays of 30 miles. An organized system for hiring hackney horses at stages along the entire route from Gravesend to Dover was in operation by early in the sixteenth century. In 1511 a traveler paid half a crown a stage. Henry VIII appointed Brian Tuke the first Master of the Posts in 1517. When Thomas Randolph took over that position in 1572, the posting (postal) system, with a chief post office in London, became a permanent institution.

Early postboys carried a horn, blown when they passed through a town, every time they met anyone and at least three times a mile to announce their coming. They carried the post in satchels slung over the shoulder. Postbags were leather, lined with good cotton or baize, and it was forbidden to carry anything in them but letters and writings. These were of two types. Packets, which could be one letter or a bundle, were the official mail and had to go out again at each stage within a quarter hour. Bye-letters were private letters rather than official mail and waited for forwarding until the next official packet ran. The most urgent letters were marked with a sketch of a man dangling from a gallows (an unofficial custom) to indicate that the postboy should deliver it with as much speed as if it were a pardon. As early as 1523 a similar message was conveyed to those postboys who could read by the inscription "Haste, Post, haste for life."

A foot post continued to be used along with post-horses, because over long distances most horses were not as fast as a well-trained man on foot. A well-cared-for horse, however, bred for distance, could carry over two hundred pounds for more than 50 miles a day. Foot posts averaged 7 miles per hour in summer and 5 in winter and usually covered 16 to 18 miles a day.

There were posts over most of England by 1628 and the postal service finally became official in 1629. At this point, letters were put into a "portmantle" which was carried on a second horse.

There were always complaints about how slow the mail was, although one letter (in 1599) traveled 193 miles in forty-eight hours, with some of the journey undertaken at night. In 1635, post-horses for a "stafetto" or packet post covered 120 miles a day. One could send a letter from London to Edinburgh and have a reply back within six days. In 1647 the coach from London to Rye cost £7. The same trip riding post would have cost a traveler 18s. The round trip from London to Bristol (240 miles) might cost a traveler as much as £8 by the fastest post-horse relay (though a royal packet went for 40s. 2d.) but riding with the regular post was only 15s.

Letters were also carried by private goods carriers, by friends and by servants. A "running footman" was part of many gentlemen's households. In one case a footman covered 148 miles in less than forty-two hours to fetch medicine, with only one stop for sleep. Until late in the sixteenth century, letters sent overseas often made better time than those sent to remote areas of England by any method. The average time for a letter to reach Calais from London was two days. Letters from Antwerp took about a week.

INNS

Although inns were still almost entirely unknown in Scotland at the end of the seventeenth century, a census of twenty-seven English counties in 1577 lists two thousand of them, along with fourteen thousand alehouses and three hundred taverns. Some few inns were large enough to house from two hundred to three hundred people at a time.

In June 1564, the maximum price an innkeeper of Norwich could charge for a meal was set at fourpence. At most inns, a meal could be had for sixpence or less. Inns were plentiful in England and had a good reputation compared to those in Europe. In Dover, which had a great deal of traffic in travelers, there were ten inns, each with between three and sixteen beds (the largest inn was the Lion), and twenty-six victualing houses. The latter were private homes licensed to offer lodging and food. Those in Dover each had three to nine beds.

Of Dover's inns, only the Angel had no stabling available. All of Worcester's twelve inns had stables. The inventory of one also boasted of ninety-five pairs of sheets for eleven bedrooms. Typical inn servants were chamberlains (rather than chambermaids), ostlers and tapsters.

ROYAL PROGRESSES

On progress, the court took everything from equipment such as wax for seals and parchment to furniture. The monarch always traveled with the royal bed. The chaplain took a portable altar. Sumpter mules and horses were used to transport all this, together with carts and wagons.

Queen Elizabeth traveled with more than three hundred carts to carry her baggage. This huge entourage rarely covered more than ten or twelve miles a day. Annual progresses were the rule for most of the 1560s and 1570s, but Elizabeth rarely went far north and only once got as far west as Bristol.

FOREIGN TRAVEL

A list of fifteenth-century travel times indicates one could get from Venice to London in twenty-seven days. This is optimistic. Just to cross the English Channel could take anywhere from a few hours to a few days. In October 1514, Mary Tudor, Henry VIII's sister and the new bride of the French king, Louis XII, left Dover for Boulogne with a flotilla of fourteen ships. A quarter of the way across, the convoy was scattered by a storm. The bride's ship managed to reach its destination but was unable to make a safe landing. Mary was loaded into a rowing boat, which brought her within wading distance of the shore. Sir Christopher Garnish then carried the new French queen the rest of the way to dry land in his arms. Queen Henrietta Maria's crossing, from Boulogne to Dover in June 1625 took twenty-four hours.

To reach the Field of Cloth of Gold in 1520, row barges with crews of sixty were used to transport courtiers and ladies. This was not a usual means of transportation. The ordinary way to reach France or the Netherlands was by packet boat. These vessels, usually around sixty tons, had single decks and cabins in their high sterns. They were in regular service between Dover and Calais and Dover and Nieuport. The usual cost to Calais was five shillings but various charges and gratuities could more than double that, especially when ferries had to be taken at both ends (these vessels did not dock). On the other hand, in 1579, John Chapman paid only 2 shillings to get from Dover to Calais in the company of "Frenchmen and English merchants."

In 1591, Fynes Morison sailed from Leigh-on-Thames. He didn't land in the Netherlands until ten days later. Once on land, Moryson traveled on foot and in disguise to reduce his chances of being robbed and to avoid calling attention to the fact that he was English. Thieves, the Inquisition, disease and wolves were among the dangers travelers on the Continent faced. In Germany, however, there were public coaches which carried six to eight people. A coach from Hamburg to Nuremberg, a nine-day journey, cost about two pounds each for six and that included both the coach fare and the coachman's food.

No one could leave England without a license from the monarch, the Privy Council or the Warden of the Cinque Ports. Travelers were not to take more than twenty pounds out of the country and were examined by the port commissioner on their return. France and Italy were the most usual destinations. In 1553 a travel guide by Henri Estienne described France as twenty-two days wide and nineteen days long. A book written a century earlier by Gilles Le Bouvier (who estimated the length of England as an eight-day journey) gave France's length as sixteen days. In 1579, John Chapman walked from Calais to Rheims, by way of Ardres and Cambrai (about 150 miles) in a week.

However long they took, most journeys combined land and water routes, and navigable riverways were augmented by canals. By the fifteenth century, one canal linked the North Sea to the Baltic. There were, however, many delays, some caused by natural hazards and others by man. By the 1500s, watercraft had to stop every 6 or 7 miles along the River Seine to pay tolls. Mountains slowed travel as well. A five-week trip from Paris to Naples took travelers across the Alps through the Mont Cenis pass. That alone took five to seven days to traverse and it was blocked by snow from November to May.

SELECT BIBLIOGRAPHY

Camusso, Lorenzo. *Travel Guide to Europe 1492*. New York: Henry Holt and Company, 1990.

Crofts, J. *Packhorse, Waggon and Post: Land Carriage and Communications under the Tudors and Stuarts*. London: Routledge and Kegan Paul, 1967.

Parkes, Joan. *Travel in England in the Seventeenth Century*. Oxford: Clarendon Press, 1968.

CHAPTER TWENTY

WITCHES, MAGIC, NECROMANCY AND SUPERSTITION

WITCHES

English witch trials were unique in Europe, principally because they had no connection to the Catholic Church and therefore lacked satanic elements until those began to be inserted by the "witchfinders" of the mid-seventeenth century. Under the Tudors, witchcraft was not even a crime from 1547 to 1563. Though there were charges (of heresy) which could be brought in ecclesiastical courts, the first English statute against witchcraft was not passed until 1542 and it was repealed in 1547.

The first person prosecuted under the statute of 1563 was Elizabeth Lowys, who appeared before the Colchester Assizes on July 21, 1564, having previously been in the ecclesiastical court of the archdeacon of Essex. The charges against her seem to have stemmed from a quarrel over her employment as a spinster, a quarrel with her husband and Elizabeth's reputation as a scold. Although the idea of a familiar imp in the shape of an animal first appeared in a case in 1530, when a toad was found in a suspect's house, Elizabeth Lowys was not questioned about one. There was no search for a witch's mark (common practice by 1579), no children gave evidence, and no attempt was made to persuade Elizabeth to name other witches. She was sentenced to death because the community found her a convenient scapegoat for unexplained illnesses and accidents.

Knowledge of what witches did was spread by the sensational pamphlets published after witch trials. They were some of the most popular reading matter of their day. By 1566 the familiar had thus become a regular feature in witchcraft trials. There was never, however, a witch cult in England. The covenant with the Devil as part of witchcraft was not included in the law until 1604, and the emphasis on stamping out devil worship did not begin until 1645, with witchfinder Matthew Hopkins. James I had been instrumental in bringing about this change. He had become convinced of the existence of witches in 1591, when the so-called North Berwick witches claimed responsibility for a storm that nearly sank the ship on which he was returning to Scotland from Denmark with his bride. James wrote his own book on the subject, *Demonology*, first published in 1597. In Scotland, witchcraft had been a criminal offense since 1563 and that act remained in effect until 1736. Between 1590 and 1700, over one thousand people were executed in Scotland and three times that many were accused of witchcraft.

Essex held more witch trials than elsewhere in England. About 250 cases were tried between 1560 and 1600, but not all of these witches were executed. Many were punished by public penance or jail time. Throughout England, the percentage of trials ending in conviction varied but the high was 42 percent during the period from 1645 to 1647. In France, it went as high as 95 percent.

Ferdinando Stanley, fifth earl of Derby, took eleven painful days to die in 1594. When an image made of wax was found in his chamber, the conclusion was obvious. He'd been bewitched to death, although no one was ever charged with this crime. Mention of such "poppets" as instruments of murder is found as early as 1537. As the wax melted, the victim's body wasted away. Sticking pins in an image of wax or clay could cause pain to the victim. If the heart was pierced, he died within nine days.

In 1618, at Belvoir Castle in Lincolnshire, the earl of Rutland's son and daughter were suffering from a wasting sickness. Another son had already died of mysterious causes. Two of the earl's servantwomen, Margaret and Philippa Flower, had recently been dismissed from his service. Their mother, Joan Flower, was well known to be a "monstrous malicious woman" and a witch. This proved sufficient cause to charge Margaret and Philippa with bewitching the children. They were tried, convicted and executed. The second son died some time later. The daughter survived. A pamphlet published after the executions maintained that Philippa had taken a glove belonging to young Lord Ross to her mother, who rubbed it on the back of her spirit, Rutterkin (a cat), put it into boiling water, pricked it and then buried it in the yard with the wish that Lord Ross might never thrive. The same pamphlet contains confessions which include a white dog, a white mouse, an owl and a kitten named Pusse as familiars.

Of all those accused of witchcraft, most were over fifty years of age and about half were women. In Lancashire in 1612, Alice Nutter of Roughlee Hall in Blackburn Hundred, a gentlewoman, was accused of being the leader of a group of witches who met in the nearby Forest of Pendle. Descriptions of their gathering sound more like a picnic than a witch's sabbat, but five men and fifteen women ended up being tried at the August assizes. Eight were acquitted. The rest were found guilty, except for Elizabeth Southerns (Old Demdike), who died in prison before the trial. She had already confessed, however, to having been a witch since 1590 and claimed to have a familiar named Tib. Of those convicted, one was sent to the pillory. The others, including Alice, were hanged on August 20.

At the same assizes, a separate witchcraft trial had a very different outcome. Jane Shireburne Southworth of Samlesbury, a widow, and two other women were acquitted when the principal witness against them, a fourteen-year-old girl, admitted she had been instructed by "Master Thompson." Master Thompson turned out to be Christopher Southworth, a priest, who had apparently been trying to punish his niece by marriage for converting to Protestantism.

In 1634, seven inhabitants of that same Forest of Pendle made infamous in 1612, including the granddaughter of Old Demdike, were indicted along with a number of others on the charges made by a young boy. Seven were found guilty. Three of them died in prison at Lancaster, but the others were eventually reprieved by Charles I when the accusations proved to be fraudulent.

MAGIC, NECROMANCY AND ASTROLOGY

Magic
Magic comes in three forms. Natural magic involves the elemental world. Celestial magic is under the influence of the stars. Ceremonial

Witches on the gallows, 1589
Chapbooks printed detailed accounts of many witch trials and were illustrated with woodcuts like the one on which this drawing is based. In England, witches were customarily hung, rather than burned as they were (for heresy) in Catholic countries.

magic involves an appeal to spiritual beings. Magical inquiry had some respectability in the Renaissance as a means of expanding knowledge. Seances, experiments with alchemy and fortune-telling were common, even though they made their practitioners liable for punishment in ecclesiastical courts.

Cunning men and cunning women were those who performed magical functions in healing and in divination. Frequently they located lost items. Sometimes they detected thefts. They were rarely accused of witchcraft. In fact, many who suspected they'd been bewitched went to the local cunning woman for protection against the witch's spell. Belief in talismans and protective amulets was widespread among all classes of society. For example, Dr. Elkes, an Elizabethan conjurer, earned a substantial sum by supplying a ring with a helpful spirit inside it to a gambler.

Necromancy

Necromancy and sorcery were not, strictly speaking, witchcraft. Under Roman law, sorcery was only a crime if it was practiced with evil intent and caused damage. However, after 1541, prognostication and other kinds of sorcery, including using magic for treasure-seeking or to recover stolen goods or to provoke unlawful love, became felonies without benefit of clergy. This law was repealed by Edward VI. The 1563 law carried a lesser penalty for similar crimes, a year's imprisonment and four appearances in the pillory for a first offense. The 1604 law restored the death penalty. Conjuring of spirits was a felony under all three laws.

Astrology

Astrology competed with watercasting (see page 77) as a diagnostic tool in medicine. The Royal College of Physicians could discipline unlicensed practitioners of astrological physic. The Anglican Church required its incumbents and churchwardens to denounce parishioners who engaged in fortune-telling or divination. At times this included astrologers. A consultation with an astrologer during Elizabeth's reign lasted about fifteen minutes and cost 2s. 6d. a session.

Henry VII consulted the Italian astrologer William Parron. Henry VIII consulted a German, Nicholas Kratzer, and an Englishman, John Robins. Jerome Cardan came to England to cast the horoscope of Edward VI. John Dee (1527–1608) was asked to choose an astrologically propitious day for the coronation of Elizabeth I. He was later called in to discuss the comet of 1577 with her. Dee was interested in alchemy as well as astrology and was popularly believed to be a sorcerer. At one point he asked King James to try him on that charge so that he could prove his innocence. His house at Mortlake was attacked at least once by mobs seeking to destroy all traces of his link to the occult.

Simon Forman (1552–1611) was not consulted by royalty, but he was the premier astrologer in London at the turn of the century. His casebooks are still extant. Testimony in trials which took place after his death (in connection with the Overbury murder) indicates that he used wax images for various magical purposes.

Forman's contemporary, John Lambe (1548?–1628), who was more fortune-teller than astrologer and ignorant even of the astrological "science" of the times, was indicted in Worcestershire in 1608 for practicing "execrable arts to consume the body and strength" of Thomas, sixth Lord Windsor of Bromsgrove. Lambe was found guilty, but judgment was suspended. Later the same year he was arraigned for having invoked spirits with a crystal ball. He was imprisoned in Worcester Castle, then sent to the King's Bench Prison in London, where he may have remained for as much as fifteen years. He received "clients" there and in about 1622 was consulted by the duke of Buckingham. At some point after that, Lambe was released, establishing his reputation as the "duke's devil." Because he was on the Thames during a violent storm on Monday, June 12, 1626, that natural disturbance was blamed on him. On June 18, 1628, as Lambe was leaving the Fortune, a playhouse in Finsbury Fields, he was attacked by a mob of apprentices and so severely beaten that he died the next day. A crystal ball was found on his body. Posters immediately went up all over London which read: "Who rules the kingdom? The king. Who rules the king? The duke. Who rules the duke? The devil. Let the duke look to it or he will be served as his doctor was served." When Buckingham was assassinated on August 23, a new rhyme was heard in London: "The shepherd's struck, / the sheep are fled; / for want of Lambe, / the wolf is dead."

William Lilly (1602–1681) was far more respectable than either Forman or Lambe and better trained in astrology. In 1644 he published his first almanac, essentially a calendar which predicted weather, the appearance of comets and so forth. Lilly continued to publish an annual almanac until his death. The 1645 edition accurately predicted the Roundhead victory at Naseby.

GENERAL BELIEF IN THE SUPERNATURAL

Folklore

In Cornwall, tommy-knockers lived in the mines and gave warnings of cave-ins. Pixies, fairies (Little People who lived in mounds and danced in fairy rings and could be malevolent) and ghosts were also part of the superstitious beliefs of the average Elizabethan. Persons believed to be suffering from a supernatural malady were "elf-shot" or "pisky-led" and someone haunted or bewitched was "fairy-taken."

Catholics in England under Anglican rule revived the story of Merlin's "Mouldwarp prophesy" (a mouldwarp staff was a stick used for killing moles). The evil Mole, the prophesy said, would be driven from the land by a dragon, a wolf and a lion, after which England would be divided into three parts. In the fourteenth century, Henry IV was accused of being the Mouldwarp. In the 1530s the term was applied to Henry VIII. In 1535, John Hale, vicar of Isleworth, was executed for making that treasonous accusation.

Ancient Druid festivals surviving in England, which later came to be linked to witchcraft, were All Hallows' Eve and the Eve of May Day. Walpurgis Night was actually the vigil of St. Walburga (Werburga), a Devonshire saint. In Scotland, witches were supposed to meet on Holy Cross (May 3) and All Saints (November 1). Seasonal festivals with pagan origins were given respectability by connecting them to Christianity. February 2 became Candlemas; June 23, the Eve of St. John the Baptist; August 1, Lammas Day; and December 21, the feast of St. Thomas.

Portents

In addition to the more commonplace portents, such as a cow in the garden foretelling a death, or a swallow nesting in the eaves bringing luck, lightning strikes, floods, earthquakes, comets and the like were all suspected of being harbingers of disaster. Hindsight provided even more elaborate explanations. The storm and floods that coincided with the death of Edward VI were spectacular, and as the stories were retold, blood-red hailstones were added to the natural downpour.

Comets tended to be blamed for any unfortunate event that happened in the same year. Notable comets were seen in England in 1500, 1506, 1514, 1518, 1527, 1531, 1533 (a blazing star foretelling the divorce of Henry VIII), 1556, 1577, 1579, 1596, 1607 and 1618. The floods in 1596 were supposed to have been caused by that year's comet.

There were earthquakes of note in 1571, 1574 and on Wednesday, April 6, 1580. The latter spawned an "instant book," published on April 8 to report on damage and speculate on divine wrath. That quake was centered in the Strait of Dover (an earthquake zone—another earthquake struck the same area in 1598) and was felt all along the southeast of England, in Flanders and in northern France. The watchtower at Calais split. A piece of Dover Castle's wall fell into the sea. Church bells in London rang of their own accord and two teenagers were killed by falling masonry. Modern experts estimate that this earthquake measured a 5.6 on the Richter scale.

This same earthquake wrecked the conversion of the George Inn into a playhouse, an act which was seen by some Puritans as proof of God's disapproval of plays and players. The Puritans also saw the hand of God in an accident on January 13, 1583, when a scaffolding collapsed, killing eight spectators at a bear-baiting.

Floods inundated the Great Hall at Westminster in 1515 and again in 1579, the same year in which there were extraordinarily heavy snowfalls. There were eclipses in 1506, 1514, 1518 and 1527 and four of them in 1544. An eclipse of the moon took place on October 7, 1576, from nine until a little after one.

In 1532, people described seeing "a flaming sword and horse's head in the sky and a blue cross over the moon." This may have been a display of the northern lights. One took place in the mid-1570s and terrified everyone. In 1580 there were reports of "a strange . . . impression in the air . . . the shape of the lath of a crossbow without the string."

The predicted nova of November 11, 1572, was a great disappointment. People saw nothing more than a clear sky after sunset and a very bright star. Another bright star appeared in 1604. The conjunction of Saturn and Jupiter at noon on Sunday, April 28, 1583, was also unremarkable, but people still watched for the next conjunctions of these two planets in 1603 and 1623.

Some days of the week traditionally brought bad luck. Almanacs printed lists of those to avoid, especially if one planned to get married or start a business venture. Unfortunately, lists printed in rival publications rarely agreed. Almost any day, it seemed, could be unlucky. Most authorities did think, however, that Fridays were especially unlucky and the age of sixty-three was particularly "fatal and climacterical."

SELECT BIBLIOGRAPHY

Macfarlane, Alan. *Witchcraft in Tudor and Stuart England.* New York: Harper & Row, 1970.

Rowse, A.L. *Sex and Society in Shakespeare's Age: Simon Forman the Astrologer.* New York: Scribner, 1974.

Thomas, Keith. *Religion and the Decline of Magic: Studies in Popular Beliefs in Sixteenth and Seventeenth Century England.* New York: Scribner, 1971.

APPENDIX

SELECT BIBLIOGRAPHY

Reader-Friendly General Histories

Bridenbaugh, Carl. *Vexed and Troubled Englishmen: 1590–1642.* New York: Oxford University Press, 1967.

Davis, Michael Justin. *The England of William Shakespeare.* New York: Dutton, 1987.

Graves, M.A.R. and R.H. Silcock. *Revolution, Reaction and the Triumph of Conservatism: English History 1558–1700.* London and New York: Longman, 1984.

Harrison, William. *The Description of England.* New York: Dover Publications, Inc., 1994. (Note: This is a readable reprint of the 1587 text, edited by Georges Edelen.)

Palliser, D.M. *The Age of Elizabeth: England Under the Later Tudors 1547–1603.* London and New York: Longman, 1983.

Reed, Michael. *The Age of Exuberance, 1550–1700.* Boston: Routledge & Kegan Paul, 1986.

Rowse, A.L. *The Elizabethan Renaissance: The Cultural Achievement.* New York: Charles Scribner's Sons, 1972.

—————. *The Elizabethan Renaissance: The Life of the Society.* New York: Charles Scribner's Sons, 1971.

Russell, Conrad. *Crisis of Parliaments: English History 1509–1660.* London: Oxford University Press, 1971.

Sharpe, J.A. *Early Modern England: A Social History 1550–1760.* London: E. Arnold, 1987.

Wrightson, Keith. *English Society, 1580–1680.* New Brunswick, New Jersey: Rutgers University Press, 1982.

Lavishly Illustrated Books

Ashelford, Jane. *A Visual History of Costume: The Sixteenth Century.* New York: Drama Book Publishers, 1983.

Camusso, Lorenzo. *Travel Guide to Europe 1492.* New York: Henry Holt and Company, 1990.

Cornish, Paul and Angus McBride. *Henry VIII's Army.* London: Osprey Publishing, Ltd., 1987.

Girouard, Mark. *Life in the English Country House: A Social and Architectural History.* New York: Penguin Books, 1980.

Hart, Roger. *English Life in the Seventeenth Century.* New York: Putnam, 1970.

Howard, Maurice. *The Early Tudor Country House: Architecture and Politics 1490–1550*. London: George Philip, 1987.

Lister, Margot. *Costumes of Everyday Life: An Illustrated History of Working Clothes from 900–1910*. Boston: Plays, Inc., 1972.

Ollard, Richard. *This War Without an Enemy: A History of the English Civil War*. New York: Atheneum, 1976.

Ross, Josephine. *The Tudors: England's Golden Age*. New York: Putnam, 1979.

Rowse, A.L. and John Hedgecoe. *In Shakespeare's Land: A Journey Through the Landscape of Elizabethan England*. San Francisco: Chronicle Books, 1987.

Smith, Lacey Baldwin. *The Horizon Book of the Elizabethan World*. New York: American Heritage Publishing Company, 1967.

Strong, Roy. *The English Icon: Elizabethan and Jacobean Portraiture*. New Haven: Yale University Press, 1969.

Trevelyan, G.M. *Illustrated English Social History, vol. II: The Age of Shakespeare and the Stuart Period*. Harmondsworth: Penguin Books, 1964.

Trevor-Roper, Hugh, ed. *The Age of Expansion: Europe and the World 1559–1660*. New York: McGraw-Hill, 1968.

Walker, Bryce. *The Armada*. Alexandria, Virginia: Time-Life Books, 1981.

Williams, Neville. *All the Queen's Men: Elizabeth I and Her Courtiers*. New York: The Macmillan Company, 1972.

————. *Henry VIII and His Court*. New York: The Macmillan Company, 1971.

————. *The Sea Dogs: Privateers, Plunder and Piracy in the Elizabethan Age*. London: Weidenfeld and Nicolson, 1975.

Note: Another excellent, well-illustrated source is the periodical *History Today*, published monthly in London. It covers all periods of history, but a good many of the articles concern Renaissance England.

A Visual Guide to Renaissance England—Videotapes

Connections, Connections 2 and *The Day the Universe Changed*, Ambrose Video (narrated by James Burke)—These have useful sections.

Discoveries Underwater: Ships of War, BBC and KCET, 1988—The *Mary Rose* and the *Vasa*, sunk in 1628, are included.

Elizabeth R, BBC

Great Castles of Europe, TLC—Use with caution.

Mary Rose: Preserving a Moment in Time, Armand Hammer Productions,

1982 (narrated by Orson Welles).

"Now Thrive the Armourers . . .", Royal Armouries at the Tower of London (narrated by Robert Hardy).

Pirates: Passion and Plunder, the History of Piracy—Use with caution.

The Six Wives of Henry VIII, BBC.

The Story of English: A Muse of Fire, PBS (1986).

Treasure Houses of Britain: Building for Eternity—Sections on Belvoir Castle, Burghley House and Hardwick Hall.

INDEX